Parenting Wisdom

for the 21ˢᵗ Century

Raising Your Children By *Their*
Numbers To Achieve Their
Highest Potential

Richard Andrew King

No part of this publication may be reproduced or transmitted in any form or by any means, electronic or mechanical, including photocopy, recording or any information storage and retrieval system now known or to be invented without permission in writing from the publisher, except by a reviewer who wishes to quote brief passages in connection with a review written for inclusion in a magazine, newspaper, online article or broadcast. Contact Richard King Publications, PO Box 3621, Laguna Hills, CA 92654.

This book and its information contain copyrighted material, trademarks and other proprietary information. You may not modify, publish, transmit, participate in the transfer or sale of, create derivative works of, or in any way exploit, in whole or in part, any Proprietary or other Material in any capacity in this work.

Library of Congress Cataloging-in-Publication Data
King, Richard Andrew
Parenting Wisdom for the 21st Century:
Raising Your Children By *Their* Numbers to Achieve Their Highest Potential
ISBN: 987-0-931872-18-1
Date of Publication: 9 August 2012

© by Richard Andrew King
Published by Richard King Publications
PO Box 3621
Laguna Hills, CA 92654
(www.RichardKing.net)

Parenting Wisdom
for the
21ˢᵀ Century

Raising Your Children By *Their*
Numbers To Achieve Their
Highest Potential

Richard Andrew King

ACKNOWLEDGMENTS

With love and gratitude to my devoted daughter, Chandra, for her exceptional and thorough editing of this work.

With appreciation to Dr. Victoria Ford, J.D. for her generous Foreword and continuing support of The King's Numerology™ system.

DISCLAIMER

This work is neither designed to extol or defame any person or entity. Its purpose is to simply correlate the relationship between life and destiny to advance the study of numerology as a science.

Parenting Wisdom
for the 21st Century

Raising Your Children By *Their* Numbers
To Achieve Their Highest Potential

Table of Contents

Chapter	Title	Page
	Author's Introduction	9
	Foreword – Dr. Victoria Ford, J.D.	11
1	For the Love of Children	13
2	The King's Numerology[tm] – Basic Matrix	21
3	The Numbers	27
4	The Lifepath (LP)	47
5	The Expression (EXP)	97
6	The Performance/Experience (PE)	141
7	Soul (Desire) Layers	155
8	Nature (Personality) Layers	183
9	Voids	209
10	Names & Letters	233
11	The 1st E-P-C Triad	245
12	The Teen Years	271
13	Parenting Wisdom & Beyond	279
	Appendix – Keywords	287
	Glossary	293
	Index	305

AUTHOR'S INTRODUCTION

*The right to search for truth and to publish and teach
what one holds to be true ... implies also a duty;
one must not conceal any part of what one
has recognized to be true.*
~ Dr. Albert Einstein

The 21st Century has brought massive changes to our world in almost every field of endeavor – science, technology, medicine, transportation, socialization, communication, publication, education and production, just to name a few. Knowledge, undiscovered, has become discovered. Mysteries, unrevealed, have become revealed. Secrets, unknown, have become known. Such is the positive progression and procession of life.

This work continues the trend of positive progression by making unknown secrets known in the field of parenting. This is done by revealing the mysteries of raising children through the systematic application of the universal laws of numbers – that body of knowledge known as numerology. Defined, numerology is the ancient science and art of numbers, encompassing their interpretation, relationship and significance to life, wherein letters and numbers serve as codes and ciphers defining and describing our lives and destinies. These letters and numbers are derived from the full birth name and birth date of the individual.

Numerology is not new age. It is ancient age. Numbers were before man was. Arguably, numbers are the most universal communication system known to intelligent life. What is there that cannot be reduced to numbers, numerical patterns or numerical structures? Numerology will come alive when people see how their lives are reflected in their numbers.

As a content note, the descriptions of the numbers offered in this work will seem redundant in various chapters. This is because attributes of numbers do not change. What does change is *how* the numbers manifest themselves in the different components of the Basic Matrix of a numerology chart. To not include a description of each number in each of the chapters describing the different components of the Basic Matrix, however redundant it may be, would be to risk the reader missing the meaning of its application relative to the specific Basic Matrix component in question. The positive note to such redundancy is that repetition reinforces the meanings of the numbers which are fundamental to the parenting wisdom process of raising children by *their* numbers.

The knowledge offered in this work is new to the masses. For those parents who avail themselves of its secrets, it will unlock mysteries of their children's lives and destines. Once equipped with such numerological insights, parents will be able to help raise their children as never before, not only generating a high level of life awareness in their children but bequeathing to them a system to help their children raise their children.

Finally, there is an underlying order to all things, including our destinies. When we know that order, we can apply it to the benefit and well-being of our most precious treasure, our children. We can raise them to be aware, balanced, whole, enlightened, evolved. The primary purpose of this work is to help parents raise their children so they, the children, can achieve their highest potential and live a life of value, fulfillment, substance and meaning.

For the Love of Children and Their Children and Their Children . . .

RICHARD ANDREW KING

FOREWORD

Dr. Victoria Ford, J.D.

This book is a must for any parent and for all parents to be. It is a necessity before you name your child, and if you have named your child, then to fully understand them. It is vital to raise our children not just from our perspective but from the soul's journey destiny each of them have.

Understanding numbers is a gift that Pythagoras gave us many years ago. It is a much simpler and scientific way to raise our children than just by "hoping" we will get it right. We spend far more time, money and energy doing it the untrained way.

As a mother of two children, one birth and one by an easy birth (adoption), I realize after reading this profoundly enriching parenting wisdom, that I could have made life so much easier for my birth son.

Now that I have read *Parenting Wisdom for the 21st Century,* I can share the information with my daughter so she will know how to name and raise her children when it is her time.

The key to understanding King's numerology method is that it does help to understand yourself, your children and even your marriage. I highly recommend that you know how to name your children, how to help the name work better for you and your husband, as well as any other family members.

It is vital to read this book now before you name your children. If you already have children, then it is just important to understand them. With understanding comes love, respect, ease of life and simply a great family bonding.

Our children have their own destiny, and in our world children and their parents simply do not get along as well as they could. As a family law attorney and a spiritual soul advisor, I see how families are hurting because they do not really "know" each other.

I had a session with Richard King several years ago to help me understand my daughter. It has brought ease and great understanding, as well as a greatly enhanced loving relationship. I only wish I had been able to counsel with Richard King's numerology method with my birth son. Life would be so different.

I honor and respect Richard King's work not just for parenting but for couples and families to truly raise the consciousness of this world. It starts with each family and each person.

I am excited to be able to read and apply the numerology methods to my life and to share with my family so their lives can improve and be their best.

Thank you, Richard King, for sharing your wisdom in this state-of-the-art parenting book. Beginning numerology does not handle it. It takes a completely educated professional to totally bring the subject of numerology all together.

Richard Andrew King should be called Dr. King. His books are of the magnitude that will be read with reverence for generations to come. I am honored to call him friend, and I am blessed to have his wisdom to help live my life.

Dr. Victoria Ford, J.D.
Counselor of Law and PhD in Transpersonal Psychology
www.VikkiFord.com

1

For The Love of Children

*Pay attention to the young
and make them as good as possible.*
~ Socrates

What is more beautiful than a new born child – innocent, pure, tender? And what job is more critical than raising a child? As sincere loving parents, we do the best we can in following the Socratic admonition – *make them as good as possible*. But how do we do that, make them as good as possible?

Certainly, we want to give our children a strong and secure foundation, good ethics and morals, a sense of independence, responsibility, confidence and self-reliance. Still, there is another powerful parenting strategy in making our children *as good as possible* and that is to raise our children by *their* numbers.

A Few Parental Questions

Are you a parent? If so, do you honestly know the answers to any of the following questions related to your child or children?

- What are their deepest needs and desires?
- What drives and motivates them?
- What is the path in life they will be traveling?
- What role will they play on the great life stage?
- What are their intrinsic strengths?
- What are their inherent weaknesses?
- What challenges will they face in their lives?
- What will their struggles be during their formative years?
- What secrets do their names contain?

Furthermore, as a parent do you know that the answers to these questions are actually contained within the full birth name and birth date of your child or children? Are you aware there is a simple and effective way to determine the answers to these questions?

The reality is that the answers to all of these questions are, in fact, knowable through your children's birth data. The final question is, *To help your children achieve their highest potential, will you help raise your children by their numbers*?

What is Raising Children by *Their* Numbers?

To be sure, raising children by their numbers is, to the modern era, a new and unknown concept. This is quite understandable. Yet, raising children in such a way is founded on the oldest of sciences – numbers.

Pythagoras, the famous Greek philosopher who lived approximately 570 to 495 BCE, said:

> *Numbers rule the universe; everything is arranged according to number and mathematical shape.*

Aside from being known as the first pure mathematician, Pythagoras has also been regarded as the first numerologist – one who studies the relationship between numbers and life.

Of Pythagoras, Aristotle commented:

> *The Pythagorean ... having been brought up in the study of mathematics, thought that things are numbers ... and that the whole cosmos is a scale and a number.*

Both Pythagoras and Aristotle are correct when they say numbers rule the universe and that things are numbers respectively. Specifically, it is the numbers associated with our full names at birth and our birth dates that create the blueprint of our lives and destinies. As such, raising our children by their numbers means deciphering the letters and numbers of their birth data and subsequently using the knowledge of what those numbers represent to guide them through their lives. It is a very simple, powerful and profound strategy and . . . it works.

Why do we stress the point of raising children by *their* numbers? The answer is simply that the numbers of children will be different from those of their parents because everyone has their own birth name and birth date. Therefore, the desires, motivations, personalities and realities represented by each person's numbers will be different. Parenting wisdom dictates that parents not look to their own numbers when raising their children but to the numbers of their children.

Granted, raising children by their numbers may seem like a crazy idea, but it isn't. It is the most natural, the most precise method of helping and guiding our children into becoming the people they are intended to be, not what we as parents necessarily want or wish them to be.

True Story

In the spring of 2009 I was asked to give mini numerology readings at a function for some graduating high school seniors headed off to college. Each reading was very short, only about fifteen minutes.

During that event, one of the mothers – a very pleasant woman who was also one of the organizers – wanted to have a reading as well. Her chart was strongly dominated by the number 8. In numerology the number 8 represents flow, involvement, social power, status, wealth, connection, commerce, business, administration, organization, orchestration, execution, management, getting things done. The number 8 is very extroverted and is the most socially external number of the nine basic numbers (1-2-3-4-5-6-7-8-9).

During the event there was a shy young man who, from a distance, kept watching all the other kids have their readings. I could tell he was very curious but reticent nonetheless. Finally, as the event was drawing to a close, he approached and sat across from me. Interestingly, the woman who had her reading earlier sat down beside me. The young man was her son and she wanted to see what numbers were in his chart.

As I made a few calculations my suspicions regarding his chart were strongly confirmed. The number 7 was very dominant. 7 is the number representing internalization, reclusion, seclusion, shyness, withdrawal, privacy, secrecy, reflection, examination, thought, study, analysis, curiosity.

When I began explaining to this young man that it was okay to be alone, to be separate, to not have to feel as if he had to be socially interactive to be acceptable to others, that it was okay to be himself (because the 7 in effect was who he was), his head lifted and a smile spread across his face from ear to ear. He was jubilant and obviously encouraged that someone finally understood who he was. For me it was exciting and rewarding to see such joyful relief and positive personal self-acceptance.

Then – and this is the main point of this whole story – his mother, who was sitting beside me and who, upon hearing me discuss her son's life with him and seeing his exalted happiness, said, "Oh my gosh, I have been raising my child the wrong way for his entire life!"

My heart, which had been soaring at this young man's joy, sank upon hearing his mother's words that she had been raising her son *the wrong way for his entire life*! It was a painfully powerful and disturbingly poignant moment for me. How might his life have been different had she actually known who her son really was from the very beginning? She was a good mom. She had her son's best interest in her heart. The problem, however, was that for her son's entire life up to that point she had been raising him by *her* numbers, her energies, not his numbers, his energies.

Of course there is no finding fault with this mom. She was a very good woman and mother doing the best she could in raising her son. The dilemma was that her energies were strongly anchored in the social attributes of the number 8, while his energies were just as powerfully rooted in the introspective attributes of the number 7.

And this is the rub – 7 and 8 are diametrically opposed! Who this young man was in the core of his very being was exactly opposite from who his mother was! 7 is the most internal of all the numbers. 8 is the most external of all the numbers. 7 is introverted, 8 is extroverted. 7 is reclusive, 8 is socially active. No two numbers could be more different, and even though this mother's heart was in the right place, the tragedy was that she did not understand her son at his core. For all of this young man's life up to that point in time, she had been raising him through her 8 lens and energies rather than through his 7 lens and energies.

Could she have avoided this dilemma of raising her son *the wrong way*, as she stated? Yes and no. On the "no" side, it was their mutual destiny for their lives to unfold as they did. On the "yes" side, had she been educated in the knowledge of numbers and that her son's life was rooted in and based upon *his* numbers, just as her life was rooted in and based upon *her* numbers, then she would have had a wider perspective of raising her son. The hope of this story is that parents will begin to see life, relationships and parenting in a whole new light, the light of numerology as one tool to help elevate their children to their highest potential.

Yes, raising children by their numbers is a relatively new concept, but just because it is new does not mean it is meritless. At one time the earth was considered the center of the universe until Copernicus proved otherwise, and Columbus destroyed the myth that the world was flat. The ideas of a heliocentric solar system and a circular globe were ridiculed, even denigrated when introduced, but their truths eventually became accepted as self-evident. Today, of course, they are not even questioned. The hope is that one day the science of numerology will also become self-evident, as will its many benefits, especially in the arena of raising our precious, priceless, children who, in turn, will share with their children the same valuable education and parenting wisdom.

Benefits of Raising Children by *Their* Numbers

The benefits of raising children by their numbers are . . .

- Parents can know their children on a deep level and guide them in ways specific to their own destinies, thus leading them on a path to their highest potential.
- Children will acquire a deeper sense of themselves and their lives, thus helping them to become more aware, self-assured, confident, happy and whole. By knowing their own paths in life, the roles they will play on the great life stage, their assets and liabilities, their desires and personality nuances, children will be able to manage their lives with confidence and assurance.
- Raising children by their numbers increases the quality of parent-child relationships. When the parent and the child act from a deep sense of knowing the particular realities of each other's destinies, their relationship cannot but be made better.
- It advances the ability of children to eventually become effective parents in their own right as they mature, themselves having benefited from their parent's wise parenting skills.
- It expands the consciousness of the human race by expanding the consciousness of each individual. The greater the knowledge of life, relationships and destiny, the greater the wisdom of the whole.

For the Love of Children

© Richard Andrew King

When I look at the smile on a child's face
I see happiness I pray will never die;
I see innocence alive and well
and . . . purity.

There is joy in that smile –
unadulterated and real.
Nonetheless, I feel the pain
of knowing it may not last,
and I am lost for words.
Secret tears fall quietly
behind the veil of my gaze.

How happy would the world be
if that smile could exist eternally?
How loving would all life be
if that purity could endure?

Why not, I ask?
Why not?
Why?

2

The King's Numerology™ *Basic Matrix*

The *Basic Matrix* in the King's Numerology™ is a general profile of the individual and his or her destiny. It is comprised of eight components, each highlighting a major aspect of the person and his or her life.

In one way the Basic Matrix can be seen as a numeric picture puzzle of these eight puzzle pieces. How each puzzle piece (number) blends and fits with the other parts of the puzzle creates the picture of each person's life, in numbers of course.

The Basic Matrix is the first major tool for raising children by their numbers. When parents understand its eight components, parenting effectiveness will be greatly enhanced.

1. <u>Lifepath</u>. The Lifepath is precisely what it indicates – one's path in life. It is determined by the birth date. The Lifepath can also be likened to the script of a person's life or to an energy world notated by one of the nine basic numbers and its attributes, both positive and negative.
2. <u>Expression</u>. The Expression is derived from the full birth name of the individual. It represents the actor or actress replete with assets, liabilities, desires, motivations and personality.
3. <u>Performance/Experience (PE).</u> The Performance/Experience (PE) is the role the individual will play on the great life stage. When an actor or actress (Expression) reads a script (Lifepath), he or she will give a performance – the reality to be experienced in life. The PE is simply a combination of the numerical values of the Lifepath plus the Expression.
4. <u>Soul</u>. The Soul is a reference to the primal needs, wants, desires and motivations of the individual. It is not a reference to the spiritual soul. The Soul is a critical energy because, as opposed to the other components in the Basic Matrix, it is hidden from the view of others. Yet, it must not be ignored because its energies are the fire in the belly of the actor/actress, driving the person forward. The Soul is derived from the vowels in the full birth name: A-E-I-O-U-Y.
5. <u>Material Soul</u>. The Material Soul references the worldly or material needs, wants, desires and motivations of a person. It is a sibling of the Soul, a secondary layer of one's innermost drives. The Material Soul is determined simply by adding the numerical value of the Soul to the numerical value of the Lifepath.

6. <u>Nature</u>. The Nature is the primal personality of the individual. It is derived from the consonants of the full birth name. The Nature also governs the way or manner in which people behave, think, act. It is a major quality of the Expression (the person).

7. <u>Material Nature</u>. The Material Nature identifies the worldly personality of the individual. It is a sibling of the Nature and a secondary layer to the basic personality of a person. It is determined by adding the numerical value of the Nature to the numerical value of the Lifepath.

8. <u>Voids</u>. Voids are missing numerical values in the full birth name. Voids play a critical role in one's destiny, and they can often create problematic conditions for the individual depending on their location in a chart. They must not be ignored.

Name and Letter Timelines

Each name of the full birth name, as well as the individual letters of each name, is a powerful component of a child's destiny. Individual names and letters have both specific time periods in which they are active, as well as specific attributes and characteristics. For parents to know the secrets contained within their children's name and letter timelines is invaluable.

The 1st Epoch-Pinnacle-Challenge Timeline (1st E-P-C Triad)

The Lifepath of an individual contains the *Life Matrix*. It is the Life Matrix that reveals the various parts of the life journey. Arguably, the most critical part of the Life Matrix is the *1st Epoch-Pinnacle-Challenge* timeline (1st E-P-C Triad) which houses a child's formative years, the period of life which can be likened to the trunk of a tree. If the trunk is strong and stable, the tree will be strong and stable, but if the trunk is weak, how could the rest of the tree be strong? Therefore, knowing what the 1st Epoch-Pinnacle-Challenge timeline holds for the child is a major numerological component of parenting wisdom.

The Parenting Wisdom Triumvirate

Together, these three components – the *Basic Matrix*, the *Name and Letter Timelines*, and the *1st Epoch-Pinnacle-Challenge Timeline* – form a powerful, foundational triumvirate of parenting wisdom and raising children by their numbers. It is these three components which are the basis of this first volume of *Parenting Wisdom for the 21st Century*.

Simple Letter Value Chart

In numerology, each letter of the alphabet has a numerical equivalent. These values will be used later when we learn how to decode a child's name. The *Simple Letter Value Chart* below is a list of the nine simple numbers and their corresponding letters.

The *letter groupings* of each number are called *genera*. Notice that the letters A-J-S all equate to the number 1. The letters B-K-T all have a numerical value of 2 and so forth. Knowing this table will be a great help in understanding your children, their lives and destinies.

Simple Letter Value Chart									
The Letters	A	B	C	D	E	F	G	H	I
	J	K	L	M	N	O	P	Q	R
	S	T	U	V	W	X	Y	Z	
Number Value	1	2	3	4	5	6	7	8	9

A Final Prenote

As you begin working with this knowledge, you will eventually come to realize that your children *are* their numbers. In fact, we are all a manifestation of our own numbers. What will also become apparent is that we do not see things as they are, we see things the way our numbers are.

Directly witnessing these truths of life will, hopefully, lead us to a deeper understanding of the nature of creation and of a power so far beyond our comprehension it can only be called divine. In the words of the greatest scientist of the 20th Century, Dr. Albert Einstein:

Everyone who is seriously involved in the pursuit of science becomes convinced that a spirit is manifest in the laws of the Universe – a spirit vastly superior to that of man, and one in the face of which we, with our modest powers, must feel humble.

The child is the father of the man.

~ William Wordsworth

3

The Numbers

The blueprint by which we can know our children's lives is derived from their full name at birth and their birth date. This entire blueprint and its process of divination is called *Numerology - the ancient science and art of numbers, encompassing their interpretation, relationship and significance to our lives.* Numerology is the device through which we can understand the connection between the internal and external forces and events in our lives as well as the lives of our children.

In numerology, numbers and their corresponding letter values serve as codes and ciphers defining and describing our lives and destinies. Established by Pythagoras, numerology offers one key to the riddle of life and one solution to piecing the knowable puzzle of life together. The purpose of numerology is to assist us in knowing ourselves and also knowing our children and helping them grow, mature and achieve their highest potential.

Numbers in numerology represent the vibrational matrix which creates the framework of a person's destiny. It is not the numbers that are primarily important but what the numbers *represent*. Each of the basic numbers, *One* through *Nine* and their many combinations, possesses special meanings, qualities and characteristics which, when translated to a person's life, define and describe that life. The letters of the English alphabet – A through Z – also carry with them a general and specific numerical counterpart which allows us, as parents, the opportunity of delving into the interworkings of our children's names to discover the secrets they contain.

The energy patterns of our children's lives, as represented by the numbers and letters of their full birth data (referred to as *natal data*), are extremely powerful elements. No person can overpower these energies, alter them, avoid them, destroy them, run away or hide from them. They are like gravity – invisible and powerful. It is these energy patterns that compel us to act in ways that manifest our destiny.

For example, one may say, "Well, if life is destined, I'm simply going to lay down on the couch and do nothing." Destiny doesn't work quite this way. Life (its conditions, situations and events) does come to us. Never do we have to go in search of it. It will find us, to be sure. In the grand scheme of the universe, and in the specific design of our lives, we are always perfectly placed in the right place at the right time. However, if we're meant to move off the couch in order to fulfill certain requirements of our destiny, some force (external or internal) will act upon us and move us off the couch in spite of our most ardent wishes, wants, demands, commands, strengths or weaknesses to stay on the couch. As Winston

Churchill clearly declared, "Destiny commands. We must obey!" And obey we will, for the forces of our lives, identified by our specific numbers, will move us in whatever ways and by whatever means necessary to fulfill the conditions of our destinies.

Number Notes

By knowing and understanding the numbers as much as we can, we assist ourselves and our children tremendously by unlocking the mysteries the numbers possess. Thus, before we begin looking into the lives of our children and understanding the foundational numeric forces governing their lives and destinies, let us begin with a few general notes regarding numbers; then we will study the characteristics and attributes of each of the nine basic numbers.

Number Note 1

Just as every coin has two sides, every number has two sides – one positive side and one negative side (polarity). Because of this polar aspect of life, every one of us walks with both the light and the dark. It's impossible not to. We each have positive and negative aspects to our lives and destinies. Therefore, it will be helpful to understand this duality when we assess the numbers in our children's charts. No number is totally good or totally bad. The "goodness" or "badness" depends on how the energies are used and expressed.

For example, the number 2 represents peace on its positive side, war on its negative side. The two sides of the number 6 are love and hate. The opposite aspects of each number are noted in the number catalogue below.

Number Note 2

Every single number (crown) has ten binary or two-digit numbers (roots) forming it. When each of the single numbers forming the binary root are added together they ultimately create a single number.

For example, the ten binary roots forming the number *One* are:

$$10 - 19 - 28 - 37 - 46 - 55 - 64 - 73 - 82 - 91$$

When any of the numbers forming one of these binary numbers are added together, the first result will be a 10, except for the number 10 itself. When the 1 and 0 of the ten are added together, the result is a 1, the crown. It's the same way with each single number and its binary roots. The ten binary roots of each single number are also included in the number catalogue.

Number Note 3

Each binary root system of each single number (crown) contains a *master number* – a binary number of the same digit. The master numbers are: 11 – 22 – 33 – 44 – 55 – 66 – 77 – 88 – 99. Master numbers are like nuclear energy. Their power can be used for good or evil. Think of a master number as eleven times its single cipher (the number forming it).

For example, the master number Eleven is 11 x 1; the master number Twenty-Two is 11 x 2; the master number Thirty-Three is 11 x 3 and so forth. This power will be expressed through the master number's crown. For example, the crown of the master number 11 is the 2 (1 + 1 = 2). Therefore, the energy of the self, genesis, leadership and action (the two 1s) will manifest in the area of relationship, partnership, competition or adversarial opposition (the 2 crown).

The crown of the master number 22 is the 4 (2 + 2 = 4). Therefore, the energy of others, relationship, partnership, support, teamwork and caring (the two 2s) will manifest as a very powerful 4, expressing its attributes of security, stability, construction, development, work and service. The master numbers of each binary set are in bold in the number catalogue.

Number Note 4

It would be impossible to list every word in the English language serving as a *keyword* to each of the nine basic numbers. Therefore, a short list of the major keywords for each single number is offered in the following number catalogue after an explanation of each single number.

The Number Catalogue

The Number One – 1

(Positive: Divine Oneness; Negative: Egomania)
10 – 19 – 28 – 37 – 46 – **55** – 64 – 73 – 82 – 91

One represents fire, the male, the *yang* aspect of the Chinese Tao, the self, the ego, independence. *One* leads. It goes first. It shows the way. *One* is the monarch, the pioneer, leader, alchemist, creator, magician, originator, instigator, aggressor. *One* stands on its own two feet and takes responsibility for itself in its higher expression. Because it governs the male energy, it is masculine, active, assertive, dominant, decisive, direct and self-reliant. It also represents the father, positive energy in motion, courage, will, force and self-ambition. *One* is also unique, seeks originality and admires it in others. It is the reflection of all things new: beginnings, events, ideas, cycles. It is the number of inception and genesis. All things start in a *One* vibration.

One is also single, solo and separate. It stands alone and apart. In its lower expression it is ego-centered, consumed with itself and oblivious to others and their needs and wants. A negative *One* is selfish, overly proud, vain, full of himself and saturated with pompous machismo. He must be the center of attention and is jealous of anyone who steals his thunder or spotlight. Negative *Ones* want only for themselves, care only for themselves, love only themselves, do only for themselves.

Spiritual *Ones*, on the other hand, represent union with *the* One Universal Source, i.e., God. When the "little One" of the ego merges with the "big One" of Source, it becomes the *All*, just as a single drop of water becomes the *All* when it merges into the oneness of the ocean.

Spiritual *Ones* understand that God is one energy, not two, and where the One exists, there can never be two. Hence, there can never be the division which creates and generates competition, conflict and strife between and amongst others.

Keywords for the number One: *fire, yang, self, male, ego, father, monarch, leader, creator, pioneer, activist, independence, separate, will, courage, action, inception, creation, genesis, beginnings, logic, reason, unique, assertive, aggressive, proud, direct, unbending, original, maverick, lone wolf, tomboy.*

The Number Two – 2

(Positive: Peace;   Negative: War)
11 – 20 – 29 – 38 – 47 – 56 – 65 – 74 – 83 – 92

Two represents water, the female, the *yin* aspect of the Tao, others, relationships, dependence, emotion, balance, equilibrium, sensitivity and the polar aspect of creation.

Two follows, supports and serves but does not wish to lead, generally. It would rather stay behind the scenes because it is, in relation to the One, non-assertive and unobtrusive. *Two* is not concerned with the self (on the surface) but with relationships, their activity and interaction. *Two*, in its positive polarity, is receptive, sensitive, intuitive, considerate, cooperative, diplomatic, agreeable, amenable, affable, passive, patient, kind, adaptable, loving, caring, sweet, gentle-hearted, peacemaking, tactful, tolerant, harmonizing, equalizing, reflective (as in the moon reflecting light, not generating light). Because *Two* rules the female energy, it represents mother, wife, daughter, aunt, grandmother, sister, girlfriend. *Two* is responsive and nurturing, and in its highest state is one of the softest and sweetest of all vibrations. *Two* flows and bends and finds its power through conciliation and diplomacy, not rigidity.

Two, however, also rules opposites and opposing forces, so within this vibration is the condition of taking sides and separating into factions and fractions. This aspect can make it very polarizing, divisive, duplicitous, competitive, argumentative, antagonistic, interfering, back-biting, resistant and overly emotional. Because of its vacillating nature, *Two* is often indecisive and can also be contrary. *Two* would not travel alone; it prefers the company of others. It does not activate or originate; it participates and supports. *Two* is the first vibration of music, harmony and rhythm.

Keywords for the number Two: *water, yin, others, female, mother, supporter, divider, partner, helper, mate, servant, follower, friend, teammate, relationships, togetherness, dependence, indecisiveness, vacillation, duplicitous, emotional, passive, tolerant, loving, kind, caring, feeling, sweet, cooperative, competitive, indirect, interfering, adversarial, intuitive, tactful, reactive, responsive, nurturing, diplomatic, divisive, polarizing, double standard, peace and war.*

The Number Three – 3

(Positive: Well-being;   Negative: Dis-ease)
12 – 21 – 30 – 39 – 48 – 57 – **66 –** 75 – 84 – 93

Three is the integration of the 1 and the 2, the combination of female and male energies – the yin and the yang. Hence, *Three* rules integrated relationship, marriage, children. *Three* expresses and communicates, most preferably with words. It loves friends, fun, social gatherings, parties, good times and pleasure. *Three* talks, gossips, is gregarious and generally happy. *Three* is the vibration most associated with health, well-being and beauty. Because of its self-expressive nature, it is fond of acting, creating, modeling, performing and writing. Individuals with dominant *Three* energy in their numerology charts smile much of the time, are cheerful, optimistic, warm, attractive, popular, easy going and good-natured.

Of all the basic numbers, One through Nine, *Three* carries the least amount of hardship, turmoil, stress and discomfort when positively aspected in a chart. In fact, negative situations which are juxtaposed with or dominated by *Three* energy are often mitigated, and conditions which would be considered discordant by normal standards are lessened considerably. In another sense, *Three* can be seen as the vibration which dilutes that which is negative, often making untoward and unfavorable situations palatable and manageable. In effect, *Three* is the easiest of all the basic vibrations. As One represents fire and Two, water, *Three* signifies air.

Three is the number of the Trinity – Father, Son, Holy Ghost; Body, Mind, Spirit; Master, Disciple, Word; Mother, Father, Child. Where *Three* exists in a chart, there are issues of self-expression, integration, image, health, well-being, communication, children, words, personal happiness or unhappiness.

Every number has two sides, and the opposite side of the *Three* of health, beauty and positive communication involves disease, dis-ease, ugliness and negative communication. When *Three* is Challenged in a chart, it portends unhappy circumstances, potential ill health, caustic words, problems with children, harsh image issues, rough exteriors and untoward communication.

Keywords for the number Three: *self-expression, personal integration, perfection, marriage, words, communication, children, ease, fun, pleasure, sex, friends, gossip, good times, health, beauty, attractiveness, joy, imagination, optimism, cheerfulness, popularity, gregariousness, sociability, Trinity, disease, dis-ease, unhappiness, misfortune, image issues.*

The Number Four – 4

(Positive: Strength/Security;   Negative: Weakness/Insecurity)
13 – **22** – 31 – 40 – 49 – 58 – 67 – 76 – 85 – 94

Four, an earth sign, offers the opportunity for more security and stability than any other number. It can also create great wealth and power because of its ability to work, build and sacrifice for what it desires. *Four* concentrates on form, foundation and transformation. It is steady, diligent, persistent. It represents the house, the job and structures of all kinds – from buildings to contracts to works of art. In short, *Four* develops and builds. It also reflects devoted, loyal friendships and partnerships. It is logical, rational, mechanical, practical and regimented. *Four* loves order, dislikes change, and loves to help and serve.

Four is the rock of the earth, always solid, perhaps even too solid for its own good sometimes. Heavy concentrations of *Four* energy can make people stiff, dull, stubborn, recalcitrant and resistant to change. Yet, life is the very epitome of change. This can make things difficult for the *Four*, which can be too attached and too rooted to tradition and structure to move with the times or adapt to new situations. Therefore, *Four* people can often get stuck within the very structure which protects them and gives them the security they love and crave. *Four* is too practical to be spontaneous, adventurous and free-spirited. Individuals with heavy *Four* energy would rather be protected and hidden from the wind than play in it.

Keywords for the number Four: *form, structure, work, service, order, duty, discipline, security, stability, conservation, construction, persistence, tradition, convention, constriction, restriction, limitation, rules, roots, regimentation, routines, loyalty, fidelity, earth, grounding, anchoring, practicality, respectability, reliability, dependability, effort, drudgery, confinement, fences, attachment, house, office, tidiness, changeless, non-spontaneous, physical body, physical strength, matter, materialism, methodology, methodical.*

The Number Five – 5

(Positive: Freedom;   Negative: Slavery)
14 – 23 – 32 – 41 – 50 – 59 – 68 – **77** – 86 – 95

Five, a fire sign, is the vibration of freedom, change, detachment, versatility, experience, exploration, movement, energy in motion, the senses and sensuality. Whereas the *Four* likes to be protected from the wind and the winds of change, *Five* loves the wind and loves to play in it, for the wind brings adventure, stimulation, excitement. Whereas the *Four* loves roots, *Five* would rather sever them and move about, like a rolling stone – gathering no moss or the dust of complacency.

Five is magnetic, loquacious, adventurous, dashing, stimulating, flamboyant, and, in opposition to its polar counterpart the *Four*, highly unconventional, non-traditional, de-rooted and detached. *Five*, because of its multi-faceted, versatile, mercurial, exploratory, fast-burning nature, wants to move and change; it gets bored easily with one thing. *Five* needs and craves stimulation and excitement more than any of the nine basic numbers and, above all, it loves its freedom and non-restriction. In fact, woe be to the person who tries to chain and restrict a *Five*-dominated person.

Five is the *Number of Man* because it is the fulcrum (midpoint) of the Alpha-Numeric Spectrum – the basic numbers One through Nine. People have more in common with the number *Five* than any other number – five fingers on each hand, five toes on each foot, five basic material senses. Therefore, *Five* loves crowds and moves well in them.

One concern with the *Five* is its potential for over-indulgence in sensual pleasures and appetites. Since it is ruled by the senses and loves to explore and be free, it harbors the potential for dissipation, engaging in a lifestyle contrary to its highest and best good.

It is true that *Five* governs the principle of freedom, but it also governs its opposite side, slavery. If those individuals with *Five* dominant in their charts are not careful, they can well be enslaved by the very freedom they demand and champion. Freedom requires temperance, discipline, restraint, self-control and wisdom. As Pythagoras stated, "No man is free who cannot control himself." This statement is further corroborated by one of the United States of America's most famous and wise Founding Fathers, Benjamin Franklin, who warned, "Only a virtuous people are capable of freedom."

However, on a positive note, *Five* has the spiritual potential for becoming truly free and detached from the senses, thereby rising above them and their controlling passion. Arguably, no concept in human history is more cherished than personal freedom, and it is the *Five* which generates it. In fact, the Lifepath and Material Soul of the United States of America – the epitome of freedom on earth – are both *Fives*.

Keywords for the number Five: *freedom, slavery, experience, exploration, change, motion, movement, mercurial, versatile, diverse, sensual, crowds, people, stimulation, enthusiasm, excitement, detachment, non-convention, non-tradition, curiosity, spontaneity, adventure, uncertainty, loss, the five senses, rebel, renegade, revolutionary, rebellion.*

The Number Six – 6

(Positive: Love;   Negative: Hate)

15 – 24 – **33** – 42 – 51 – 60 – 69 – 78 – 87 – 96

Six, a water sign like the *Two*, rules all matters of the heart, hearth and home. Therefore, it is the vibration of domesticity, family and community, whether that community is a home, a neighborhood, state or nation.

Six is also the vibration of adjustment. *Six* is personal love. It is warm, nurturing, mothering, fathering. It also governs romance, sex, heartaches and heartbreaks. Because *Six* is a higher octave of the *Two*, it has the same potential tender compassion of the *Two*. It can be soft, gentle, attentive, kind, caring, conscientious, conventional, comforting, peace-making, sacrificing, responsive, responsible, dependable, devoted, understanding, sympathetic and empathetic. *Six* loves with open arms and a tender heart. It thrives on the personal touch and is prone to giving hugs and kisses.

Six, because it is also an octave of *Three*, is artistic, creative, harmonious. It loves beauty, harmony and symmetry. Many famous singers maintain *Six* in their charts, for their hearts and souls are filled with the rhythm of the *Two*, the expression of the *Three* and the love of the *Six*.

Six not only loves personally but passionately. It accommodates, reconciles, harmonizes and balances. Because of its loving, sacrificing and nurturing nature, it is important that those ruled by its vibration not allow themselves to be used or abused by those who would take advantage of them.

The opposite side of love is hate, and a negative *Six* can potentially be hateful, heartless, jealous, envious, possessive, vengeful, lustful, resentful and certainly personally unloving. A negatively aspected *Six* can be highly unpleasant, unappealing and excessively emotional to a fault.

In its purest form, *Six* rules love – pure, unadulterated, real love on a personal level. In its lowest form, *Six* is pure lust – lust for sex, money, fame, name, power, position. This negative aspect can manifest as addiction to sex, drugs, alcohol, partying.

Keywords for the number Six: *personal love, domesticity, romance, heart, hearth, home, family, community, nation, adjustment, harmony, music, sympathy, empathy, devotion, beauty, loyalty, balancing, peace-making, attentiveness, sexuality, responsive, artistic, sacrificing, nurturing, accommodating, protective, responsible, dependable, hate, jealousy, envy, passion, lust.*

The Number Seven – 7

(Positive: Nobility; Negative: Ignobility)
16 – 25 – 34 – 43 – 52 – 61 – 70 – 79 – **88** – 97

Seven, an air sign, represents the rise and fall of the spirit. It can carry one deeply inside the hallowed halls of life's most guarded secrets, into the inner worlds of mysticism and spirituality, or usher one into the wretched abyss of ignominy, despair, shame and chaos.

Seven is the cipher directing all to move *inward,* to move *within.* To accomplish this, it places people in isolation and separation, either physically, emotionally, financially, socially, mentally, philosophically and spiritually so they can think, ponder, reflect, analyze, philosophize, scrutinize, cogitate, meditate, pray.

Basically, *Seven* turns us away from the outer world of materialism, redirecting our attention to the inner world of spirituality. This it does regardless of whether we are willing or unwilling subjects, which is why it can be a harsh number. Being caught between the polar extremes of the dense, magnetic, attractive, familiar world of materialism and the equally magnetic, but stark, pure, non-sensually pleasing and unfamiliar realm of the spirit, its energies can be extremely discomforting, especially in the beginning. If we resist the inward pull, we end up fighting, struggling, suffering. The key is to accept, adjust and acquiesce to the *Seven's* inward pull and go with its flow.

Because of its bi-directional composition, *Seven* can be the stately, elegant, royal monarch or the indigent drunk in the gutter. It is king or courtesan. It moves us *up* or *down* in glorious or ignominious style. *Seven* can bring great peace or great chaos, pure perfection or impure imperfection. *Seven*, indeed, is the double-edged sword of the spirit.

Seven is the student, teacher, thinker and the great inquirer. A perfect image of the *Seven* is Rodin's masterpiece, *The Thinker*. *Seven* seeks answers, it wants to know and moves inward to find what it seeks. Therefore, in order to inwardly find what it seeks, it seeks reclusion, separation, solitude and isolation so it can do what it does best, think, which it cannot do in a crowded environment.

One negative aspect of the *Seven* is to not think at all or think too little. People can be *penny wise and pound foolish* under the 7's influence. It is not uncommon for intelligent people to be extremely foolish, their folly sometimes leading to their demise. Such foolishness is usually witnessed when *Seven* is voided in a chart.

Potentially, *Seven* is the most noble, holy, sensitive, sacred and spiritual of the nine basic numbers. No number can lead one to greater heights than the *Seven* because no number takes one deeper than the *Seven*. Therefore, *Seven* rules saints.

Contrastingly, because all numbers have two sides, *Seven* also rules that which is ignoble, unholy, insensitive, profane and unspiritual. Therefore, *Seven* also rules sinners. Ruthlessness, betrayals, adulteries and compassionless behaviors can be a reflection of the *Seven's* negative side.

Keywords for the number Seven: *introspective, intuitive, secretive, reclusive, sensitive, wise, private, isolated, sequestered, alone, alienation, analytical, metaphysical, spiritual, reserved, indifferent, shy, retiring, withdrawing, gracious, royal, stately, poised, serene, calm, chaste, patient, perfect, deep, mystical, inward, tragic, stressed, suffering, turmoil, chaos, despair, lonely, ignominy, disturbance, nervous, foolish.*

The Number Eight – 8

(Positive: Management;   Negative: Mis-management)
17 – 26 – 35 – **44** – 53 – 62 – 71 – 80 – 89 – 98

Eight, an earth sign, represents the vibration of involvement, interaction, connection, disconnection, inhibition, flow, business and commerce. As *Seven* moves the individual *inward*, *Eight* generally moves him *outward* into the consciousness of worldly and material success.

Eight is that number which connects polarities, positive and negative, buyer and seller, idea and completion. Because of this characteristic, *Eight* is often present in the charts of commercially successful entities, businesses and individuals.

It is the *Eight* energy which coordinates, manipulates, administrates, directs and manages and, hence, *Eight* is often found among high level leaders, administrators, generals, athletes, managers, executives, performers and people who must bring together various components of a system – be those systems political, military, physical, emotional, educational, financial, mechanical, social, scientific, clerical, artistic or cinematic. It is the number 8 which integrates the individual parts of the whole and makes them work efficiently. If the master number 44 is present in the 8's root system, and there are no voids in either the 4 or 8, the individual will generally operate at a high level of administration and orchestration.

Just as the *Seven* energy influences one to ascend or descend, the *Eight* cipher can disconnect as efficiently as it connects. It also maintains the ability to inhibit and retard the flow of success. Some people may work extremely hard during the entire course of their lives and still end up with nothing to show for all their efforts. This is not because they're unlucky or incompetent. It is most probably because they maintain a negatively aspected *Eight* in their life's blueprint, or no 8 at all, which disallows them from making a successful connection.

In its highest aspect, *Eight* connects man with his most noble ideals and his Soul to its Source. However, because man is mostly interested in connecting with the material world, *Eight* is generally seen as being the vibration of worldly success, wealth, riches, comfort and status.

Keywords for the number Eight: *involvement, interaction, connection, disconnection, continuity, comfort, success, money, wealth, riches, status, social power, influence, coordination, flow, management, administration, orchestration, execution, generalship, leadership, commerce, business, manipulation, external focus.*

The Number Nine – 9

(Positive: Benevolence; Negative: Malevolence)
18 – 27 – 36 – 45 – 54 – 63 – 72 – 81 – 90 – **99**

Nine rules. In the King's Numerology^{tm} system, *Nine* is the *Grand Elemental* and the most universal of all numbers. It is the vibration which includes all other vibrations within it. If a person were to add the single ciphers *One* through *Eight* together and reduce them to a single digit, the final result would be *Nine* (1+2+3+4+5+6+7+8 = 36; 3 + 6 = 9). If the basic numbers *One* through *Nine* were added together, the result would be 45, also a 9 in reduction.

What this means is that *Nine* identifies and is a part of all numbers, all people. In effect, *Nine is* all numbers. Individuals with the *Nine* dominant in their charts, therefore, understand the masses (either consciously or unconsciously) who are governed by the nine basic numbers. Simply stated, *Nine* dominated people understand and have an intrinsic connection with the masses; the masses understand and have an intrinsic connection with them.

Thus, *Nine* has the distinction of being all-inclusive and all-encompassing. It is this aspect of its nature that makes the *Nine* universal, representing the macrocosm, the world, the public stage.

Where *Nine* exists, there is generally fame, recognition or notoriety of some degree. *Nine* is the vibration which makes people charismatic, dynamic, powerful, dominant and connected to "the many" in some capacity. Often, *Nine* dominated people are involved in entertainment, education, medicine, law, politics, music, media, theater, religion, public speaking and all things of a communicative and universal nature.

As *Six* is the number of personal love, *Nine* is the cipher of impersonal, universal, public love. This is why *Nine* is also seen in the charts of humanitarians, philanthropists, philosophers, theologians and public personalities. *Nine* is the most public vibration of the Alpha-Numeric Spectrum. More than any number, *Nine* carries people into the public eye and onto the public stage.

Because of its universal characteristic, *Nine* is the chameleon of the basic numbers. It can become anything and anyone, harmonize with anything and anyone. *Nine* can just as easily be a great ruler or a great wolf in sheep's clothing, pretending to be the exact opposite of what it actually is. Therefore, individuals with a *Nine* in their charts must be careful of not falling into the wrong crowds or the wrong mindset. We become known by the people with whom we associate, be those people good or bad; decent or indecent; noble or ignoble. *Nine* can be just as nefarious and ignoble as it can be magnanimous and noble.

As *One* represents beginnings, *Nine* represents endings, completions, conclusions. Under *Nine* conditions, things draw to a close, they end, terminate, come to a resolution or are finalized. It is not wise to begin new projects under a *Nine* influence because energies are working to conclusion, not genesis. New projects should, generally, be initiated in a *One* vibratory period.

Keywords for the number Nine: *rulership, macrocosm, universality, completion, finality, endings, conclusions, art, theater, music, public, the stage, education, broadcasting, expansion, impersonal love, charisma, power, dominance, domination, domineering, philanthropy, philosophy, humanitarianism, artistic expression, drama, selfless, the 'All', the 'Many', the masses, the chameleon, benevolence, malevolence.*

Number Power

© Richard Andrew King

Numbers tell the time;
as well, they tell the tale;
numbers calculate the voyage
of life in its detail.

Numbers, just like coins,
incorporate two sides –
positive and negative,
as in the turn of tides.

Numbers are the codes of life;
they gauge, describe, define
the framework and the structure
of a life that is divine.

Numbers are life's basis
and, as cosmic law avers,
the blueprint of our destiny
has its design in numbers.

4

The Lifepath

The Lifepath is exactly that – the path of life, a roadway of individual destiny. Derived from the day, month and year of birth, the Lifepath can also be seen as the *script* of each person's life, the storyline of a personal play in which the individual takes center stage as the star attraction.

The Lifepath script contains all the conditions, circumstances, events, lessons, experiences, scenarios, themes and challenges – both positive and negative – the individual will face in life as he travels down the road of his life or performs the script laid before him at his birth.

The Lifepath compels us to move and act in manners commensurate with the unfoldment of our destiny. The Lifepath brings people, events and circumstances to us. It magnetizes us to every deed our destiny calls for us to experience. The energy patterns of the Lifepath and its inner structure comprise one of the two main vibratory structures of our lives. The full birth name (Expression) and its separate names account for the other.

There are nine Lifepaths, each designated by a simple number 1 to 9. Every person has his own Lifepath. Parents have theirs; children have theirs. The important thing to understand is that the Lifepath of the children may not be the same as that of the parents and, in fact, it can be very different, if not totally opposite from the Lifepaths of the parents.

For example, one parent may have an 8 Lifepath, her child a 7 Lifepath. We discussed this earlier. The numbers 7 and 8 are diametrically opposed. Such a discrepancy can create problems. However, when parents are aware of the situation, management becomes easier.

The energies of our Lifepath will move us to manifest our destiny. For example, we may choose to go on a camping trip in the woods. However, if the woods catch on fire, we will have to abandon our plans and move to safety, lest the forest fire consume us in its heat and fury.

Similarly, we may choose to have a pleasant swim in the ocean, but the currents of the ocean will determine the pleasantness of our swim, not us. In fact, those currents could, because of their strength and overpowering force, pull us out to sea or drown us entirely, taking our life in the process. Likewise, we may build a fortune in the stock market but lose it all because of financial influences beyond our control.

Just as the forces of the forest fire, the ocean's currents and the financial climate compel us to move against our will, so the forces of our Lifepath compel us to move in ways appropriate to the fulfillment of our destiny, some of which may be against our will, too.

If we spend just a little time analyzing our lives, we will see that we were forced to make many of our past decisions because of conditions, events, people and circumstances extraneous to us. The things that happen to us come through the vibrations of our Lifepath. When we can learn to *accept* this reality, we can *adjust* to our lives, allowing life to run its course without us becoming neurotic, imbalanced, discomforted or stressed out in the day-to-day process of living, which will surely happen if we try to force our will upon the massive vibrational tides of our Lifepath.

It is no different for our children. They have their Lifepaths which will move them according to their destinies. As parents, when we know what the Lifepath is for our children we can guide and help them through their lives, especially their early lives, where our responsibility to them is critical.

Lifepath Analogies

There are five analogies that will help us understand the Lifepath:

1. Path/Roadmap
2. Script
3. Automated Theme Ride
4. Energy World
5. Hand of Cards

We've already discussed the Lifepath as being analogous to a path or road and the *script* of a play or movie. In fact, were we to extend our study of the Lifepath beyond the purpose of this work we would find that the Lifepath contains other features likened to the acts and scenes of a play. These are discussed in *The King's Book of Numerology II: Forecasting – Part 1*.

A third way of perceiving the Lifepath is to consider the analogy of an automated theme park ride. In the beginning of the ride, our vehicle is hooked up to a chain which pulls us along its course through various aspects of the ride until the ride is completed. Once aboard the ride, we have no choice but to stay on until the ride is over. We cannot safely exit the ride until the ride is over.

Likewise, when we're born, our soul is hooked up to a physical body and chain of events which pull us along until our life ends at death. Once we are attached to this life through the process of birth, we are hooked up to a series of events, experiences, circumstances, situations and relationships that are beyond our control. These events and experiences become our destiny. We may weep or laugh as we move through them but, to be sure, we will experience what our Lifepath holds in store for us.

A fourth analogy for the Lifepath is that of an energy world. Picture a solar system of nine planets, each planet represented by one of the nine basic numbers. At the time of our birth we are born onto one of these nine planets where we will live for our entire life, involved with the attributes and characteristics represented by the number of the planet we inhabit. If we are sent to Planet #1, our lives will be focused solely in its vibratory field with lessons of Yang (male) energy, independence, identity, action, leadership and the self. If we are sent to Planet #2, we will experience the lessons, attributes and characteristics of Yin (female) energy, dependence, others, relationships, teamwork, partnership, competition, opposition, conflict, peace and balance. So it goes throughout the entire spectrum of the nine energy worlds.

Once sent to a particular planet and its vibrations, we cannot move to another planet. We must live on the world to which we were sent and make the best of it. It may not be the world of our choosing. We may not like it and it may be extremely uncomfortable. On the other hand, we may love it and find it quite fulfilling. The point is, all of this is beyond our control. Once born, the date of birth establishes the number of the energy world we will inhabit for this lifetime.

Furthermore, to wish to live on or in someone else's world, to be envious or jealous of them, their life style or experiences, or, on the other side of the coin, to ridicule or deprecate others and their existence on another world because we see them as inferior or less fortunate, is unhealthy and dangerous. We each have our own destiny and no one can change it. The key is that we must learn to understand and appreciate our own energy world and learn its lessons through the Lifepath.

A fifth analogy of the Lifepath is that of a hand of cards, the 'hand' we were dealt at birth. The cards within our 'hand' are exclusive to us and like no other. We may be dealt four aces and experience a worldly life of riches, wealth, success, power, fame, pleasure and happiness, or on the other hand, we may be dealt a bunch of cards having seemingly no value whatsoever. For most of us, our 'hand' falls somewhere between the two extremes. The point is, however, we cannot change the 'hand' we were dealt at birth. We must play it. It's just the way it is. In doing so, like every card player knows, we need to keep a poker face throughout the game, stay balanced, poised and calm as we play out the 'hand of cards' that is our destiny.

Calculating the Lifepath

The calculation of the Lifepath is extremely simple and literally takes seconds. Simply write down the day, month and year of birth in numeric form, add left to right and reduce to a single digit. Let's take some examples.

Example A

Birth date: 8 January 1960 [January is the 1st calendar month]

8 January 1960

$8 + 1 + 1 + 9 + 6 + 0 = 25: 2 + 5 = 7$

The Lifepath is 7

[Note: For example purposes later on, we'll associate this birthdate of 8 January 1960 with a fictitious person, Mary Jane Smith.]

Example B

Birthdate of 14 August 1985 [August is the 8th calendar month]

14 August 1985

$1 + 4 + 8 + 1 + 9 + 8 + 5 = 36: 3 + 6 = 9$

The Lifepath is 9

[Note: For example purposes later on, we'll associate this birthdate of 14 August 1985 with a fictitious person, John David Doey.]

Now it's your turn as a parent. What is your child's Lifepath number? Those of your children?

Child's Date of Birth: _____ / _____ / _____

    Day: _____ + Month: _____ + Year: _____ = # _____ Lifepath

Child's Date of Birth: _____ / _____ / _____

    Day: _____ + Month: _____ + Year: _____ = # _____ Lifepath

Child's Date of Birth: _____ / _____ / _____

    Day: _____ + Month: _____ + Year: _____ = # _____ Lifepath

Lifepath Descriptions

Now that we've learned how to calculate the Lifepath, let's take a look at what each Lifepath represents. Please keep in mind the Lifepath is not the person. The Expression, which we'll discuss in the next chapter, is the person. It's based on the full birth name of the child. The Lifepath is the script of life, as we've discussed. It contains the lessons, circumstances, events, obstacles, situations and so forth that will confront the child from cradle to grave.

The One (1) Lifepath

The number One represents the yang aspect of Nature. A fire sign, it is masculine, assertive, creative. One likes to go first and show the way. Therefore, it can lead, and in the Lifepath position, your child will be learning to do and to lead, not to follow; to create, not subordinate; to stand alone, not hold hands with others or follow another; to act, not react. One is the vibration of self-reliance, not reliance on others. It is also the energy of that which is original and unique.

All of this taken into consideration, the One Lifepath will find your child striking out on his or her own. Situations will occur during the life journey which will compel the individual to take the lead – the lead in relationships, the lead in the home as the matriarch or patriarch, the lead at work, at school, in church, in the community and possibly in the business environment as an entrepreneur, manager or leader.

Because the element of the One is fire, it heats things up, takes action, initiates, grabs hold of the standard and, while standing out front, says, directly or indirectly, "Follow me!" Therefore, a person with this Lifepath lesson will learn to lead – voluntarily or involuntarily. And, furthermore, when these opportunities present themselves, the One Lifepath individual should take charge and not generally relinquish the lead to someone else unless the other person is a leader too.

The One Lifepath is also one in which your child could create, particularly in the realm of mental and artistic self-expression. Any occupation using the mind, words and communication skills would be important in harmonizing with this Lifepath, especially if strengthened by Three (3) and Seven (7) energy elsewhere in the chart, particularly in the Basic Matrix. Three rules words and communication, while the Seven represents the mind and spirit.

Because One stands alone, people under this vibration make excellent pioneers and adventurers. One is intrinsically solo by nature and generally unencumbered by the need to socialize or survive in groups. Being bold, daring, courageous, willful and adventurous are qualities the One Lifepath person would be wise to engender because they are the exact lessons to be learned under this dominant fire sign of individuality.

The cautionary yellow flag for the One Lifepath is the possibility of the child becoming too self-oriented, self-consumed, self-possessed, self-centered and ego-maniacal. Huge egos can be destructive, arrogant, imperious, unyielding, unbending. Fire warms and gives life. But too much fire burns, maims, incinerates and destroys.

Thus, it is pride that may be a major hurdle and stumbling block for the One Lifepath person to overcome. How many conflicts have been generated, how many wars fought, how many people hurt, how much blood spilt, how many tragic tears have been shed because of the weakness and disease of human pride? And, yet, from a spiritual perspective, what is there in this life to be proud of? It is this negative quality of the One Lifepath that should warrant a close eye in the child's development.

Finally, when One operates at its zenith, it is the beacon of light illuminating the way for others. From a spiritual perspective, One is union with the divine. For those with a One Lifepath the goal is self-reliance, standing on one's own two feet, being counted, having courage, going first, often flying solo, playing the role of the maverick, the lone wolf and illustrating, ultimately, what it means to be a pioneer, leader and initiator.

- <u>Parenting Wisdom for the One Lifepath</u>: Teach your children the value of being independent, unique, different, taking action; being doers, not followers; taking responsibility for their actions and being accountable for them. Teach them to have courage, strength and appreciate their identity as a whole person. Be cautious, however, that they do not become arrogant, over-bearing, too willful, full of themselves and ego-centric. Teach them that humility is the highest form of strength and that arrogance is the highest form of weakness. The One Lifepath will place the individual in a position of leadership or taking charge in some capacity. Therefore, children must learn to stand alone, have a backbone and be the maverick or the lone wolf if need be. The One Lifepath is not about holding hands. It is about going first, taking charge, being the leader, pioneer, manager, executive, employer, star and, most importantly, being self-accountable and self-responsible.
- Famous People with a One Lifepath: *Billy Graham, Ernest Hemingway, George Washington, Larry King, Napoleon Bonaparte, Steve Jobs, Tiger Woods*

The Two (2) Lifepath

The Two Lifepath addresses the yin, the female aspect of creation. Whereas the One Lifepath focuses on male energy [yang] and the self, the Two Lifepath focuses on female energy [yin], others, relationships, support, balance, harmony, rhythm, equilibrium, receptivity, sensitivity, cooperation, compromise, teamwork and working together.

The Two is the first vibration of the nine basic numbers which addresses social issues for, in progression, the One is now moving beyond itself into the domain of duality and discovering that other people, other entities, other points of view, other philosophies, other cultures and so forth do exist, and in order to live harmoniously and in balance with one another, one must consider and embrace other Ones as well as itself. As John Donne said, "No man is an Island, entire of itself; every man is a piece of the Continent, a part of the main." It is the Two Lifepath in which this thought comes to life and showers lessons upon the child so that the reality of others is received and embraced.

When your child is born into the Two Lifepath, his or her life will be spent predominately in a support capacity. Under this vibration, the lesson is not necessarily to lead but to follow, maintain, corroborate and support those in the lead. Although society often gives over-enthusiastic high praise to leadership, followership is just as important. After all, without followers there could be no leaders, and without efficient, competent, strong, dedicated, devoted, intelligent, loving support, nothing could ever get done by those who may have the vision to create but not the wherewithal to accomplish or carry out the plan or the task at hand.

For example, although officers are the decision makers in the armed forces, it has been said that *Sergeants run the army, not officers.* In other words, it is the sergeants who, after receiving orders from their commanding officers, implement those orders and ensure their execution.

In like manner, it can also be said that secretaries and personal assistants, not presidents or chairmen, run the business world. Like sergeants, they are the ones responsible for carrying out the plan and seeing that the detail work is done.

Just a little thought here will reveal how precious and uncompromisingly critical a sergeant, secretary, personal assistant or support person can be to the success or failure of any enterprise. As the yin and yang form an integrated whole, so leaders and followers must work together in the concept of wholeness. Neither can exist without the other. Therefore, although the Two Lifepath is one of support, it is by no means unimportant. Nor should a child think less of himself or herself if either is placed in a support role.

In the Two Lifepath, music may well be a major aspect of the life experience. All rhythm is composed of an up-stroke and a down-stroke – a two-stroke cycle. Reflective of this concept is point-counterpoint, consonance-dissonance, fast-slow tempos, etc., all factors which create contrast in music and appreciation of one factor for the other. Generally speaking, women have more natural musical rhythm than men. It is no coincidence that women are ruled by the Two vibration and men by the One vibration, the latter lacking in the bi-polar ingredient to make it rhythmical. This is not to say that men do not have rhythm. It is to say that it is the female principle in Nature that engenders rhythm more than the masculine ray. Furthermore, 'feminine' does not necessarily mean 'effeminate,' although one who is strongly feminine will naturally be effeminate. All of us, whether we are male or female, have some aspect of the opposing polar energy in us in the form of the 1 or the 2, just as in the yin/yang symbol of the ancient Tao where there is a white dot in the black hemisphere and a black dot in the white hemisphere, signifying that within the masculine, there is feminine and within the feminine, there is masculine. Nothing is totally black or white, positive or negative in this dimension of duality.

The positive aspect of the Two Lifepath is perfect balance and loving support. The earlier children learn this vital concept of the 2 the better. In life, balance is absolutely critical if one is to experience a fulfilling and meaningful life. Balance includes all aspects of life – mental, emotional, familial, physical, financial, social, professional, sexual.

The number Two represents duality. This duality is further represented by the teeter-totter going up and down, just as the pendulum sways back and forth and the ocean's tides flow in and out. When each of these actions is given its proper respect, measure and attention, there is perfect balance. Harmony, peace and love will result. When an overemphasis is placed on one polarity or the other, imbalance occurs. Strife, struggle and discomfort are the result. It is difficult to achieve balance because we often spend too much time focusing on one polarity or the other. The issues of self importance often stand in the way. Pride and ego create imbalance by not recognizing others, others of all kinds – people, issues, concerns, feelings, animals, etc.

It is the Two Lifepath which brings into focus these issues and concepts of others. Hence, qualities of compassion, consideration, compromise, cooperation, companionship, sharing, togetherness (as opposed to "I-ness"), diplomacy, patience, tolerance, kindness, giving, sweetness, harmony and equilibrium become the positive focus of this lifescript for children.

On the negative side of this Two Lifepath is destructive imbalance and contention. Since Two rules others, the individual will be placed in life arenas, circumstances, situations, environments and predicaments where he or she can learn and experience what this 'others concept' is all about. Often, competition is found within this vibratory field, for it is competition which places one against other *ones* in a field of comparison and contrast, e.g., the playing field, the court, the debate facility, the forum, the legislature, etc. Learning not to dominate or subordinate is the ultimate goal of the peace-seeking Two. Rather, the goal is to cooperate and compromise for the peace and balance of all.

Oftentimes, we see strong egos in the competitive arenas of life, and it is the competitive environment which exists to lift the ego-driven soul into a place of balance and harmony where winning and losing, victory and defeat are each seen in their proper perspective – as opposite polarities of the same issue. Ultimately, each is insignificant, and one must learn under this Two Lifepath vibration that the ultimate winner is neither the victor nor the vanquished, but the balanced! Why? Because where there is balance one can walk the tightrope of life without falling off and jeopardizing his life or the lives of others and therefore cross the chasm of life from beginning to end successfully and meaningfully.

Thus, under this Two Lifepath, one must be aware of competition taken to levels of unhealthy contention, confliction and war. Absolutely no good will come, or can come, from a situation in which ego-driven dominance, not tolerance, is the end result. When the pendulum swings one way, it must by its very nature swing the other. No one wins forever. The way of the warrior is death. He who wins will lose and he who loses will win. It's as axiomatic as the rising and falling of the tide, as certain as the inflow and outflow of air to and from the lungs, as predictable as the coming and going of the seasons or the revolution of the earth from night to day and day to night.

Another caution of the Two Lifepath that we parents would be wise to instill in our children is the possibility of negative duplicity, deceit and deception. Because Two represents polar extremes, it is easy under this vibration to show two sides: one true, one false. Showing two sides can be deceitful, and the deception generated will create negative reactions and guarantee their return to the 'generator'. What goes around certainly will come back around. Here again, balance is the key, for in a balanced state, one can see both sides of the teeter-totter at once because it is straight and true – one line with two aspects in one elevation.

In life, there are sins of omission as well as sins of co-mission. Because Two is dual by nature, there is the distinct possibility in this Lifepath of vacillation, of swaying back and forth and not coming to a definitive conclusion. Hence, one can become bogged down and make no progress vis-à-vis definitive action. Vacillation may be good at times, but it can also cause problems. Thus, under this Two Lifepath, it is suggested that one learn not to vacillate if such vacillation generates an imbalance thwarting success. Again, it is best that the teeter-totter remain still and balanced so that there may not be any chaos or disruption caused by a state of imbalance.

The positive lesson for the Two Lifepath is, therefore, balance. Where balance exists, the energies of life flow smoothly and freely for everyone to share and experience equally. Imbalance may create excitement, but it can never create peace.

Because Two rules support and governs women in general, it is natural that oftentimes throughout history it has been a woman who has been "the power behind the throne." Simply because Two rules support it does not mean that the Two is less intelligent than the One. Leaders are not necessarily smarter than followers. They may have more directorial presence, more will to survive, more arrogance, more ego involvement, but these qualities do not equate to intelligence. Therefore, leaders must not patronize followers or speak down to them but rather seek their support and be grateful for it.

- Parenting Wisdom for the Two Lifepath: Teach your children that balance is critical to their lives, that all things have two sides, that people can have differences and still be wonderful people. Explain to them the importance of having followers as well as leaders, and that to be a good leader, one must also be a good follower. As well, teach them that leaders need followers and followers need leaders and neither is more important than the other. All souls originate from the same Source, the same Flame. Show your children the dual aspect of life in its various forms, pointing out that all coins have two sides, that a full revolution of the earth has both a day and a night, that there is both health and sickness in the world, as well as joy and sorrow, smiles and frowns, joy and sadness; that there is both peace and war in the world, victory and defeat, winners and losers. Teach them that everyone has feelings and that to have successful relationships everyone's feelings should be considered. This will assist them in manifesting harmony in their lives, creating equilibrium and fostering diplomacy. The Two Lifepath focuses on others, sharing, togetherness, partnership, teamwork, support, competition, division, opposition (remembering that everything has two sides). Success in the Two Lifepath rests in understanding the dual aspect of life and keeping all things in balance, especially the self, emotions and relationships.

- Famous People with a Two Lifepath: *Amelia Earhart, Bill Clinton, Bob Hope, Duke of Wellington (Arthur Wellesley), George Armstrong Custer, Prince Charles, Prince William*

The Three (3) Lifepath

As One represents the yang, the male principle of Nature, and Two, the yin, the female principle, Three personifies their union, their blending and integration. Spiritually, Three denotes the Trinity, the Divine Relationship of Father, Son and Holy Ghost; Master, Disciple, Word. On a different level, the trinity is reflected in other structures such as actor-script-role, body-mind-spirit, man-woman-marriage, father-mother-child, idea-development-product, concept-materialization-expression.

Therefore, the Three Lifepath is one which focuses on this triune relationship and its different forms. On a personal level the Three, represented by the triangle (the symbol of perfection), manifests itself through individual expression in many forms – physically as beauty and health, vocally in song, communicatively in speech, mentally through the creative arts, professionally as a member of the media or theater, socially as good times with friends, romantically as marriage or intimate relationship.

As we can see, the Three Lifepath is rooted in the vibration of self-expression and personal integration. If there is a preponderance of Three energy in the chart beyond the Lifepath itself, the more intense the expressive factors will be.

Invariably, concentrated Three energy means a lifescript where words may play a major role in some type of communicative activity, interest or employment. Personal image may also be a dominant theme. This may translate to a career in writing, art, law, language, teaching, acting, singing, reporting, commentating, etc. It may also equate to careers in health and beauty where personal integration with the body is important, or in a modeling career where one uses the body as the vehicle of self-expression.

Generally speaking, the Three Lifepath affords the easiest and most fulfilling of all the life scripts. Because it is the vibration of integration and expression, people are usually more happy and relaxed under its influence. There is, as compared with the other life lessons, little stress with this Three sojourn through life as long as the Three is not negatively aspected in a chart, i.e., voided, challenged, or both.

If any Lifepath vibration could be called the 'vacation Lifepath', it would be the Three. This energy field generally brings ease, pleasure, good times, friends and overall enjoyment. Of course, it does have its problems like all life scripts. This dimension in which we live is not paradise and is not problem-free. Everybody dies. Everybody gets sick from time to time. Everyone experiences stress. However, the intensity of life's problems have a tendency to be mitigated under this vibratory pattern, and problems just don't seem to carry the weight and burden they can carry compared with other numerical vibrations.

The triangle, the geometric symbol of the Three, integrates. When there is a positive connection between the three apexes of the triangle, there is free-flowing expression and fulfillment because the energy of the vibration is flowing within a completed circuit. But if the circuit is broken, disruption occurs and the expression becomes negatively aspected.

Therefore, the other side of the coin for the Three is not integration but disintegration. Where there was health on one side of the coin, there is now sickness. Where there was positive self-expression, there is now negative self-expression. Where there was the positive usage of words, there is now the negative usage of words and language. Where there were friends, there are now enemies. This will not happen, however, unless the chart is negatively aspected or if the person becomes too self-indulgent, self-centered, self-consumed, entitled, vain or arrogant, which is a possibility with this vibration since it is so highly charged with the energies of image and self-expression.

When we experience our children being expressive to a level of self-preoccupation, there is always the possibility they will get a big head and lose perspective of their true place in the social framework of life. As parents, we would be wise to monitor our children's behavior so it does not become too vain or self-important. Our children should enjoy their Three Lifepath, embrace it but not flaunt it, abuse it, or take it for granted, emitting an attitude of entitlement and arrogance.

The admonition here is that the Three Lifepath, being one primarily of self-expression and personal integration, should be used positively to promote one's spiritual integration. Negative expression, or a saturation of material and excessive self-expression, will do nothing meaningful for the child.

At its zenith, the Three Lifepath directly addresses an integrated connection with all that is divine, spiritual, ethereal and eternal. This is the higher ground for this vibration and the wise person will follow its road. . . uphill.

Yet, if used inappropriately the Three energy will force the individual downhill, often in an uncontrolled spiral of self-destruction, self-mutilation, self-degradation, disease, dis-ease, partying, drug and sexual abuse. The number Three rules pleasure as well as its flip side, disease. Too much material pleasure such as alcohol consumption, recreational drug use, sexual indulgence and culinary intemperance will create an imbalance leading to sickness, disease and loss of personal well-being and happiness.

Another major caution of the Three misuse is ego-saturation and entitlement, as touched upon already. While the number One rules identity, the number Three rules image, and an image carried to the extreme point of excessive vanity creates a maelstrom of problems. A study of the lives of those individuals whose egos are commonly viewed as quite large, who carry a sense of entitlement, and who are infatuated with themselves will verify this fact.

Because Three rules words and communication, the Three Lifepath may well give its owner experiences reflecting both positive and negative words and communication such as expressions of love and hate, support and interference, harmony and anger. Expect both with this Lifepath but keep balanced throughout the journey. Keep in mind, too, that Three rules health and disease, so it's best to focus on the health issues and avoid the excesses that create not only physical disease but mental and emotional dis-ease.

The number Three also rules children, so the Three Lifepath may well bring issues of children into focus for our children at some point in their lives. Depending on other aspects in the numerology chart, these may be good or bad. Positive aspects would be the support, encouragement and honoring of children and their well-being. Negative aspects would be child neglect and abuse including but not limited to emotional abuse, sexual abuse and physical abuse.

Ultimately, the highest goal of the Three Lifepath is to express the love and beauty of life. In keeping with this, we should teach our children to have gratitude for all things while remaining humble for the gifts and advantages they received in their lives. In many ways, this journey through the Three territory offers a rest for the soul and mind. It is a journey, however, that must not be abused, taken for granted, nor disrespected lest it be taken away.

- <u>Parenting Wisdom for the Three Lifepath:</u> The heart of the Three energy focuses on self-expression, image, art, joy, children, happiness, health, words, communication, sickness, disease, and the triune nature of life – body, mind, spirit; father, mother, child; teacher, student, subject; master, disciple, Word. If the Three is not void in the person's birth name (if there is a C, L or U in the name then there is no void), the Three Lifepath journey will be, generally speaking, the most joy-filled, happy, self-expressive and pleasurable of all the nine Lifepaths. Children under this energy will be benefited by parents who teach them the value of words, art, images, communication and expressing themselves in music, song, plays, paintings, modeling and theater. The caution with the Three energy is in vanity, thinking too much of oneself to the detriment of others. As the child grows, beware of excessive partying and untoward sexual activity. The Three rules pleasure, and if there is any number which has led people down the wrong path more than any other number, it is the Three. Partying, sex, alcohol and drugs are an aspect of a life that can get out of control. The opposite side of pleasure is pain. This must never be forgotten. We reap what we sow, and if we sow an over-abundance of pleasure, the reaping will be an over-abundance of pain. Keeping things in perspective is important for the Three Lifepath. Another issue to curb is the potential of self-entitlement.

Sometimes life can be so easy for someone walking the Three Lifepath that they take things for granted and in the process acquire a cloak of entitlement and superiority. Parental wisdom teaches children to be wonderfully expressive but wise enough to remain healthy and not let one's excesses turn to ill-health, sickness and disease. Be happy and make others happy too. This is a good message for the parent with a child following the Three Lifepath.

- Famous People with a Three Lifepath: *Cameron Diaz, Danica Patrick, John Wayne, Peter Jennings, Phil Mickelson*

The Four (4) Lifepath

The Four Lifepath addresses everything related to structure – physical structure, spiritual structure, emotional structure, mental structure, marital structure, material structure, employment structure, social structure, creative structure, financial structure, ethical structure and foundational structure. Obviously, the key word for the Four is *structure* and a lifescript maintaining this energy field will deal in the arena of *form* and *foundation*.

A Four Lifepath will be one of constancy and little change. Four is strong but it does not like to move, be adventurous or generally explore new things. Four likes to stay right where it is. It loves roots and avoids being uprooted in any way – physically, mentally, spiritually, socially, emotionally, financially, etc. Four loves to be secure because it is the vibration of security and stability.

Because the Four energy plants itself in one place, a person under this vibration would do well in situations and environments where there is little change and, in fact, the life under this vibration will not be filled with much change at all unless there is a dominant amount of Five energy elsewhere in the chart. The person may change and be changeable; his or her nature may be changeable, but the Four Lifepath calls for a grounding, a sense of stability, a rootedness in life or lessons involving stability and rootedness where there exists a fair amount of transformation or a changing and metamorphosis of form.

Because the Lifepath is the structure dealing with life lessons, the person living the Four Lifepath will be forced, voluntarily or involuntarily, to learn the importance of structure in life, relationships, activities and projects. There will be work under this vibration, constant and enduring effort. One will be placed in situations where issues broached will relate to order, rules, regimes, laws, discipline, duty, devotion, fidelity, constancy, loyalty, effort, reliability, service and security.

Because Four is symbolically represented by the square, one may find himself either confined within the walls of the square, as if imprisoned, or standing on top of the square, free from the confining limitations of the square but, nonetheless, rooted, grounded, magnetized, stuck, even chained to it.

The positive thing about the Four is that it is solid. The negative thing about the Four is that it is solid, sometimes too solid for its own good. In effect, its asset is its liability. Life changes, and if one is to be successful in life, one must be willing or able to change with the times, tides or events of life's ever changing currents. If one cannot change, or if one doesn't want to move when he or she should move, or refuses to move, one may come to severe harm, even die for being too solid, i.e., too stubborn for one's own good. It is good to be strong. It is good to be faithful. It is good to be secure. It is good to be disciplined. It is good to be controlled. But it is not good to be anchored to the ground when a hundred foot tidal wave is rapidly approaching and one refuses to move in stubborn defiance of the laws of Nature and in celebration of man's strength and courage. Such stubbornness is not strength; nor is it courage. It is glaring and lethal stupidity. Discretion is the better part of valor, and if there is a fault to the wonderful stability of the Four, it is that it does not recognize when it should move, change and alter the conditions of its form. Even snakes shed their skin. So must we all if we're to grow and evolve. This is a powerful message that children with a Four Lifepath should be taught – be strong but be flexible.

The positive aspect of the Four Lifepath has solid, spiritual import. Spiritual success is founded upon purity of the spirit. Purity of the spirit cannot be achieved unless one exercises discipline, sacrifice, restraint and control over the internal and external forces of the world which are constantly urging and importuning the individual to be undisciplined, unrestrained, uncontrolled, unfaithful, if not down right wanton and dissolute. Thus, it is good to be rooted in the onslaught of such negativity, otherwise one might well be destabilized, moved off course, and, thereby, denied the opportunity of achieving spiritual success. It is strength, courage, determination, sacrifice and an absolute conviction and set of actions, behaviors and conducts which support a spiritual focus.

Squares have sharp corners and defined edges. While this can be an advantage in some circumstances, having sharp edges in a social instance can be damaging to all parties. Because Fours can be stubborn and resistant, it's advisable to, when appropriate, soften the corners and edges of the square, being more forgiving, less stubborn, less dogmatic, less opinionated. Therefore, the admonition of the Four is: "Be strong but have a soft and tender heart, and round edges."

The lesson of the Four Lifepath is to learn to be constant, faithful, devoted, strong, courageous, determined, unrelenting, hard-working, service-oriented and secure. Be the rock. Be solid and enduring, but. . . have enough sense to move and comprise when it is appropriate and ensure the edges of the square are soft and harmless when they need to be.

- <u>Parenting Wisdom for the Four Lifepath:</u> Teach your children the value of order, work, service, constancy, convention, tradition, honesty, reliability, practicality, functionality, ethics, being strong, faithful, helpful, devoted. The Four Lifepath is about being the rock. Under its energy people will work and be put to task. There is the possibility of financial security if the laws of service, loyalty, devotion and honesty are followed, especially if one of the roots is the master number Twenty-Two, referred to in numerology as the *master builder*. Therefore, teach your children to construct, build, develop, design, organize. Discipline and self-control are also an aspect of the Four energy. Pressing on, being unrelenting and never giving up are vital to the Four. Strength is the ability to endure to the end. Sometimes we have to toil to succeed, dig in and hold our ground. One of the main challenges for parents to consider with children who have a Four Lifepath is that although it can create great strength, it must learn to be malleable enough to bend when appropriate. Sometimes the Four can be so stubborn and recalcitrant that it refuses to move, change and adapt when it should in order to secure its survival. Thus, children under the Four Lifepath must learn to transform their lives when needed and not be detrimentally anchored to a sinking ship. All in all, the Four Lifepath is one of strength, security, service and work. Whatever helps children learn these principles will be of great assistance to them in their lives.

- Famous People with a Four Lifepath: *Arnold Schwarzenegger, Babe Ruth, Bill Gates, Dolly Parton, Frank Sinatra, Oprah Winfrey*

The Five (5) Lifepath

The Five Lifepath is the most fluid of the nine basic life scripts. Under this vibration, there is constant motion, movement, change, exploration, shifting, variety, diversity, detachment, freedom and an underlying feeling of uncertainty because of the Five's ceaseless, unrelenting motion. Whereas the Four Lifepath is one of roots and stability, the Five Lifepath is almost devoid of roots unless they are in the wind. The Five Lifepath will definitely bring change to the person's life, and such change will be intensified if it is corroborated by other Five energy in the chart. Do not think of big, stable, secure rocks with this vibration. This is the energy of a fire wind, the constant ever-changing tidal action of the sea, and the amorphous form of mercury on the move.

The Five Lifepath gives the freedom of movement so longed for by the one rooted and bound by the walls of the Four and who longs for a less restricted life. However, too much change, too much movement, too much variety, too much freedom can be a prison in itself, an ever-changing hurricane where one longs for some anchoring, some stillness and security in the dynamic motion of the wind. As the English Romantic poet, Richard Lovelace, wrote in his poem *To Althea, From Prison*: "Stone walls do not a prison make, nor iron bars a cage. . ." Certainly, every Lifepath has its freedoms as well as its prisons, and the walls and bars of the prison come in many forms, sizes, shapes and intensities.

One of the challenges of the Five Lifepath is managing the coming and going of events, people, projects, activities, fortunes and relationships, for all of these have a habit of changing regularly and often. This creates a sense of uncertainty because nothing ever seems to stick, to stay in place, to remain still. But it's not supposed to. The great lesson of the Five Lifepath is freedom, but not in the way we normally think of freedom. All of the movement, change and motion of the Five Lifepath is designed to detach us from that which anchors us down and paralyzes us.

Normally, we think of freedom as the ability to do whatever we want, whenever we want. But this definition is restricted because true freedom demands great discipline, great control, great restraint and great regulation. The Five Lifepath gives us a certain level of unrestricted movement, action, fun, friends, a variety of opportunities and enjoyable experiences to see if we can truly learn the lesson of what freedom really is.

We can think of this freedom issue in another way. If one wishes to be a concert pianist, one does not simply sit down at the keyboard and play staggeringly beautiful and exquisite music. Such great piano talent, such total freedom, comes at the expense of almost ruthless incarceration within the walls of discipline, practice, determination, restriction, constriction and long-suffering. There is a price to pay for real freedom, and that price is not freedom, it is slavery, slavery to that regimentation, restraint, discipline, control and toil that sets us free. Any great artist can testify to the horrendously long and tedious hours of practice and patience where there was no freedom of escape from the torment and/or love of creating the skill necessary to be free. A great musician can generate great music with effortless effort in a rich tapestry of complete freedom, but such freedom was the child of adherence to rules and regulations, not their absence. Thus, the great lesson of the Five Lifepath is – true freedom is the child of slavery. It is such a beautiful paradox – that which gives us freedom is anchored in discipline.

The vibration of the Five Lifepath often places us squarely in the middle of the Valley of the Senses. This is critical for parents to understand. The mistake of the Five Lifepath is to think that this is a time, place and opportunity for saturating one's experience in sensual pursuit. Nothing could be further from the truth. The Five Lifepath is the time for our children to learn that resistance to overt sensual experience is liberating, that indulgence in such experience, which is what is most commonly perceived, does not lead to freedom but material and carnal bondage. It is in this Five Lifepath that the individual is often placed in the Valley of the Senses and given a choice to see if he or she can truly learn freedom or be captivated and imprisoned by a false concept of it.

Thus, not only is great strength required of those who walk the Five Lifepath and who would be free, but they must also maintain a strong sense of discernment and discretion. Within this Five life script, situations will be placed before the individual in which tough choices will have to be made regarding one's health and progress. Restriction or indulgence will be the fabric of these choices, and whatever the choices made, there will be consequences because freedom is not action devoid of consequence. Real freedom is action taken in awareness, acceptance and consideration of consequence.

For example, under the energy veil of the Five Lifepath, our children may think they can do whatever they like and that freedom has no boundaries, no limitations, no restrictions, no consequences. And because Five rules the senses and diverse experiences, if children adopt this non-consequential philosophy they may become too involved in the indulgences of drugs, sex, gambling and other activities which ultimately enslave them, leading them into a valley of despair, rather than onto the avenue of freedom and liberation. It's always a double-edged sword with the Five Lifepath, just like every other Lifepath.

Within the framework of the Five Lifepath, one will come in contact with a large number and variety of people. Thus, one's experiences will be enlarged and expanded. As Five is the numerical vibration which rules the senses, it is also the *Number of Man*. Therefore, Five can be translated into the single word, *people*, and under the Five veil there will come and go many people, many relationships, many experiences. A person with a Five life script will find his or her life's vocations (plural on purpose) concentrated in those jobs and areas of employment which cater to and deal with many people.

Another aspect of the Five Lifepath is the variety of talents the person will possess. Five rules variety, and the Five's mercurial energy will grant opportunities to use many talents in many ways. Remember, in all ways Five moves. It does not remain concentrated or fixed to one thing or activity. This can be exciting and stimulating and, certainly, the Five Lifepath is never boring. Fast cars, boats, planes, horses, dancing, martial arts – anything pertaining to motion and movement come under the umbrella of the Five vibration.

Buddha said that attachment is the root of all suffering because when we're attached to something or someone and we lose it or them, we suffer. The Five energy is designed to detach us from the shackles of this world and make us free by giving us so much change that we learn not to cling to things, people, events, conditions, pets, interests, etc. True freedom equates to total detachment, never attachment unless it is to God. Of all the nine major Lifepaths, it is the Five Lifepath which teaches us this lesson of detachment leading to true, spiritual freedom. Furthermore, this freedom is not based in a theory of "license carte blanche" but in discipline and control.

The bottom line for parents with children who have a Five Lifepath is to teach them to enjoy their talents and the diversity of their lives but to also instruct them as to the critical virtues of discipline and self-control so their lives do not get away from them but remain under their self-regulated jurisdiction. Freedom is not free. It comes at a price. Furthermore, the opposite side of freedom is slavery. Wise parenting will embrace this truth.

- Parenting Wisdom for the Five Lifepath: The best thing a parent can teach children with a Five Lifepath is that the only true constant is change, for their lives will constantly change, bringing them assorted adventures, multiple talents, diverse skills, detachments, losses and a life that will never be boring. To teach a Five Lifepath child that his life will be like that of the Four Lifepath child is to do potentially great harm because the Five moves, changes, detaches. It loves adventure, speed, doing new and exciting things. The number Five is not traditional like the Four but non-traditional, even unconventional. The Five Lifepath is about freedom, change, detachment and experience more than anything else. Fives don't care about what is practical. They care about what is adventurous and fun, even risky. Regardless of who they are as noted by their Expression, their Five Lifepath will not bring them rootedness but change. Therefore, they must be taught to adapt, adjust and develop a moving sense of balance rather than a rooted sense of balance. Because Five rules change, it can bring detachments in the form of short term or broken relationships of all kinds. Remember, Five rules diversity and variety. If your children under the Five Lifepath energy seek to do many things, let them, within wise limits. That's what their life is forcing them to do – not to be still but to move. A critical parenting wisdom note, however, is that children must be taught that seeking too much freedom, adventure and experience of the senses can cause enslavement. Cause and consequence, self-control, discipline and temperance are concepts that must be taught and learned if children under this vibration are to have balanced lives. On another note, change can be a good thing, allowing us to let go of concepts, principles and relationships that no longer serve our highest and best good. Therefore, the Five Lifepath is a path of liberation and freedom. It just must be lived wisely and within the proper boundaries of control, and if there is any vibration that needs to control itself, it is the Five. Yes, it can be fun and free, but it must also be disciplined and controlled lest its energies run a way with the individual, causing a wreck or leading the person to become a wreck. The admonition of the parent to the Five Lifepath child is have fun, enjoy your freedom but be wise lest you become enslaved by the very freedom you seek.

- Famous People with a Five Lifepath: *Abraham Lincoln, Angelina Jolie, Charles Darwin, Helen Keller, Jack LaLanne, J.K. Rowling, Michael Phelps, Peyton Manning, Thomas Jefferson, United States of America* (not a person but an entity), *Walter Cronkite*

The Six (6) Lifepath

Heart. Hearth. Home. Personal love. Artistic expression. Devotion. Domesticity. Community. Beauty. Adjustments. Responsibility. Nurturing. Attentiveness. These are characteristics of the Six Lifepath, and a child transiting this Lifepath will be involved in all that involves *ticker*, the beating of the heart as it relates to people, home, community, nation.

Six, a higher octave of the Two, is potentially the warmest and most personally loving of all the basic numbers. Positively expressed, it reflects that which is artistic, soft, sweet, tender, gentle, kind, caring, tolerant, patient, nurturing, supportive, beautiful, warm and harmonizing. The Six demonstrates these qualities primarily in the home and community environments. Individuals with this Six Lifepath will, no doubt, be heavily engaged in caring for others [people, homes, animals], parenting and parenthood, and the bulk of the life lessons will center in and around the family and domestic environment.

A child with a Six Lifepath will be learning about the Six energy. This is a critical point regarding the Lifepath vibration because the Lifepath focuses on learning and being involved with its vibration. It doesn't mean the person himself naturally exudes the number characteristics identifying the Lifepath. "Exuded qualities" would be found in the individual's name at birth, the Expression. Qualities of the Lifepath vibration are *learned qualities*, not *exuded qualities*. Therefore, having a Six Lifepath doesn't necessarily mean a person will express the qualities of the Six on a personal level, although Lifepath energies may cause one to acquire and manifest their essence in some way.

As we recall, the Lifepath is the script of someone's life. It is not the actor [the person] living life from the core of his being. It is rather life being lived, i.e., acted out, through a script, i.e., the Lifepath. As we look upon the Lifepath as the "hand" we were dealt at birth which must be played out, or as the curriculum of our life which must be studied, we realize that 'studied' or 'learned' qualities, although possibly being incipient in the life because of the Lifepath energy, may not necessarily be inherent in the person. This is an important distinction when analyzing a child's life.

In the Six Lifepath one will generally learn to make others happy, do for them, support them, love and nurture them. In its highest expression, the Six Lifepath is about unconditional personal love. On the other hand, it can reflect a life of personal, selfish gain and irresponsibility. Because it can be loving, the caution is for the individual not to sacrifice him or her self beyond what is individually healthy; not to become so nurturing that he or she becomes a doormat allowing people to walk over him or her.

This Six Lifepath vibration often involves music – the giving of love through melodious sound. Many musicians and singers have the number Six dominant in their charts. Beauty and art can also come under this cipher, especially the type of beauty that is loving and harmonious, sweetly flowing and warmly pleasing.

Because Six rules the domestic environment, occupations involving the home and community come into focus. Nurses, teachers, doctors, interior decorators, architects, veterinarians, politicians, landscapers, gardeners, homecare practitioners, childcare specialists, insurance agents and community organizers are some of the careers contained within the Six environment.

Sex is also a major function of the Six vibration because it is the sharing of personal physical love. Unfortunately, this love is often degraded into less than the true, caring, physical, emotional and psychological interaction that it represents in its highest expression and becomes lust instead. Sex may be an expression of physical love, but sex is not love and love is not sex, nor is the phrase "making love" a true manifestation of love in its highest form. When love is equated to sex, the sanctity of love is lost.

The polar opposite of love is hate. Thus, with the Six Lifepath it would not be unusual for a person to experience hate, anger, jealousy, envy and bitterness at some point during the life. Individuals manifesting a spiritual outlook in life will be loving, kind, patient, attentive, considerate, tolerant, sweet and harmonious. However, those with less than a spiritual outlook run the risk of fulfilling love's negative side.

This is why it is critical to have a spiritual outlook in life and, furthermore, a life which manifests spirituality in action and deed, not merely in words. Where hate is present, discord, disease, destruction and death prevail. One cannot be high-minded and lead a low life. One simply cannot live in the fire of hell and feel the soothing, sweet ambrosial waters of heaven. Until we teach our children to live in a spiritually positive manner, they will continue to suffer from and experience the negative energies of the Six.

Given the sacred subject of love, a person with a Six Lifepath has much important work to do in focusing upon and manifesting love, true love. Six can be a wonderfully warm, nurturing and spiritual vibration, but its manifestation requires purity of thought, purity of motive, purity of action, purity of commitment, purity of duty, purity of devotion, purity of promise. As Saint Dadu Dayal, a 16th Century mystic stated: "Hold pure, stay pure, say pure, take the pure, give the pure."

It's impossible to miss the operative word in Dadu's statement. When thought, motive and action are muddied and adulterated, love is not pure and loses its sweet nurturing essence, potentially turning vile with discord and hate. Therefore, it's critical for parents to teach their children to be purely focused with the Six Lifepath. No vibration is sweeter or more loving than the Six when given the care and concern it deserves and demands.

- <u>Parenting Wisdom for the Six Lifepath:</u> Teach your children to love purely, without expectation. Love only gives. It asks nothing in return. To care for others, nurture them, be attentive to them, help them, be kind to them, be devoted to them, to be compassionate toward them and give warmth to their lives is the mission of the Six. Be sure as the children grow they understand the difference between pure love and lust and to be careful of equating sex to love. Love transcends sex. Sex is not love; love is not sex. Love exists beyond the realm of form and mind. Love is a pure vibration of compassion and care. It is not a commodity housing a return on investment. Love is its own reward. Beauty and harmony are an aspect of love. Let these shine through in all forms of art. Caution children to be careful of too much partying and enjoying the material pleasures of life because uncontrolled pleasures can lead one down a very dark and troublesome road. The Thirty-Three master root of the Six can lift one to great artistic heights, but it is, arguably, the master number causing more heartache and heartbreak than any other number. The Thirty-Three is nuclear pleasure. It has destroyed many lives because of its unchecked pleasure-seeking quality (33 is 11 x 3). There is great power in the Thirty-Three, so be wise if this number occupies the Lifepath.

- Famous People with a Six Lifepath: *Albert Einstein, Howard Hughes, Jackie Evancho, Michael Jackson, Sam Walton, Sarah Palin, Sylvester Stallone, Warren Buffett*

The Seven (7) Lifepath

The Seven Lifepath is the most internal of all the nine Lifepaths, and in many ways it is the most critical of all. The inward-dwelling energy of the Seven will take the child on a life journey of examination, analysis, research, investigation, study, and any activity that involves the mind and its thought processes. Professions and activities which can involve the Seven Lifepath are: science, education, engineering, medicine, acting, accounting, research, writing, religion, metaphysics, spirituality – all activities involving the *internal* aspect of life. However, regardless of an individual's profession, the Seven Lifepath will draw the individual inward, not outward.

In social gatherings, when others are mixing and interacting, it is the Seven which stands or sits off to the side – alone, quiet, pensive, seemingly distant and cool. Seven is not a social mixer. It is an internal dweller. It thinks, reflects, cogitates, meditates, muses, observes, questions and analyzes. For externally focused souls, it may be "hip and happening" to be socially gregarious, but for the indwelling Seven, it's all happening on the *inside*, and socializing is as dull and boring to it as the inner existence is to those seeking social interaction. Individuals with a Seven Lifepath can therefore expect to be placed in settings and environments where they are isolated and separated, giving them an opportunity for reflection and self-examination.

Although Seven can bring great peace and tranquility, that peace is usually the result of great stress, trial, tribulation, isolation, sorrow, pain, suffering, anxiety, frustration and disruption. When one lives in 'heat' for extended periods, one learns to adjust to it, accept it and remain calm and unaffected by it. After all, diamonds are made under extreme heat and pressure over an extended period of time, not by a mere and casual blowing of an intermittent wind. If we or our children are to be diamonds, we and they will have to be baked in the furnace of the world. This is not a pleasant experience, but the result is that we all become diamonds in the process, a price worth paying for becoming a substantive soul. In the words of the Lebanese-American artist, poet and writer Khalil Gibran, "Out of suffering have emerged the strongest souls; the most massive characters are seared with scars."

The metaphor of the hurricane is a perfect depiction of the Seven Lifepath – destructive outer winds circling a perfectly calm center. Its message: when we experience the tumultuous winds of life, the key is to use their force to force us inward to the center, to the eye of the storm, the center of our purest being where all is calm, centered, peaceful and still.

The poignant suggestion for those on the Seven Lifepath is, Go Within. Don't fight the battle on the outside. The battle must be fought on the Inside. This is what the Seven is forcing us to do. We must not mask or cover our frustration, pain or sorrow with intoxicant stimulants and negative acts which poison our mind and spirit and inhibit us from feeling the very heat, fire and pressure which exist to cleanse and purify our mind and spirit. The Seven Lifepath is the door to great mystical and spiritual illumination. Utilized properly, it will lift us to the zenith of our greatest and noblest good.

Because the Seven is internal by nature, a child with this life script may find himself during parts of his life feeling separate, alone, isolated or private. There is the potential of some degree of tribulation with this energy. Divorce is not uncommon, nor are alcoholism, personal betrayals, even adulteries. This is why it is critical the child learn to be centered and whole early on in life, to learn to manage personal challenges with aplomb, a positive mindset, pure behavior, ethical conduct, nobility, courage and most of all, a spiritual outlook. Without a spiritual foundation, the Seven Lifepath can be daunting. With a spiritual foundation, the Seven Lifepath will find itself right at home.

- <u>Parenting Wisdom for the Seven Lifepath:</u> The way out is In. A child with the Seven Lifepath will be well-served to learn this early on. No Lifepath is more inwardly driven than the Seven Lifepath. It houses experiences of the mind and spirit. It is a thinker's and mystic's Lifepath, not a socialite's Lifepath. The Seven is the most powerfully sacred and spiritual number of the Alpha-Numeric Spectrum. It holds great promise for great internal achievement. However, parents must be aware that the greatest accomplishments in life demand the highest price, and their children will be tested during their Seven Lifepath experiences, as we all are. One way to explain this is to compare their path in life to school. In order to pass from one grade level to another we have to be tested. The same is true of life. In order to elevate to a higher height in consciousness, thinking and behavior, one must be tested and pass the tests to graduate to the next level. And please know there will be testing of one's character, ethics, morals, honesty, devotion, fidelity, trust and wisdom in the Seven Lifepath. There is no way around this. Therefore, parenting wisdom mandates children with a Seven Lifepath be taught that their lives are very special because they are being given an opportunity to acquire secrets of life available to very few souls because their Seven Lifepath is the journey of the inwardly-directed consciousness and mind. They very well may, at some point(s) in their lives, find themselves in isolation or separation from life's normal social environments in order to allow them to think, ponder, reflect, cogitate and examine life's purpose and meaning. Being true to that knowledge and personal conduct which is pure, ethical, honest, moral and upstanding will be their shield against the possibility of experiencing a fall from grace and living a life of ignominy. The Seven Lifepath has the ability to take one to great noble and spiritual heights, but it also has the ability to force one into a deep, dark and unforgiving abyss. When we are not honest, ethical, moral, pure or upstanding in our personal conduct or dealings with others, we fall, and sometimes we fall from a very high place. This is a simple fact of life. By not helping our children understand this, we do not serve their highest and best good. As parents, we need to guide them properly, and keeping the truth of life from them is not serving them well. Knowledge is power, and ignorance of knowledge that is powerful can lead to powerfully negative results. Ignorance of the law is no excuse before the law. Children following a Seven Lifepath have been blessed with a great opportunity, a chance to elevate their minds, consciousness and souls to the next level, but if they're not aware of this opportunity it may go to waste, and painfully so. Therefore, as parents, let us help our children grow and succeed as they embark on the great inward journey of the Seven Lifepath's spiritual lessons and ultimate ascent.

- Famous People with a Seven Lifepath: *Dr. Phil McGraw, George Foreman, Jackie Robinson, John Fitzgerald Kennedy, Marilyn Monroe, Muhammad Ali, Patrick Swayze, Princess Diana, Queen Elizabeth II, William Shakespeare, Winston Churchill*

The Eight (8) Lifepath

The Eight Lifepath is the script of social involvement, status, marketing, management, generalship, interaction, administration, execution, connection, disconnection, circulation, orchestration, coordination, commerce and all that is involved in the principle of *flow*, be it smooth or rough, graceful or clumsy, swift or slow. Eight connects polarities: positive to negative; male to female; buyer to seller; management to labor; concept to completion; product to consumer; past to present. Traditionally, the Eight has been regarded as a money number. But in reality it is not. Money, ruled by the number Two, is the substance of the flow of commerce, but it is not the flow itself. Eight is the flow. It is the path or tube through which the money flows.

The Eight Lifepath is about interactive efficiency. The energies of this life script will manifest many circumstances, conditions, events, problems and people into the life of the person in order to teach him or her what works and does not work in making life successful, not just in business or commerce, but in social, domestic, personal and professional arenas.

The Eight cipher is unique. When turned on its side it becomes the ancient lemniscate representing infinity, beautifully symbolizing the flow of energy between polarities. This image of the Eight laying on its side is called the Lemniscate Eight Loop.

As Seven is the most intrinsic of vibrations, Eight is the most extrinsic, the highest octave of the external social quatrain of the vibrations

2-4-6-8. Eight likes to mix, manage, mingle, manipulate, orchestrate, organize, interact, involve and connect. It is not generally a deep, mystical, reflective, thoughtful number. It is, however, a powerfully social and commercially connective number. What Seven is to the inner worlds, Eight is to the outer worlds, for it flows and connects and/or disconnects people, energies, ideas and things of one polarity to other people, energies, ideas and things of the opposite polarity.

Eight and Seven are opposites. Eight, an even number, loves to mix, seek the outer world of material success, wealth, riches, property, titles and all the accouterments and status money can bring. Eight generally cares little about the inner worlds, inner realities and activities requiring introspection, aspects we have learned are vital to the Seven.

Children who carry Eight as a life lesson, therefore, will be compelled to focus their attention generally on external, social, worldly, material matters. But not always. There are exceptions to every rule. As every number has a positive and negative polarity, so does it have a spiritual and material aspect as well. Eight can be a very spiritual number, seeking to make a connection between God and man, the inner worlds and outer worlds. But, generally, Eight can be thought of as worldly.

Individuals compelled to operate under the Eight Lifepath vibration can make very good executives, managers, leaders and administrators because the specific function of these positions demands a coordination of all parts of the whole. From top to bottom, low rung to high rung, basement to penthouse, janitor to president, the leader, manager or executive is the one who insures that all is flowing efficiently, smoothly, properly and, hopefully, fairly, humanely and lovingly to assure that the whole organization or institution is successful. And let it be said that the most successful of these individuals will be the ones who see themselves as servants – not bosses, big shots or rulers. The Great Eight works with others to achieve an efficient and harmonious flow within the structure of the organization it serves. And that is the operative word – *serve,* for the Great Eight serves, not subjugates.

High-level athletes and performers often carry the Eight cipher in the Lifepath. Athletes must be coordinated, and it is the Eight energy that creates a condition of coordination. Having the ability to get the ball in the hoop, the pass to the receiver, the puck in the net, the kick to the target, the parry to the punch, the car to the finish line, the skis over the moguls, the feeling of the song or the meaning of the message to the audience and so forth is all a matter of coordination, orchestration, interaction and connection – a function of Eight energy.

Eight seeks success or that which is traditionally regarded as success – money, social power, recognition, wealth, fame, authority, status, possessions. The non-traditional Eight seeks success in terms of a connection with a higher power. Regardless of the focus, they both want to make that connection which integrates the flow of an idea, impulse or desire with its manifestation, yielding that state of being or accomplishment we regard as success.

Although Eight integrates, administrates and coordinates, it can also manipulate. Eight governs flow. It doesn't govern purity, ethics or morality. It simply moves between polarities, creating connections or disconnections in the process. As money moves through all types of hands, so does the Eight energy move through and between all types of people with all types of motives and intentions. It is only when operating within the sphere of a spiritually elevated consciousness that we can trust the Eight's goodness, sincerity, purpose and truthfulness.

As the actor or actress plays out the Eight Lifepath script, the life lessons will revolve in, through and around the Eight loop – the connective path between polarities. It may be a smooth path, a bumpy path, an intermittent path, but it will be a path of interaction to some degree.

- <u>Parenting Wisdom for the Eight Lifepath:</u> The key here is to teach children the importance of understanding the interrelationship of how things work from start to finish, beginning to end, concept to completion regardless of the system, device, network or paradigm. The key word for the Eight is *flow*. When all parts of the whole are connected and integrated, things run smoothly. When they are not connected or integrated well, things don't run smoothly. A child with an Eight Lifepath will need to learn to be an integrator, a manager, planner, executor, administrator, marketer, orchestrator, coordinator. The Eight is not an internal number, so it would be unwise for a parent with strong Seven energy in his or her chart to directly or indirectly try to sculpt their Eight child into the ways of the Seven. The same is true in reverse. For a parent with strong Eight energy, it would be unwise to raise a Seven dominated child in the ways of the Eight. Such methods would be counterproductive and potentially harmful. This is exactly why parents need to know their children's numbers. Another thing of note relating to Eight Lifepath children is that they will be learning the lessons of social interaction. If their Expression is a Seven, they will have a natural tug-o-war going on between their life's lessons of externality and their intrinsic nature of internality. They will need to learn to balance these opposites so they do not feel conflicted, which often happens when the Lifepath number is in opposition to a personal number such as the Expression, Soul or Nature energies. The bottom line of the Eight Lifepath is that it will involve the child in lessons, circumstances, events and activities related to social involvement, orchestration, coordination, business, commerce, management, interaction or execution on some level.

- Famous People with an Eight Lifepath: *Anna Nicole Smith, Bob Dylan, Edgar Cayce, Edna St. Vincent Millay, Elizabeth Taylor, General Douglas MacArthur, General George Patton, Marion Jones, Martha Stewart, Naomi Campbell, Rudyard Kipling, Tom Brady, Tommy Lee Jones*

The Nine (9) Lifepath

Nine is the Lifepath of the macrocosm, the big picture, the universal stage. In contrast to the personal, loving vibration of the Six, the Nine represents impersonal love. It is compassion, caring, concern, involvement and service in the arena of the 'many', the masses, the public.

Nine often finds itself as the humanitarian, philanthropist, philosopher, teacher, educator, doctor, nurse, singer, actor, writer, performer, volunteer, newscaster. Its universality makes it charismatic, magnetic and attractive but it is not as personally warm and loving as the Six. Nine is public, not personal.

All of the basic numbers are encased within the Nine, including the Nine itself. If all the single digits One through Nine are added together, the reduced result is Nine! Because of this aspect, Nine is referred to as the *Grand Elemental*.

$$1 + 2 + 3 + 4 + 5 + 6 + 7 + 8 + 9 = 45: 4 + 5 = \mathbf{9}$$

Therefore, Nine is all-inclusive and complete. It instinctively understands all vibrations, all people. This is why it is popular and charismatic – everyone can identify with it. It is also why Nine 'rules' and is the cipher of sovereignty.

Nine is magical. If it is added to any single digit, that particular digit is duplicated upon reduction. For example:

$$5 + 9 = 14: \ 1 + 4 = \mathbf{5}$$
$$8 + 9 = 17: \ 1 + 7 = \mathbf{8}$$

Thus, Nine is chameleon-like. It blends with all numbers, all energies, without altering their basic vibration. Therefore, it might be said that Nine is non-judgmental, open-minded and fair.

Because of its chameleon aspect, the Nine faces challenges the other numbers don't. Individuals possessing a Nine Lifepath will be placed in situations where their life will blend with all people. This becomes problematic because the Nine can blend with forces of light or forces of darkness. A person can become absorbed into societies, movements, organizations, groups or cultures that are constructive or destructive; benefic or malefic. Hence, the caution flag must be raised with the Nine.

Because of its universal appeal, Nine often brings fame and fortune. Fame is nothing more than mass recognition, and since everyone can identify with the Nine, it becomes universally known, i.e., famous. In spite of how popular the individual with the Nine Lifepath may or may not be, it is certain that he or she will be involved with the public and the mass of humanity in some way. An individual may even be cast into the limelight. What happens when he gets there is another issue.

As the highest octave of the Three, Nine is extremely artistic, communicative, expressive. With its indigenous universal energy, it therefore often finds its way to the stage, podium, lens, movie camera, courtroom, classroom, hospital, magazine cover or care center. The Nine Lifepath, because of its universal compassion, may compel one to seek the distant, foreboding environments of the jungle, desert, forest or mountains to help those in need. Nine acts, and usually with compassion unless negatively aspected. After all, in its highest octave, Nine is universal love, and the word *love* is, itself, a Nine vibration: L(3) + O(6) + V(4) + E(5) = 18: 1 + 8 = 9.

As love is universal, so is music. The Nine Lifepath often carries one into the profession of music and its performance. No one needs words to understand music because music is felt and experienced. Music is a universal language.

Nine also rules endings, conclusions, completions and terminations. Thus, one with a Nine Lifepath may find himself involved with many endings, resolutions and finalizations in his life.

The universal aspect of the Nine Lifepath renders it the perfect vehicle for travel. Individuals playing out this script of life will often find themselves traveling to other places, counties, states, regions or countries – physically or vicariously.

- Parenting Wisdom for the Nine Lifepath: The main lesson for children with the Nine Lifepath to know is that they will be involved with the 'many', the masses, the public in some capacity. Serve, perform, rule, but do so with great care, responsibility and caution. Cause and effect is forever working in this creation. Great actions bear great reactions, and when a person is spotlighted on the great stage of life, the consequences can be critical to one's evolution because seeds sewn in the realm of the masses yield massive harvests. If the seeds are good, the harvest will be good. If the seeds are bad, the harvest will be bad. Take heed and act accordingly. There is no way the Nine Lifepath will be solitary or small. The Nine rules everybody and everything the world over. Travel – vicarious or real – is quite possible. Mixing with all types and kinds of people is a given. Careers involving education, politics, law, medicine, modeling, theater, music, travel, entertainment, media, art, television, radio and transportation are more than probable. The Nine Lifepath is the biggest of the nine Lifepaths. One of the critical things to teach children with this life script is because their life is big, they must be careful not to be too dominating or imperious. An over-the-top Nine can be extremely arrogant and prideful. Parenting wisdom requires teaching children of the Nine Lifepath to be kind, caring, considerate, compassionate and benevolent, avoiding the malevolent expressions of the dark side of the Nine.

- Famous People with a Nine Lifepath: *Albert Schweitzer, Charles Lindbergh, Elvis Presley, Garth Brooks, Gisele Bündchen, Heidi Klum, Henry Wadsworth Longfellow, Mohandas Gandhi, Mother Teresa, Serena Williams, Shaun White, Whitney Houston*

The Lifepath Challenge

Every Lifepath generally contains at least one built-in Challenge – an issue or concern that can be considered a cross we have to bear in life, an obstacle we have to overcome, a problem we have to solve, or circumstances requiring careful management.

The Lifepath Challenge is simply determined by subtracting the two ciphers appearing in the binary root structure of the Lifepath from one another. For example, the Lifepath of Mary Jane Smith is a 7; its binary root is 25; its Challenge is 3.

Birth date: 8 January 1960: Lifepath Binary Root is 25: 7
$8 + 1 + 1 + 9 + 6 + 0 = 25: 2 + 5 = 7$ Lifepath

When the 2 is subtracted from the 5 in the 25 binary, the result is 3, the Lifepath Challenge.

Applying the same formula of subtraction of the Lifepath binaries of John David Doey's Lifepath, we see that his LP Challenge is also a 3.

Birthdate of 14 August 1985: Lifepath Binary Root is 36: 9
$1 + 4 + 8 + 1 + 9 + 8 + 5 = 36: 3 + 6 = 9$ Lifepath

When the 3 is subtracted from the 6 of the 36 binary, the result is 3, the Lifepath Challenge.

However, even though both Mary and John have a 3 Lifepath Challenge, each 3 is derived from a different binary: Mary's from the 25 and John's from the 36. This single number 3 in the Challenge position, derived from a process of subtraction, is called the *Subcap* [the *capstone* from subtraction]. The single ciphers derived from the addition process are referred to as the *Addcap* [the *capstone* from addition]. Therefore, Mary's Lifepath houses a 7 *addcap* while John's Lifepath has a 9 *addcap*.

For both of these individuals, the 3 Challenge indicates they will each confront issues and concerns during their lives with some [but not necessarily all] of the attributes associated with the Three energy: self-expression, image, words, art, communication, joy, friends, pleasure, children, health, beauty, well-being, disease or dis-ease.

What is your child's Lifepath Challenge? What is the Lifepath Challenge of all your children? To discover the Lifepath Challenge, simply add the numbers of the Lifepath together and if there is a binary root [in most cases there will be one], subtract the ciphers to derive the single number, the Subcap, which will be the Challenge, and then cross-reference this number with the *Keywords* of each number listed in Chapter Two, *The Numbers*, to assess the meaning of the Challenge energy.

A Final Lifepath Note

A final note regarding the Lifepath: the Lifepath is not the individual, as is sometimes erroneously believed. The Lifepath is the *script* of one's life, the *energy world*, the *hand of cards*, the *theme ride*, the *road* the child will travel from birth to death, replete with lessons, events, experiences, issues, circumstances, challenges, relationships and so forth the child will face during his or her entire life. Parenting wisdom encourages parents to know each of their children's Lifepaths and help them understand the journey they will be taking. This will be an enormous gift in helping them create a personal sense of well-being, confidence, health and self-image.

Cards Of Life
© Richard Andrew King

These are the cards your life has dealt,
so these are the cards you play.
There's no use weeping over cards
that were not dealt your way.

Life is destined to the breath –
a truth we must accept
if we're to find some peace of mind
and live without regret.

We all are actors on a stage,
but the Director sets our role.
Our life performance is a script –
it's the nature of the show.

Therefore, we mustn't be distressed.
No two hands are just the same.
When all is finally said and done,
in the end, it's just a game.

So play the cards your life has dealt,
but play them straight and true,
and, remember, from the Lord's own hand
your cards were dealt for *you*!

It is a wise father that knows his own child.

~ William Shakespeare

5

The Expression

As the Lifepath can be regarded as the script or screenplay of our lives, the Expression is us, the actor or actress, who will read and 'play out' the script of the Lifepath on the great stage of life. While the Lifepath is determined from the birth date, the Expression is derived from the *full* and *complete* birth name.

The Expression is the composite self, replete with assets, liabilities, strengths, weaknesses, potentials, possibilities and talents. Within it are also contained the individual's basic needs, desires and drives, as well as the basic nature, personality and manner of doing things. In fact, the Expression also carries factors, characteristics and time periods of one's destiny, just as does the Lifepath. Together, the Lifepath and Expression comprise the two major components of a numerology chart.

The Expression, as represented by our full name at birth, is a complex tapestry of interwoven energy patterns with each individual letter and name of the full birth name forming its own distinct energy field. The separate names of the full birth name create distinct *Name Timelines* (NTL), and the separate letters of the full birth name create distinct *Letter Timelines* (LTL). The number, variation and arrangement of the Expression's individual names and letters create the uniqueness and individuality we see in ourselves and our children.

In very simple terms, the Expression represents our children as the individuals they are. As the Lifepath is non-personal, i.e., the life script, the Expression is completely personal.

- *Parenting Wisdom for the Expression*: As humans, we are all like snowflakes – generally similar but specifically different. As no two snowflakes are exactly alike, so no two children are exactly alike. Even identical twins will not be completely identical. Therefore, it's important for us parents to recognize the special uniqueness in each of our children, honor that uniqueness and teach them to honor themselves and their own lives. Too often, children do not see themselves as individually special, but they are, each and every one. By appreciating, honoring, applauding and reinforcing the original distinctiveness of each child, the child will grow into a sense of wholeness and completeness and avoid the trap of not feeling worthy. It is parental folly to compare one child against another. Pointing out positive traits and characteristics of each child allows them to see themselves in a positive light. Thus, they grow strong and beautiful with a healthy sense of confidence, self-worth and self-assuredness.

Calculating the Expression

Calculating the Expression is just as simple as calculating the Lifepath. All we're going to do is add some simple numbers together and reduce them to a single digit. First, however, we have to translate the letters of the name into numbers. Use the full and exact name at birth. Don't miss a single letter. Some people have just two names, some three or more.

The *Simple Letter Value Chart* below shows the value of each letter in the alphabet within their different letter *groups* or *genera*. For example, the letters A-J-S are contained within the numerical group representing the number 1; the letters B-K-T comprise the genera of the number 2, and so forth. For birth names in other languages simply translate them into English. To find the number associated with the name, follow the three simple steps beneath the chart. Examples follow.

Simple Letter Value Chart

Simple Letter Value Chart									
The Letters	A	B	C	D	E	F	G	H	I
	J	K	L	M	N	O	P	Q	R
	S	T	U	V	W	X	Y	Z	
Number Value	1	2	3	4	5	6	7	8	9

The Process of Calculating the Expression

1. Write the full birth name down on a piece of paper.
2. Place the number associated with each letter under it.
3. Add the numbers from left to right and reduce to a single digit.

Example #1: Mary Jane Smith

Version A. Full Name

This is the simplest method. Using the *Simple Letter Value Chart* above, add all the letters of the full name together and reduce to a single digit.

M	A	R	Y	J	A	N	E	S	M	I	T	H		
4+	1+	9+	7+	1+	1+	5+	5+	1+	4+	9+	2+	8	=	57
57: 5 + 7 = 12 which becomes 1 + 2 = 3													
The Expression of Mary Jane Smith is a 3													

Version B. Separate Names

This method allows us to see the separate value of each name. After each name is reduced, simply add the values of each name together. The final value will be the same as Version A.

M	A	R	Y			
4+	1+	9+	7	=	21: 2 + 1 = 3	Mary is a 3

J	A	N	E			
1+	1+	5+	5	=	12: 1 + 2 = 3	Jane is a 3

S	M	I	T	H		
1+	4+	9+	2+	8	24: 2 + 4 = 6	Smith is a 6

[Mary] 3 + [Jane] 3 + [Smith] 6 = 12: 1 + 2 = 3

Example #2: John David Doey

Version A. Full Name

J	O	H	N	D	A	V	I	D	D	O	E	Y		
1+	6+	8+	5+	4+	1+	4+	9+	4+	4+	6+	5+	7	=	64
64: 6 + 4 = 10: 1 + 0 = 1													
The Expression of John David Doey is a 1													

Parenting Wisdom   King

Version B. Separate Names

J	O	H	N			
1+	6+	8+	5	=	20: 2+0 = 2	John is a 2

D	A	V	I	D			
4+	1+	4+	9+	4	=	22: 2+2 = 4	David is a 4

D	O	E	Y			
4+	6+	5+	7	=	22: 2+2 = 4	Doey is a 4

[John] 2 + [David] 4 + [Doey] 4 = 10: 1 + 0 = 1

Your turn. What is the Expression of your child or children? Below is a practice grid. Place the number value of each letter below it, add the numbers together and reduce to a single digit. For more in-depth analysis, check the transition binary if there is one. For more information on single numbers, double numbers and root systems, study *The King's Book of Numerology, Volume I – Foundations & Fundamentals*.

Letters								
Numbers								

Letters								
Numbers								

Letters								
Numbers								=

The Expression of _____ is a ____

Expression Descriptions

The One (1) Expression Child

Children reflecting a One Expression will definitely be their own persons. They like to do things their own way. They like to lead, not follow. In the family they may be a dominant force. As adults in business or commerce, they will need to be out front as the boss, manager or employer. They may also be entrepreneurs and pioneers, following the beat of their own drum, exploring concepts unknown to the rest of the masses.

One Expression children have ideas and can generate them, for they are ruled by the element fire, which is always active, alive, vibrant, warming. Ones are unique, and there is great potential for them to be especially creative with their minds, talents and words.

Ones are doers, activators, initiators. They are the ones who get the ball rolling and the project underway. They do like to be out front and in the lead where all can follow them or be in the center where they are the focus of attention. One Expression children do not like to share the spotlight as a general rule.

As parents, you will discover that in One Expression children there is great emphasis on the self, themselves. This is fine if they do not allow the dominant, powerful, creative, vibrant One energy to become too self-absorbed and individually all-consuming. The highest expression of the One is union with the Divine. The lowest expression is negative egomania where one feels the entire world and universe revolve around him or her – a totally self-centered, self-consumed, self-absorbed, arrogant, imperious, egomaniacal, overbearing, unbending dictator. To keep the One humble, it must be remembered that there is only one true One – that divine power from whom all other Ones originate.

Because of their dynamic nature, there is noticeable responsibility placed on the shoulders of a One Expression child, especially if the child is also the first-born sibling. Therefore, self-responsibility and accountability are important principals for all Ones to learn and express.

One children generally have strong wills. This is important from a leadership position. As a leader, One must take a stand and lead, not bend and break or worse, descend into the flock where confusion and chaos will possibly reign if there is no leadership, if there is no one with the strength, conviction, wherewithal and basic guts to stand up and take charge.

Leadership is always a lonely, frightening, uncomfortable, solitary experience because the leader is out front for all to see, acclaim or defame. However, it's easy to criticize from the pack, especially if the burden of leadership is on someone else's shoulders. Being a leader means making tough decisions and having the courage to stick by them. Leadership is additionally difficult because it is impossible to please all the people all the time. It's a rough and tough job but society must have leaders, and this is one of the potential roles for any child who reflects the One Expression.

The strength of will of the One Expression becomes negative when the One becomes so rigid it does not bend. However, One must bend at times, just not break. Take, for example, the solitary and beautiful willow tree. It stands strong and alone but its branches bend to accommodate the wind. In other words, it gives in where it has to. This does not diminish it, for the tree sustains no damage from the wind. Its inherent structure simply allows it to bend and survive.

Another aspect of the One Expression is the self, the ego. Self is an important concept but, once again, the self has two sides: one positive, one negative. The positive self is the one 'at one' with its Source. The negative one is the one separate from its Source and acting independently without acknowledging a higher power.

This may seem enigmatic but it is not. In the realm of separate entities, as all of us are in the worldly scheme of things, we naturally possess a unique individuality. But we are nothing without a common Source uniting us all. To illustrate this, we can simply see each of us as a separate light bulb – unique, separate, individual but, nonetheless, a bulb like every other bulb which receives its brilliance from one source – the electric current. Without the current, each bulb, each of us, is lightless and lifeless. Yes, we are individuals, but we all run on the same current and derive our life energy from the same Source.

Another example is that we are all bubbles floating on the surface of the ocean. Yes, we are separate but not dis-separate from our Source, once again. Furthermore, as a bubble our life span is not very long. Thus, why get too involved with our fleeting individuality which is temporal? It is best, therefore, to identify with the one Current which gives us life, to identify with the vast Ocean of the Spirit from which we gain our true identity, our true self. It's important for a One Expression child to understand this concept as they mature.

The One Expression is a masculine energy. Does this mean that a female maintaining a One Expression is not feminine? Of course not. Quite the contrary. It simply means that she will tend to be more logical and reasonable than she might otherwise be, as logic and reason are male/yang characteristics. She will, as a One Expression, naturally possess energies of leadership, creation, initiation and action. She will be self-motivated, will take charge and get things done without being told to if she is in a support role as a secretary, assistant or helper of some kind. If she is in a prime leadership role as a manager, president or executive, she has the inherent ability to lead exceptionally well by infusing her One Expression male/yang energy with her inherent Two female/yin energy. Male One Expression leaders run the risk of being too overbearing and dominant because of their natural concentration of One energy. A female, on the other hand, can balance the male yang energy of leadership with her intrinsic female yin energy of support, caring, nurturing and compassion. She must simply avoid being too vacillating, which is a general female/yin characteristic. Leaders of any sex may change their minds, but they cannot be vacillatory nor illogical or overly emotional if they choose to be effective leaders. Leadership requires action and courage, and the best of all leadership is that which is balanced by both male and female energies.

- <u>Parenting Wisdom for the One Expression</u>: Teach One Expression children to enjoy their uniqueness, for they are unique, original and independent. No number is more solo than the One. These children should also be encouraged to enjoy their creative abilities and embrace opportunities to take action and to lead. Not everyone can act, create, generate, initiate and lead as Ones do. Yet, they should be taught not to look down on others because they (others) are not leaders or because they cannot create or take action. Leading and initiating action, taking responsibility and being accountable are primary principles of the One. A leader needs followers; followers need leaders. Neither is more important than the other. It's all part of the whole polarity scene of this creation. Caution your One children to be wary of becoming too self-centered. It is best to be divinely Self-Centered, i.e., acknowledging a divine presence as the source of all true action.

This will prevent One Expression children from falling into the trap of egocentricity.

- Famous People with a One Expression: *Dr. Phil McGraw, Heidi Klum, Helen Keller, Jackie Robinson, Philip Mickelson, Steve Jobs*

The Two (2) Expression Child

Children with a Two Expression are those who innately support, help, care for and sustain others. On the positive side of the Two, they have compassion, kindness and a gentleness of manner. Their passive nature allows them to be unobtrusive, soft, friendly, congenial, agreeable, cordial, conciliatory, cooperative and comprising. Because they are ruled by the Two, they can generally see both sides of an issue and often serve as a peacemaker, arbitrator or diplomat. Their emotional energy brings feelings to situations where pure logic and reason are found lacking. They tend to be intuitive and receptive, flowing and working with situations rather than attempting to impose their will and ego on others. Two Expression individuals are considered peacemakers of the Alpha-Numeric Spectrum.

The Two Expression is governed by the female yin energy of the universe. Therefore, children under this vibration are supporters by nature, giving those dominated by One energy a chance to lead and experience the lesson of the self. They tend to be subordinate and possibly submissive, but this does not make them less important in the least. After all, cosmic, universal structure is comprised of two distinct energies – the One and the Two, the yang and the yin. Neither is more important than the other. They both comprise the whole. Yet, they do have different qualities and characteristics – in fact, qualities and characteristics opposite and oftentimes contrapuntal, if not contentious by their very nature. Truly, what could be more contentious than fire (1) and water (2)?

The Two Expression is centered in relationships. This is why women, and men with a Two Expression or other dominant Two energy in their charts, are more in tune with relationships than men in general or women dominated by a strong One influence. Females are ruled by this number Two energy of relationships whereas males, who are ruled by the number One, live in the world of ideas, logic and action. Women live in the world of others, emotion and reaction. One is day. Two is night. Both are ends of the same continuum. Both are critical to cosmic structure. However, neither men or women are purely yang (male) or yin (female). Both sexes are a blend of One and Two energy, although One energy is generally associated with men and Two energy with women.

The Two energy is powerful in its ability to support. This is why women have often been characterized as the "power behind the throne," especially in the past. But all that is changing. Women are now moving to the forefront of society and becoming the "power on the throne" (see *The Age of the Female: A Thousand Years of Yin* at RichardKing.net).

Two Expression children will obviously harmonize with the energies of this Second Millennium. As the Two Expression is focused in the realm of *others*, so the Second Millennium will be one of *others* as well. This will not be a time glorifying the sovereignty of isolated and separate nations and people. This will be a time of interacting with others, learning to get along with others, to share our world, to be concerned about what others do in the scheme of world balance, health and equilibrium. Relationships will be important, relationships that have the potential to engender peace and harmony (the 2's positive aspects) but, hopefully, not war and conflict (the 2's negative aspects).

One of the cautions of the Two Expression rests in its quality of duality. At its spiritual zenith, Two rules balance, peace, compassion, equilibrium and harmony. However, at its negative nadir, it is a vibration of opposition, division, competition, contention, conflict, imbalance, hostility, antagonism, disunity, separation, argumentation, interference and friction. The number Two can be viewed as a tug-o-war with both sides, both polar extremes, pulling equally from opposite directions. The Two can also be viewed as a teeter-totter in constant imbalance, rising and falling in almost perpetual motion. This is why the Two is viewed as emotional – it lacks one continuous, direct, steady motion.

Thus, a Two Expression child should be taught to guard against this polarization creating imbalance, inharmony, disruption and contention. Two Expression children have the intrinsic ability to generate great peace, harmony, kindness, diplomacy and compassion, but like all vibrations the Two also has its opposite side, and the opposite of harmony is inharmony; the opposite of balance is imbalance; the opposite of peace is war.

The number One unites; the Two separates and divides. In our society today we probably have more separate and distinct factions than at any other time in world history, and the number seems to be growing. Under the Two vibration, people divide into groups and take sides. These sides oppose each other and will oppose each other until everyone learns that harmonious life is the result of balance, the positive aspect of the Two, not destructive opposition, its negative aspect.

The beauty of the Two lies in expressing unity, not disunity. This is the challenge of the Second Millennium. It is also the challenge of the Two Expression. Make peace, not war. Think of others, not of self. Respect those who support and serve, not just those who lead while being maintained by the support of others. Cooperate; don't dominate.

Compromise. Talk. Adjust. Find the Golden Mean, the middle ground between polarities. Create peace. This is the great calling for the Two Expression.

As an aside, an interesting cosmic note regarding the number Two is that, from a numerological perspective, our earth has entered the Second Millennium – a thousand years of Two energy which is an energy of socialization, not pioneering, as is the One energy. Thus, a person with a Two Expression will feel more comfortable in this millennium than in the First Millennium where the number One dominated. The cosmic pendulum has now swung the other way. We have experienced a thousand years of the One male energy of the yang, and it is now time for the earth to experience the Two female energy of the yin – a very opposite polarity with opposite attributes and characteristics.

This polar shift is one of the main reasons we see such confusion in our world today. All of us alive at this time, particularly those born before the year 2000, or who have parents or friends who were born before the Millennia Shift, are experiencing, either directly or indirectly, both of these contrasting polar vibrations of the One and Two! As explained in *The Age of the Female: A Thousand Years of Yin* [available at www.RichardKing.net and online retailers], those souls born after the year 2031 will have only the polar vibration of the Two anchored in their final Epoch, Pinnacle and Challenge locations (E-P-C Triad) of their Life Matrix (more on the E-P-C Triad in *The King's Book of Numerology II: Forecasting – Part 1*). Given this fact, they will not know by *direct* experience the vibration of the One except vicariously through the eyes and tongues of those of us who were born in the nineteen hundreds.

Thus, individuals born after the year 2031 will not have the understanding of having lived in both yang and yin vibratory periods.

That gift, if it can be called that, is reserved only for those who were born in the Twentieth Century and whose lives have carried them into the Twenty-First Century, quite a distinction when one thinks about it. What other souls in creation can claim this unique experience?

For information regarding major females of the 2nd Millennium and their contributions to the world, read *The Age of the Female II: Heroines of the Shift* available at RichardKing.net.

- <u>Parenting Wisdom for the Two Expression</u>: One of the first things to implant in Two Expression children is that they have great capacity to be the peacemakers of the world, for they possess the ability to see both sides of issues. Therefore, they can be exceptional diplomats, negotiators, arbitrators, ambassadors, personal assistants, secretaries, intermediaries, team players, business partners, supporters, nurses, attendants, and service personnel. It would be wise, however, not to portray individuals in a support capacity as secondary to leaders or those in charge. Our society has a tendency to extol leaders more than followers, but leaders need followers and vice-versa. As we have discussed, leaders and followers are all part of the same whole, all are generated from the same flame. On a numerical note, the master number associated with the number 2 is the 11 which is saturated with 1 energy. In fact, the number 11-2 (the cipher depicting the master number reduced to a single digit) is often found in the charts of individuals who have achieved great things in life. The reason for this is that these achievers employ relationships (2) to create (1). In other words, the Two can achieve within the environment of relationship while the One achieves as the solo pioneer. The thing to impress upon Two Expression children more than anything else is that they are the peacemakers of life, the keepers of the balance in society, and if they employ the Two's positive characteristics of togetherness, compassion, equality, caring, tenderness, friendliness, partnership, support and teamwork, there is nothing they are incapable of accomplishing in the realm of relationship.

- Famous People with a Two Expression: *Danica Patrick, General Douglas MacArthur, Patrick Swayze, Shaun White*

The Three (3) Expression Child

Three Expression children are definitely expressive. Pleasant to be around, they smile a great deal of the time, are friendly, easy to know, and emit a positive attitude. Generally, they like to talk, and as they grow, visiting with friends and socializing will be commonplace. Words will eventually very likely be an important part of Three Expression children. They may like to write, especially if they also maintain some dominant Seven energy in their chart.

The number Three rules beauty and therefore it's highly probable that children under this vibration will grow to be very attractive. If a Nine is prevalent in their charts, they could well find themselves as models because the Nine is the energy of the public stage.

There is an excellent chance these children will be associated with the arts in some capacity – this to fulfill their personal sense of self-expression and communication. Radio, television, theater, movies, magazines, video, photography, dance, design, and acting are excellent avenues for the Three individual.

Writing is quite common with Three children because through their self-expression energies, they can share their thoughts and deepest feelings on paper as journalists, playwrights, sports writers, composers, authors. Their mental skill with words could also propel them into the television milieu as commentators, news-anchors, reporters, hosts or announcers. As a Three Expression, communication in some capacity is vital to their very being.

The key word to describe Three Expression children is exactly that – self-expression. Even if they do not use words as much as other Threes, they may find themselves visually expressing and communicating their talents in the health and beauty field, perhaps as a beautician, makeup artist, clothes designer or hair stylist.

Since all vibrations have their negative side, as certainly as the Three can bring integration, ease, health and beauty, it can also bring disintegration, dis-ease, sickness and ugliness of one sort or another. Negative self-expression, self-harm, self-mutilation or self-destruction are possible with a negatively aspected Three, as well as being unlikable in a social sense. What can be perfect can also be imperfect. Beauty, like sickness, does not last forever. Happiness, in a worldly context, is as ephemeral as sadness. Remember, the cosmic pendulum swings both ways, and where there is health, there is also the potential of disease or dis-ease.

There are three cautions with the Three Expression:

1. <u>Excessive vanity</u>. The number Three rules image, and if one's personal image is not controlled it will expand to destructive degrees. It is important to have a healthy self-image, no doubt, but when carried to extremes that image becomes very distasteful and socially problematic.

2. <u>Entitlement</u>. Three rules ease of living, comfort, joy and good fortune. Such things are wonderful blessings, but they should not be taken for granted or expected. Sometimes having too much of a good thing can be a curse as much as a blessing. Such good fortune should not be flaunted or imposed upon others with thoughtless disregard and egocentric abandon. We do reap what we sow, and sowing entitlement and ingratitude will result in good fortune being taken away.

3. <u>Over-indulgence in pleasure</u>. Three rules pleasure of all kinds, but when that pleasure is focused too much in the material world, the results will be painfully tragic. Over-indulgence in alcohol, drugs, sex and personal power is the harbinger of a great fall. Numerology archives are filled with cases of individuals whose lives were destroyed because of unchecked, wanton self-indulgence.

- <u>Parenting Wisdom for the Three Expression:</u> Children ruled by the Three energy should be encouraged to create, sing, write, paint, debate, act, sculpt, compose, model – in effect, to express themselves in positive ways. These children are intrinsically joyful, positive, artistic, happy, good-natured, fun, approachable and embraceable. Teaching them that their positive energy will help others and be of benefit to them will create a sense of confidence in who they are. They should be encouraged to shine – not to dominate social situations but simply to be happy and let their joy radiate to others. A major caution with Three Children is to insure they do not become too vain, self-important, entitled or arrogant. They should also be cautioned, as they mature, of the risks involved in becoming too involved with partying, drug use, sexual indulgence and excess. It must not be forgotten that the Three is a powerful energy of joy and pleasure, but its power can equally manifest as sorrow and pain.

- Famous People with a Three Expression: *Elizabeth Taylor, Ernest Hemingway, Frank Sinatra, Mohandas Gandhi, Muhammad Ali, Serena Williams, Thomas Jefferson, United States of America* (not a person but an entity)

The Four (4) Expression Child

Four Expression children are the rock and salt of the earth. Four is the vibration representing the structures of our lives – physical, mental, emotional, social, marital, financial. If the number Four is not negatively aspected in a child's chart, he or she will quite likely be a solid, dependable, reliable, responsible, hard-working, trustworthy, devoted, service-oriented individual who is more rooted than any of the other nine vibrations. Four children are anchors, and people may depend on this anchoring to anchor them and give them strength. The ultimate expression of the Four energy is one of service, work and effort, moving, sometimes plodding, along with undiminished regularity and dogged persistence.

Your Four Expression children may express themselves in the creative field as a painter, sculptor, designer, photographer, teacher. The Four energy designs, constructs and builds, especially in the world of matter and form, so their artistic abilities may take shape as great works of tangible or visual art. Beyond the world of art, Four children will be the builders, contractors, developers and keepers of the order. Organization is key to their nature. They will be conventional and traditional, so do not expect them to be free spirits, rebels or world-shaking iconoclasts. Fours are the standard bearers of time-honored traditions and institutions.

The symbol of the Four is the square and represents the foundations and structures of our lives. Depending upon our perspective, we can stand on top of the square, using it as a foundation; be protected and guarded by it by dwelling within the security of its walls, or be crushed by its weight when existing below it. Therefore, how Four energy is used is vital to the child's sense of strength, security and well-being. All of these locations in relation to the square can give security. However, they can also give a sense of limitation and imprisonment because the Four, unlike the Five, does not move or change. It stays put, rooted in place like the Rock of Gibraltar.

In the top position of the square, Four children are anchored to life but free enough to experience the world around them. In the center position, they are situated within the square. Depending upon their makeup, this may be comforting or confining. In the lower position, they are burdened by the weight of the Four, perhaps even feeling crushed by the mass of its vibrations. They may even experience all three positions at once or at separate times. The point is that they will feel the strength, weight and gravity of the Four, positively or negatively.

Positive Four children are very secure, rock solid and oozing with control, dependability, reliability, service and trust. They love to help. Negative Four children often violate the principle of structure in their lives and become imprisoned or pressed down by its weight. For example, if a Four child grows into an adult who is not trustworthy, reliable, dependable, faithful, disciplined, controlled or principled, then only trouble can ensue.

The great vibration of the Four Expression demands persistence, effort and sacrifice of action and behavior characteristic of the long-suffering of Noah and his family during the forty days of rain upon the earth and the forty days of the Flood; of Moses and his people in the desert for forty years; of Moses himself on Mount Sinai for forty days and nights and, of course, Jesus in the wilderness for forty days.

Forty, whose crown (single cipher) is the Four, is the vibration representing purification through discipline, determination, restraint, continence, toil, limitation, regimentation, regulation, rules, order, sacrifice and unrelenting tenacity. When these qualities are learned and expressed, the result is ultimate strength and security. But make no mistake, there can be no strength and security without the aforementioned virtues. Strength is, itself, a virtue but it cannot be manifested without those qualities which comprise its structure and which give it form.

One of the hazards for the Four Expression child is being so overly consumed with the principle of structure that one becomes stuck in the mud, unable to move and change when one's best interest may call for some type of adaptation to the structure, maybe even to abandon the structure altogether. The Four energy can be so recalcitrant and resistant at times that it gives new meaning to the word stubborn.

If, for example, one believes in loyalty, he is under no obligation to jump off a cliff at the behest of another person, taking his life in the process, however strongly he believes in loyalty. A person, however, who is overly saturated with a misguided sense of devotion may not have the good sense to see outside the box and make the proper adjustments to protect himself. It is good to be rooted but not so immovably rooted that one jeopardizes his health and well-being, or that of others, in the process. No one is obligated to sacrifice his soul for the soul of another. We are each responsible for ourselves. Thus, the balanced Four Expression child needs to reflect practicality.

- Parenting Wisdom for the Four Expression: Encourage your Four Expression children to continue developing their sense of strength stability and security; living in a practical way; exercising discipline and diligence; being reliable, trustworthy, loyal and faithful. Compliment their ability to help, to be responsible and accountable. Help them realize that in a strong work ethic there can be no excellence without effort, that living by a code of life is critical to happiness. Service to others is vital to the Four, and Four Expression children, arguably more than any other Expression number, can be the great servants to the masses. This should be applauded and encouraged. As these children grow and mature, teach them to guard against being too stiff, stubborn, opinionated, recalcitrant and unyielding. Being rooted can be a good thing, but being too deeply rooted may keep them from moving, changing or adapting when they should. This said, teach them to be what they intrinsically are . . . the rock!
- Famous People with a Four Expression: *Babe Ruth, Bob Hope, Charles Lindbergh, George Foreman, Jackie Evancho, J.K. Rowling, Marilyn Monroe, Napoleon Bonaparte, Peyton Manning, Princess Diana*

The Five (5) Expression Child

Five Expression children are the epitome of motion, movement, change, experience, adventure, diversity, versatility, excitement and wildness. They can't seem to be still, love their freedom and do not like to be restricted. Unlike the Four Expression which plants roots and seeks a grounded stability, Five children generally have few roots and prefer to be on the move. Their love of freedom makes them seem unstable at times but stability is a relative concept. An airplane in flight, for example, is not stable in a grounded sense but quite stable in a moving/flying sense. In fact, it needs the movement of the air over its wings to keep it stable. Motion and movement are critical to its balance, health and well-being. Without such motion, the plane would crash and burn. Five Expression children are much like an airplane – motion not only makes them free, it keeps them stable.

Change is important to Five children. The movement they need in their life is not simply physical movement, it is psychological, social, vocational, emotional, and spiritual as well. These children thrive on stimulation and new experiences because these feed the Five's desire to know more, explore more, do more. Change, constant change, is the vehicle through which these children acquire experience.

This need for stimulation and experiences makes Five Expression children talented in many areas. Doing one thing is not enough for them. Their very being needs the input of varied stimuli to keep them alive and excited. If they receive this stimulation, they feel complete and satisfied. If there is too little stimulation, they wither and wane. Five children are not meant to be the rock, confined to one place or one activity their whole life. They are meant to be the eagle – to fly, soar, be free and ride the ever-changing winds of life, enthralled with the majesty of motion in flight.

Five Expression children may definitely have many talents and be a person for all people. Unless there is a dominant amount of the Seven energy of seclusion in their chart, they will be an individual who loves to socialize with friends, seeking pleasure and good times. They will possibly enjoy exploring things mentally, psychologically and spiritually if their Five Expression maintains a Seventy-Seven master root, the energy of seeking the inner path.

As they mature, Five Expression children must guard against over indulgence in sensual pleasures of all kinds. The Five loves to experience and explore, but some things are better left unexplored and unexperienced. Who, in their right mind, would ever want to be sucked into the dark abyss of a black hole? Yet, there are many black holes in this world. Not all experiences or adventures are positive, and many experiences lead to incarceration and slavery, not freedom. Alcohol, drugs, gambling, excessive risk-taking and illicit sexuality are black holes to the soul. Free and unrestricted indulgence in them leads to imprisonment in the world of materialism and the senses from which escape is extremely difficult.

In effect, nothing is free. Everything has a price. Five Expression individuals must never forget that. In spite of contemporary thought and wishful thinking, there is no such thing as free love, free drinks, free anything. We must simply, and truthfully, pay for everything we get in life. Neglecting spiritual law and its edicts of discipline, self-control and temperance lead to imprisonment, and imprisonment is not a pleasant, comfortable or enjoyable experience. If Five Expression individuals are not careful, they will one day rue the day they sought too much experience after demanding too much freedom, lamenting their over-indulgence in sensual appetites when they should have exercised more discipline and restraint. More than any other number, the Five individual needs to heed this lesson.

Therefore, for Five Expression children, discretion and a positive sense of discrimination – the ability to discern what is healthful or harmful, is critical for these freedom-loving, experiencing-seeking explorers and adventurers. Learning to make right choices to advance one's spiritual evolution is more important than simply making a choice to be free and adventurous. If we can <u>progress</u> in our life's journey, we can <u>regress</u> as well. Where we go and where we will be tomorrow depends upon the choices we make today, now, in the present, for as certain as the sun shines, there will be consequences to our every action, and we will have to pay the price for the things and experiences we choose to buy and bear.

The Five vibration must be seen and understood correctly from a spiritual perspective. The Five loves freedom, but true freedom is based on and is the product of extreme discipline, regulation, restriction and self-control. Unrestrained, unregulated, undisciplined action does not create freedom because all actions have their consequences, and the consequence of unrestrained behavior is captivity and destruction. Freedom is not license-carte-blanche. True freedom is action taken in consideration of consequence, not in ignorance or denial of consequence.

Five Expression children must carry this truth with them throughout their lives, for the choices they make today will determine where they are tomorrow. The Five offers great freedom of choice, but its choices demand discretion because of the freedom/slavery polarity. Five children must be taught to look ahead at the possible consequences of their actions *before* they take them, remembering that those choices promising fulfillment and satiation of the senses, although pleasurable and easy to make, often take the soul down a nether road to a dark and sorrow-filled land where freedom, even as a word, doesn't exist.

Five Expression children must be careful also of becoming too scattered and too free, just as Four children must be careful of becoming too stable and too rooted. Balance is the key in all things. Because the Five moves at breakneck speed, it must be careful it doesn't fall and break its own neck. It is not uncommon for Fives to be accident-prone because they are doing so much so quickly they forget to concentrate on the task at hand. They must never engage in an action before their mind is engaged. It's fine to move fast, but one cannot afford to lose one's concentration, just as a race car driver cannot afford to lose his. Fives do like to take risks, and they do like speed, so the speed issue must factor into their decisions.

Five Expression individuals can be very personable. They like talking and visiting with others and can be extremely animated, charismatic, charming, spontaneous and dashing. Therefore, they would do well in fields involving the public and/or where they could move freely with little restriction. A nine-to-five job sitting in some back room or cubicle is not for them. Leave that to the Fours. Fives need a job in which they can be free to move about experiencing and sharing their talents with others. This does not mean they are irresponsible. Irresponsibility has nothing to do with freedom. It has to do with personal integrity. Fives can be as responsible as any other person. Nor does it mean Fives should lead a wanton, sensually-driven, libidinously-saturated life in violation of spiritual law. Fives just cannot be constricted or restricted if they are to do their best work and be at their optimum health.

- Parenting Wisdom for the Five Expression: Five Expression children must be free to move, fly, change, experience and explore within careful limits. Their very nature demands stimulation, and attempting to restrict them too much can become problematic because severe restriction and limitation could result in an eventual volcanic eruption of destruction. Therefore, as these children grow and mature they need to be taught the difference between true freedom and license-carte-blanche. Bad choices made under the superficial pretense of freedom can be painfully binding and bonding, relegating them, not to fields of freedom but to dungeons of despair and bondage. When living a life of temperance, discipline and self-control, Five Expression children will enjoy their wonderful versatility and array of talents. Encouraging them to develop and hone their skills will prove fruitful. Since they love to be on the move, they should be given opportunities to do multiple things and participate in various activities until they find their niche. Remember, they love speed, excitement, spontaneity, diversity and adventure. Five Expression children must be loved with open arms. Holding on to them too tightly will create unwelcome restriction and not promote the essence of who they are at their core . . . free spirits.

- Famous People with a Five Expression: *Albert Schweitzer, Cameron Diaz, Larry King, Peter Jennings*

The Six (6) Expression Child

For Six Expression children their entire being revolves around and is centered in their heart. Love of family, romance and close friends is extremely important to them. On a social level, they may well have a concern for their community. There is a softness about them, a gentleness which makes them the nurturer, the one who gives to others, embraces and supports them, keeping them warm and secure. As a female, they are the Mothers of the Earth; as males, the Fathers of the Earth. Loving matriarchs and patriarchs are the title reserved for Six Expression individuals. For them, their hearts remain at home.

Six Expression children will most likely be lovers of beauty and harmony. Six is a higher octave of two (the vibration of balance) and of three (the energy of beauty and integrated perfection). Six, therefore, is an amalgamation of these energies, expressing beauty, balance, creativity, harmony and sweetness.

As they mature, Six Expression children will most probably enjoy music very much and may even be exquisite and exceptionally expressive performers. They may love to sing, creating beauty and harmony with their voices and words, giving joy to others through song. Many great singers and performers have Six dominant in their numerology charts, although the Six may not necessarily be in their Expression. Some of these great singers and performers are: Elvis Presley, Whitney Houston, Michael Jackson, Celine Dion, Michael Grimm, Frank Sinatra, Sarah Brightman and Mariah Carey.

One of the attributes associated with the Six vibration is adjustment. Personal lives change, and as lives change during a Five period, the subsequent Six period brings opportunities of adjustment to return conditions to a state of balance.

One red flag for the Six Expression is that while Six is the vibration of pure, personal, nurturing love, the opposite side of the coin is hate and its affiliate attributes of jealousy, envy, bitterness and resentment. Love and hate are the positive and negative warp and woof of the tapestry of the Six vibration. In this dimension where one occurs, the other must also be present. Being aware of these opposites will help parents give their children a greater understanding of the dual nature of love.

Six rules love. One expression of worldly love is lust, i.e., sexual gratification. Since Six is two times three and Three is the energy of pleasure, another red flag emerges. If one's romantic passions are not held in check, trouble can and often does arise with the Six Expression. It can even be far greater than that caused by the Three's misuse. Loving relationships, not lusting relationships, demand responsibility to both parties. However, one's passion for sexual gratification may often override one's loyalty to his or her significant other, the family and the community, bringing a wave of negative feedback, pain, sorrow, destruction and tears in the process. This is where the responsibility and devotion factors of the Six must come into play. Where there is responsibility, there is balance and beauty. Where there is irresponsibility, there is imbalance and ugliness.

It is, therefore, important to separate love from lust, love from passion. While many people say they are in love, they are really only expressing their passion and carnal desires, which are self-serving. Love is selfless and would never jeopardize the health and well-being of another.

Why is this important? Because Six Expression children have the ability to bring true personal love into manifestation as they grow and mature. They can be the great mothers, the great fathers, the great nurturers of mankind; the true, devoted and loyal lovers who embrace the love of all in their hearts. Or. . . they can be the depraved and wanton libertines who use others to satisfy their own carnal and depraved appetites. As the Five Expression walks the road between freedom and slavery, the Six Expression walks the road between love and lust. We all have choices at every step, and those choices will determine our future.

One of the primary attributes of the Six energy is the concept of home, where home may reference a personal domicile, a community or even a nation. Arguably the greatest president in the history of the United States of America was Abraham Lincoln. His Expression was a Six. In a like manner, Great Britain's great leader, Winston Churchill (Winston

Leonard Spencer-Churchill), also had a Six Expression. These men were leaders of their respective homelands, i.e., nations. They had a deep and abiding sense of family on a large scale. They cared. They had compassion, but at the same time, they made the kinds of hard decisions great fathers and leaders are responsible for making. It is safe to say that without Lincoln and Churchill America and England would not be the same today.

- <u>Parenting Wisdom for the Six Expression</u>: The purity of true love, heart, hearth and home are key to the well-being of children with a Six Expression. These souls will have an affinity for family and the domestic environment. They are the sweetest nurturers of the Alpha-Numeric Spectrum. Their domestic reach may extend beyond the environs of their personal home to the larger environments of their community or even their country. Music and harmony may also be a large part of the Six Expression's life experience. Three things parents can help their children be particularly aware of as they mature will be: 1. the dual aspect of true love and lust; 2. the avoidance of hatred, jealousy, resentment and anger; 3. the desire to help others to such an extent that they become used, abused and unappreciated. There is such a thing as loving too much, nurturing too much and enabling too much. Therefore, having tough love can be positive love. Too, because Six people want to love, nurture and care for others, they run the risk of being walked on and walked over by those with little compassion. Thus, Six children should be taught that loving others is good, but they should never love so much they place themselves in jeopardy of usury. On the positive side, Six Expression children are wonderfully warm, attentive, nurturing, compassionate and responsible, and it is these qualities that should be reinforced.

- Famous People with a Six Expression: *Abraham Lincoln, Angelina Jolie, Billy Graham, Charles Darwin, Duke of Wellington (Arthur Wellesley), Edna St. Vincent Millay, General George Patton, Martin Luther King, Jr. (born Michael), Sam Walton, Sylvester Stallone, Winston Churchill*

The Seven (7) Expression Child

Still waters run deep, and Seven children are the most inwardly driven and potentially deepest thinking and feeling of the nine basic numbers. As they mature, they will become the thinkers of society, the ones who ponder, reflect, analyze, scrutinize, assess, examine. As children, they are too young to have mature insights about life. However, as they grow into their adulthood, they will not generally care to be connected to the outer world because their connections are with the inner world. Therefore, they will tend to be on the more thoughtful and reserved side of the social spectrum.

Howard Hughes, the famous billionaire of the Twentieth Century who referred to himself as being shy, had a Seven Expression. Amelia Earhart, the iconic aviatrix and heroine had a Seven Expression, as does media icon Oprah Winfrey. The greatest playwright in history, William Shakespeare, had a Seven Expression, as did arguably the greatest scientist in history, Sir Isaac Newton. Henry Wadsworth Longfellow, the great American poet and Harvard professor had a Seven Expression. Nobel Peace Laureate and world-renowned Catholic nun, Mother Teresa, had a Seven Expression. These are just a sampling of Seven Expression individuals who have made profound achievements in their lives. They had depth, and they gave depth to their lives. Thus, parents of Seven Expression children would do well to take note of the power inherent in their children.

This depth is manifested in their spiritual, religious, metaphysical, scientific, educational, industrial and literary behavior. As our list of the previous Seven individuals reflects, their world is substantive, internal, private, reclusive and deep. Their need is to be separate from others; to think, meditate, ponder, cogitate, examine, study and reflect.

Because most of the world is socially oriented, it does not understand Sevens and their need to internalize. But Sevens do understand themselves and that is all that is necessary. This separation from others appears to them (others) that Sevens are cold, aloof and distant, but Seven individuals are not cold, distant or aloof from the fiery spirit permeating their every pore. There is a reality within Seven individuals that those who live on the outside simply cannot understand nor appreciate. Therefore, Sevens create their own private space to pursue their interests and find their own peace.

These deep connections do not come without a price. That price is often the censure, criticism, ridicule and ostracism of others. Therefore, Sevens must be calm and serene to balance this unknowing of others and their possible untoward behavior toward them. In truth, we don't see things the way they are, we see things the way our numbers are, and Seven Expression individuals view life from an internal, not external, perspective more than any other number in the Alpha-Numeric Spectrum. They have internalized and inquisitive minds. They live *within*, not without.

Thus, Seven Expression children often find themselves alone. This state of isolation, and perhaps alienation, can be painful because even though they are deeply connected, they are still human, and although they do not require the same external contact that others crave, it is difficult to be an isolated island within the stream of humanity.

We all need contact with others, and we have an intrinsic need to touch and be touched – not necessarily physically but emotionally and mentally. And here is where the Seven's special vibratory pattern shines. Because of its inward-dwelling sense of life, it has the ability to make the internal connection which those living in the external world cannot make. This is one of their special gifts.

Therefore, the admonition of Seven people is – *make the internal, eternal connection*. When this connection is made, there will be no more isolation because there will only be oneness, Oneness with the divine energy of life.

Seven individuals love to have their space, and no number needs its own space more than the Seven. Others in its world need to know this so they can make the proper adjustments and keep the relationship harmonious. It is not that the Seven is not connected to others, it's just not connected to others in an external sense. Its depth of knowing can be a great anchor in other people's ocean of turmoil.

Seven is the vibration of supreme peace. Its opposite polarity is the vibration of supreme chaos. The Seven may be exhibiting one or the other polarity, but the end to which it must aspire for its spiritual ascendancy is, of course, peace.

Pythagoras, the father of numerology, said Seven is the most sacred of all numbers because it's a synthesis of the trine of the spirit [ruled by the number Three] and the square of matter [ruled by the number Four]. Other world religions corroborate this fact of the Seven's sanctity, which is mentioned often in the Bible, especially in the Book of Revelation. In fact, the 3-4-7 triad is, arguably, the most powerful number set in the Bible. Thus, a Seven Expression person is saturated with the potential of spirituality.

Carrying this further, it is worthy of note that one of the two numbers most often prevalent in the charts of substantively famous people whose reputations have stood the test of time is the number Seven. This is because Seven rules the spirit and it is the Spirit that every living soul has in common by divine decree. The Seven energy sensitizes us and makes us feel deeply, connecting with others in a way that is impossible for any other number. The other number prevalent in the charts of famous people is the Nine, the energy of universality, without whose energies it is difficult to obtain recognition and notoriety on the public stage.

Seven is not only the most potentially spiritual of all the numbers, it is also the most secretive and private. Sevens will always seek some degree of privacy. If they can't get it, they will create it by possibly starting a confrontation which they can use as a reason for some temporary separation. It's critical that people associated with a Seven person understand that the Seven person needs time alone because it's in their isolation that the Seven recharges and re-centers itself.

As far as secrecy goes, the Seven individual should be judicious and discerning. Some things are best left private, but secrecy can also create suspicion and have a negative effect on relationships. The foundation of all relationships is trust, and if the trust between people is destroyed because of secretive and untoward behaviors, the relationship may well be destroyed too.

Seven people can be overly meticulous. This is good for jobs requiring exactness, precision and perfection such as science, engineering, accounting, mathematics and editing. The problem arises when other people are not as meticulous and perceive the Seven person as being overly critical. Therefore, Sevens need to be cautious when dispensing help to others, and if they have to offer positive suggestion to do so with warmth and tenderness to avoid being perceived as ruthlessly critical.

The Seven is a very special number. It is intrinsically different from the other numbers in the Alpha-Numeric Spectrum. Its goal is to be patient, appreciate its love of isolation and separation, seek perfection softly and go *within* where it is most at home and at peace.

- Parenting Wisdom for the Seven Expression: The key to these children is the inner path. Do not expect your Seven Expression children to be social phenoms. Do expect them to be thinkers, possible loners. They may well be reclusive, shy, and desirous of being alone and to themselves. They are not extroverted socialites. They are introverted internalites, for the most part. More than any other number, these children are different. They live in the world of ideas, dreams, thoughts, and it is through their inner path that they will be moved to act. It was the Seven that drove Shakespeare to use his mental power to become not only the greatest playwright of all time, but also the most quoted author of all time. It was the Seven energy that made Isaac Newton a genius among geniuses. The Seven's internal power gave Amelia Earhart the courage to gain recognition as the most famous solo aviatrix in history and to become the first person, not just woman, to fly the Pacific Ocean alone. This could only be done by a person who was comfortable with being secluded. Why did the brilliant Howard Hughes alienate himself from society, becoming the most reclusive eccentric billionaire of all time? How could Longfellow have given us his famous poems such as *Paul Revere's Ride*, *The Song of Hiawatha*, *Evangeline* and others were it not for his deep imagination? And what of the spiritually attentive life of Mother Teresa and her sacrifice in helping the sick? Through these extremely successful Seven Expression icons, we receive a clear picture of what the Seven energy is capable of manifesting. The bottom line for Seven children is this – let your child have the space (physical, emotional, intellectual, social) they need to think, be alone, dream, reflect, ponder, analyze and express themselves inwardly. Let them know it is alright to be who they are, and that while popularity is for the masses, their beauty and gifts to the world are internal, for they are the thinkers of society. They are also the ones who can connect deeply with the spiritual realms, for no number is more inwardly connected and involved than the Seven whose internal energies are integral to their very essence.

- Famous People with a Seven Expression: *Amelia Earhart, Anna Nicole Smith, George Armstrong Custer, George Washington, Henry Wadsworth Longfellow, Howard Hughes, Martha Stewart, Michael Phelps, Mother Teresa, Oprah Winfrey, Isaac Newton, Walter Cronkite, Warren Buffett, Whitney Houston, William Shakespeare*

The Eight (8) Expression Child

Eight Expression children are individuals who love to connect, interact, be involved and integrate. As they mature, they generally will be success-oriented, social, enjoy material comforts, love money, wealth, status, power, position and social prominence. They can lead and manage well. Eight Expression individuals are not reclusive and introspective like the Seven, but outwardly driven, seeking to make themselves a worldly success or be involved with the world. They can also work hard and efficiently, seeing what needs to be done and doing it. Eights are not just workers. They are managers, the ones who orchestrate and coordinate the work, making things run smoothly – like a well-oiled machine. If they are an athlete, they are, no doubt, very coordinated and most likely successful in their sport. As a performer, they know how to connect with their audience and with their subject matter. They are quite skilled at interacting with others, which gives them a powerful social presence. They mix well with just about everyone. Success is vital to their well-being.

In many cases the Eight Expression individual will function smoothly in the world of business and commerce, focusing its energies in the fields of management, marketing, sales, advertising and finance.

The Eight Expression wants to integrate, connect and interact. As the highest octave of the 2-4-6-8 quartet, it is socially focused and likes to be involved in the external, worldly, social loop of success, wealth, riches, fame, name and power.

This interconnective attribute is expressed in the ancient lemniscate, the symbolic figure Eight representative of connection and 'flow' between the polar extremes of positive and negative charges. The lemniscate represents the cosmic energy loop connecting opposite polarities: male/female; buyer/seller, idea/manifestation, product/market, etc. A smooth flow is well-coordinated and efficient. When polar charges are brought together, there is success, a normal attribute of the Eight energy. It is the Eight Expression which reflects the function of this ancient symbol more than any other number. Eights love to be on the move, flowing in the loop of success, making the connections needed to realize and manifest their desires and goals. Whether it's the loop of business, the loop of high society, the loop of the artistic world in its many varied forms, the loop of government, the loop of the athlete in perfect coordination – the Eight Expression is there. The energy flow of the loop is its lifeblood.

The Eight also represents the principle of continuity and continuation. This is one reason why successful people often have the number Eight prominently aspected in their charts. The Eight creates a continuous flow of energy from person to person, a flow that is invaluable in the process of social interaction and involvement.

However, not everything connects under the Eight vibration. As things can connect, they can disconnect as well. This disconnection characteristic is the natural opposing polarity of the connective attribute of the Eight. As we recall, all numbers have a positive and negative charge within them. The negative disconnective aspect of the Eight is why people under this vibration can be just as disconnective in their personalities and behavior as those who are quite noticeably connective and successful.

Success and failure are opposing poles of the same continuum, opposite sides of the same coin, opposite ends of the teeter-totter. Therefore, the Eight Expression may create success – actions which connect, integrate and interact, as well as create failure – actions which disconnect, disintegrate and are non-interactive, if not inhibitive and even destructive. This explains why some people under the Eight are successful with money, personal relationships and financial management and others are not. In the latter case, such inefficient use of money and an inability to maintain relationships may be exacerbated by a lack of Hs, Qs and Zs in the natal name (the Expression). These letters carry an Eight value numerologically and a lack of them oftentimes manifests as difficulty in the process of making and maintaining connections and integrating the flow of energy between polar extremes or between people in general. Many single people are often found missing Eights because this is the vibration which connects, and where there is no energy of connection, there is disconnection or inhibition.

Another concern with the Eight lies in the concept of negative manipulation. Because Eight seeks to connect and be successful, it may tend to do so at the expense of moral and ethical behavior, manipulating everything and everybody to get what it wants. The worldly lure of power, wealth, riches, fame, name and success, which fuels the engines of the Eight Expression, very often overpowers the individual's spiritual vision and good sense, entrapping the person in a web and loop of dishonesty, deceit, illusion, fraud, usury, misrepresentation and general untoward behavior, a spiritually tragic scenario. The Great Law of Sowing and Reaping – the pure embodiment of cosmic law – brings back to everyone that which is generated and perpetrated. Manipulation for personal gain, therefore, only spells trouble for the manipulator. He may be successful in the short run, but his negative karma will catch up to him eventually. It is interesting to note that the word "karma" is itself an Eight.

$$K\ (2) + A\ (1) + R\ (9) + M\ (4) + A\ (1) = 17: 1 + 7\ =\ \mathbf{8}$$

The Eight Expression would best be served to focus on making positive connections which yield positive results for itself and others. Eights need to be the movers, doers, connectors of society, and in fact they will be. Therefore, Eight Expression children should be placed on notice that they have the potential to be the CEO, executive, leader, manager, commander, general, principal, president, organizer, orchestrator, coordinator.

John Fitzgerald Kennedy, the 35th President of the United States, Michael Jackson and Sarah Palin, Governor of Alaska, all are Eight

Expression individuals. They were each very connective in their roles in life. The critical thing of note, however, is for Eight people not to misuse or violate the special integrative, interconnective, managerial, social skills and talents inherent in their Eight energy. Eights need to walk a karmically tight line. What the Eight person does will eventually return to him or her in spades. Therefore, the admonition is to play the connective game of life well, but play it honestly and ethically and never forget the age-old saying that, *What goes around, comes around.*

- <u>Parenting Wisdom for the Eight Expression</u>: Raise your children with the insight that they have tremendous potential to be leaders, doers, executives, managers, administrators, marketers, generals, commanders, presidents. Teach them they have a wonderful innate ability to connect and understand the flow of things and actions better than most people understand them. Because they have this ability, they therefore have the talent to manage, in effect to connect the dots of whatever they are doing. It is almost uncanny how Eight Expression people can "see" the flow of things and get things done. This is what makes them special. They may not be the great thinkers of society, but they certainly can be the great managers of society. The caution for them is not to abuse their managerial talents. Eight is the most powerful of all the social numbers and with that power comes a responsibility to use it for the good of all, not just themselves. Misuse of the Eight energy often leads to greed, and the accumulated weight of such greed will eventually sink them. Eight is the number of the executor – the one who executes. Such an individual must be able to see how all the parts of the whole are interconnected and then bring those parts together so they work in harmony with each other. Whether the Eight Expression individual is a mechanic, an artist, movie director, self-employed business owner, president of a company, events coordinator, school administrator, wedding organizer, thespian, general or president, he or she must know how to integrate all of the parts of the whole. This talent is best reflected in the Eight energy, and so the primary wisdom of parents with Eight Expression children is to teach them the process of integration, organization, coordination, execution all wrapped up in the garments of efficient *flow*.

- Famous People with an Eight Expression: *John F. Kennedy, John Wayne, Marion Jones, Michael Jackson, Naomi Campbell, Rudyard Kipling, Sarah Palin*

The Nine (9) Expression Child

The Nine Expression manifests a power and charisma unlike any of the other eight basic vibrations. Nine is the final vibratory experience of the soul as it journeys through the numerical *Avenue of Crowns* – the single digit numbers One through Nine, aka, the Alpha-Numeric Spectrum. Since Nine is the Grand Elemental, being a composite of the nine single digits, it contains all vibrations within it and, therefore, understands, identifies and is understood and identified by all (see *The King's Book of Numerology, Volume I: Foundations & Fundamentals*). Thus, Nine is the vibration of all people, the 'many', the masses, the public stage, the universal theater of man.

The Nine Expression spans many areas of life's universal theater and is, in fact, a prime vibration within the specific arena of the artistic theater, drama, radio, and television. But it is also present in the healing arts, literary arts, language arts, educational arts, musical arts, metaphysical arts, martial arts, mechanical arts and all creative and performing arts in general. Notice the word 'Art'. Nine is definitely artistic, and it is no accident that it spans all cultures, all races, all geographical, financial, social, ethnic, environmental and governmental boundaries. Therefore, a Nine Expression child will intrinsically emanate a universal energy, giving him or her a sense of magnetism.

The Nine Expression maintains an expanded focus, often national, international and global in dimension. Nine Expression children are individuals for all people because they understand all people and all people, consciously or subconsciously, identify with them. They have a natural charisma that radiates even when they just stand still. They don't even have to pretend to be charismatic. Their vibratory essence rules. They are strong, dominant, powerful.

This natural power and strength of the Nine is one of its greatest assets. However, it is also one of its greatest liabilities. Although Nine dominates, it can also be domineering to its detriment. No one likes a bully or one who abuses his power, authority or position. As Lord Acton wrote in a letter to Bishop Mandell Creighton (5 April 1887), "Power tends to corrupt and absolute power corrupts absolutely." Charles Caleb Colton declares, "No man is wise enough, nor good enough to be trusted with unlimited power" (1825). Percy Bysshe Shelley, the famous English poet of the Nineteenth Century, muses in *Queen Mab*, "Power, like a desolating pestilence, pollutes whatever it touches." This is one of the dangers facing Nine Expression individuals: it can be corrupt, arrogant, imperious, overbearing and powerfully destructive. Therefore, Nine children need to learn early to keep a tight rein/reign on the natural power that emanates from them, and their parents will be wise to teach them that it is always important to take the high road but the low ground.

As the Six Expression loves personally, the Nine Expression loves impersonally. Its focus is on the masses, not the solitary individual, save the fact that each person is a part of the great whole. Nine is not primarily a domestic energy. It is a public, universal energy. It moves on the public stage of life, which is its true and natural home.

When its energy rises to its highest level, the Nine Expression is the humanitarian, the universal giver, the loyal, devoted, committed servant of the people and the common good. Nine is often seen, therefore, in the charts of teachers, religious leaders, doctors, nurses, dentists, social workers, philanthropists and all types of occupations in which contact with the public is standard operating procedure. Nine touches all people, serves all people, embraces all people because it is all people.

- <u>Parenting Wisdom for the Nine Expression</u>: Teach your Nine Expression children to enjoy their charisma, talents, power and strength. Enjoy the grand stage of life; enjoy mixing and moving among the world's many and varied peoples; love their artistic side; embellish their humanitarian nature and be the gracious, grand, magnanimous, generous, universal giver. This is the reflection of Nine Expression children at their best. Teach them to rule well and remember that true rulership is based on service, not dominance; on meeting the needs of others, not satisfying their own. Instruct them to educate, entertain, help, heal, uplift, serve, rule. As Saint Charan Singh states, "Only the highest can help the lowest." Nine is the highest of all the nine vibrations. All numbers are contained within the Nine and the Nine reflects all numbers to themselves. Likewise, Nine Expression individuals are all people and reflect all people to themselves. This is why the Nine is unique and universal. The critical key, however, is to teach these innately powerful Nine children that their power must not be abused, but rather used for the good of all. Their life goal should be one of benevolence, not malevolence; humility, not arrogance; love, not hate; light, not darkness and nobility, not ignobility.

- Famous People with a Nine Expression: *Albert Einstein, Arnold Schwarzenegger, Bob Dylan, Dolly Parton, Edgar Cayce, Elvis Presley, Garth Brooks, Prince Charles, Prince William, Queen Elizabeth II, Tiger Woods, Tommy Lee Jones*

Children are our most valuable resource.

~ Herbert Hoover

6

The Performance/Experience

As the Lifepath represents the script of our children's lives, and the Expression denotes them as actors or actresses, the Performance/Experience (PE for short) represents exactly that, the *performance* or *role* they will give on the great life stage. If one hundred thespians were given the same script, when each performer acted out the script, the performance each would give would be different from all the rest because of the individual personalities, talents, traits and attributes each actor/actress brings to the script. So it is with life scripts. Two people could have the same Expression number and the same Lifepath number but their performances would be different. This is because of differences in the root systems of the Expression and Lifepath. For more on root systems of numbers, read *The King's Book of Numerology, Volume I – Foundations & Fundamentals*.

To reiterate, the Performance/Experience is the *role* our children will give in life. It is not the script of their lives. Nor is it them. The PE is the performance the child, as actor or actress (Expression), will give while reading a script (Lifepath).

Calculating the Performance/Experience

The PE is determined very simply by adding the number of the Expression to the number of the Lifepath (PE) and reducing to a single digit if necessary.

The PE Formula

Expression + Lifepath = Performance Experience (PE)

Therefore, the performance our children give in life becomes their *reality*, just as the character in a play or movie becomes the reality for the actor or actress playing the part of their specific character. But when the part is over, when the movie or play is done, the actor or actress moves on to other roles, other scripts, other screenplays.

In numerology, the ability of distinguishing individuals (Expression) from their roles in life (PE) is noteworthy. In most instances, the person and the role are two very different entities. For example, a child's Expression number may be a 5 but his PE a 4. These are contrasting numbers and easy to differentiate. However, if a person has a 9 Lifepath, the Expression and the PE will be the same because of the 9's unique properties. As we remember, when the 9 is added to any number the outcome is always that number. Therefore, when a 3 Expression child has a 9 Lifepath, the PE will be a 3 (9 + 3 = 12: 1 + 2 = 3). A 9 Expression child with a 9 Lifepath will generate a 9 PE (9 + 9 = 18: 1 + 8 = 9).

As another example, let's assume a child maintains a Six (6) Expression and an Eight (8) Lifepath. Through addition of these two components the PE would be a 5 [6 + 8 = 14: 1 + 4 = 5]. The 5 PE would showcase this person in a *role* of freedom, movement, change and adventure in contrast to the attributes regarding family, domesticity, personal love, home and community – all characteristics of the 6. Therefore, there will be a marked difference between the child and his 6 attributes, and his role in life (PE) marked by its 5 attributes. However, in the case of a 9 Expression child with a 9 Lifepath and its subsequent 9 PE, one may have difficulty distinguishing the person from the role he is giving because he and his role in life are identical.

The Expression-PE Filter/Funnel

Continuing the discussion of the PE Formula, the Lifepath can be regarded as the funnel or filter through which the Expression passes to create the PE. In the previous example, the 6 Expression merged with the 8 Lifepath to create a 5 PE. Therefore, the 8 is the filter/funnel in the equation. This is important because it illustrates that when the love and domestic energies of the 6 Expression pass through the 8's Lifepath energies of connection, involvement and interaction, they create the 5 PE energy of freedom, detachment and adventure.

However, this 5 PE generated from the 6 Expression and 8 Lifepath would be different from, for example, a 5 PE whose Expression and Lifepath were both 7s (7 + 7 = 14: 1+ 4 = 5). See the difference? A 5 PE springing from two 7s would be still be free, detaching and adventurous, but it would be saturated and colored with the energies of internalization, study, knowledge, privacy, seclusion, spirituality, philosophy, reflection and analysis – qualities of the 7.

In like manner, a 5 PE generated from a 2 Expression and 3 Lifepath would have a fabric composed of relationship energies (2) and self-expressive energies (3). Therefore, it is important when understanding the composition of any PE number to know the numbers forming it – the Expression and its Lifepath filter/funnel.

In the case of the 5 PE, it can be generated from any of the following combinations:

Numerical Combinations for a 5 PE

1 and 4
2 and 3
5 and 9
6 and 8
7 and 7

Whether a person has a 1 Expression and a 4 Lifepath to create a 5 PE, or in reverse, a 4 Expression and a 1 Lifepath to also create a 5 PE, is important. As we've been discussing, the filter will be different and will *color* and influence the *outcome* 5 PE. A 1 Expression with a 4 Lifepath (LP) will create a 5 PE where the 4 Lifepath is the filter, but a 4 Expression with a 5 PE will have a 1 Lifepath. A 4 Lifepath filter is much different from a 1 Lifepath filter. The 4 Lifepath filter references life lessons involving structures, rules, regulations, order, effort, work, service, security and duty, while the 1 Lifepath filter references life lessons involving independence, leadership, action, self and personal identity. Therefore, regarding the PE Formula it is important to understand the relationship of the numbers, especially the number acting as the filter or funnel because the filter colors the outcome of the PE.

Expression vs. PE Opposites

There are three sets of opposites between the Expression and PE that should be noted because these opposites can potentially create an internal struggle which children will experience for their entire lives. When a person's Expression is one energy but their PE is an exact opposite energy, there can be a dilemma unless the parents understand the inherent situation and can teach their children that it is okay to be one number while playing the role of another number, just like an actor or actress.

Either number in each of these three sets of the Expression and PE opposites can be in either position (Expression or PE). The opposites are:

$$1 - 2$$
$$4 - 5$$
$$7 - 8$$

These three oppositions are not uncommon in numerology charts. However, when the differentiation is made between the Expression and PE, it is much easier for the child to understand, especially as the child matures. In fact, it will also be easier for us parents to raise our children who possess these oppositions in their charts because we'll know what's going on within our children and their life blueprints. When a numerical opposition is present in our children's charts and is *known*, management of the situation is much easier.

1 – 2 Opposition

The 1 is a fire sign; 2 is a water sign. Fire and water obviously don't mix. The 1 is masculine; 2 is feminine. 1 is direct action; 2 is indirect action. 1 governs reason; 2 governs emotion. 1 leads; 2 follows. 1 likes to be the star and center of attention; 2 likes to assist and work from behind the scenes. 1 is highly independent; 2 is dependent.

When a child's Expression, therefore, is a 1 and his PE is a 2, it is easy to see from the opposite qualities of these numbers in the preceding paragraph the internal conflicts that could easily occur within the child.

There are two variations of the 1 – 2 opposition. These involve the number 1 as a filter and the number 8 as a filter.

$$A.\ \mathbf{1}\ \text{Expression} + 1\ \text{Lifepath (filter)} = \mathbf{2}\ \text{PE}$$
$$B.\ \mathbf{2}\ \text{Expression} + 8\ \text{Lifepath (filter)} = \mathbf{1}\ \text{PE}$$
$$(2 + 8 = 10:\ 1 + 0 = 1)$$

When a 1 Expression child has a 1 Lifepath, there will be a 2 PE. The filter is the 1 Lifepath. When a 2 Expression child has an 8 Lifepath (filter), there will be a 1 PE ($2 + 8 = 10: 1 + 0 = 1$). Both instances generate a 1 – 2 opposition, but as we see, the filters are different.

A 1 Expression child with a 1 Lifepath creating a 2 PE will be strongly independent, self-oriented and wanting to take the lead because of the two 1s in his Expression and Lifepath. In contrast, a 2 Expression child with an 8 Lifepath will give a life role involving independence and leadership (1 PE) but it will be a much softer 1 because of the social energies of the 2 and 8 which are rooted in relationship and personal involvement respectively. Therefore, although a 1 – 2 opposition exists in both cases, they will be very different.

In the 1-1-2 pattern, the person will be intrinsically self-oriented but will be ultimately placed, through the energies of destiny, in a support role. This could be a person acting as a nurse, for example, where her personal duties are to care for others.

In the 2-8-1 pattern, the person may not be independent at all, nor wish to be a leader or manager. Yet, the forces of her destiny will place her in a role where she is the leader, manager, organizer, teacher, boss, employer, star.

Both the 1-1-2 and 2-8-1 patterns house potential conflicts because the energies of independence and identity (1) are juxtaposed with the energies of dependence and support (2). Regardless of how the lives are specifically manifested, the opposition exists. Knowing this will definitely help parents raise their children more efficiently.

One solution to this 1-2 pairing is to explain to children who have this combination in their charts that they are both the 1 and 2, and therefore they, unlike other children, have the advantage of expressing the qualities of each number and their specific pattern, whether it's a 1-1-2 or a 2-8-1. The key is to explain and teach the positive aspects of each combination, giving more knowledge to the child as he grows.

4 – 5 Opposition

The number 4 is an earth sign; 5 is a fire sign. Earth and fire certainly don't blend. 4 governs all things of structure; 5 is freedom and lack of structure. 4 rules roots; 5 rules movement. 4 is regular; 5 is irregular. 4 is logical; 5 is adventurous. 4 rules form; 5 is formless. 4 is the rock; 5 is the rolling stone that gathers no moss. 4 conforms; 5 rebels. 4 loves its security; 5 loves to take chances. 4 is traditional; 5 is non-traditional.

This 4 – 5 opposition houses two different Lifepath filters, the 1 and 8, creating patterns of 4-1-5 and 5-8-4. Here again, the outcome PE is colored by the same Lifepath filters operating in the 1 – 2 opposition pattern.

A. **4** Expression + 1 Lifepath (filter) = **5** PE
B. **5** Expression + 8 Lifepath (filter) = **4** PE
(5 + 8 = 13: 1 + 3 = 4)

In the 4-1-5 pattern, the 4 Expression child will be a worker, love her roots and security and enjoy being of service to others. However, if she has a 1 Lifepath compelling her to learn lessons of self, independence, leadership and personal identity, the outcome will generate a reality of freedom, change, motion, movement, adventure, excitement, loss and detachment – the 5 PE. Therefore, if she is to live a balanced life, she will have to learn early on to not expect her life to be stable and secure, attributes intrinsic to who she is. Her life's role and reality will be quite mercurial, not the kind of experiences which give her a sense of comfort.

The 1 and 5 are both fire signs, and these offer formidable challenges to her 4 earth sign. She will need to be taught the values and benefits of being independent (1) and free (5) because these will be a dominant aspect of her life, while not ignoring her own internal energies.

In the 5-8-4 pattern, the 5 Expression child will be placed in a reality of structure, service, convention (4 PE) courtesy of the 8 Lifepath lessons of socialization and management. Such a 4 reality will rub against the 5's innate love of being free, detached and unconfined. Yet, that is the reality of this 5-8-4 pattern.

However, as in the 4-1-5 pattern, the 4 can serve as an anchor to the 5's freedom-loving energies. This is a good thing because if the 5 is left to itself, it can be led down a path of excesses due to its desire for adventure, experience and exploration, especially in the arena of the senses and sensual gratifications. Thus, there is a silver lining in this 4 – 5 opposition.

7 – 8 Opposition

Like the 1 – 2 and 4 – 5 opposition pairings, the 7 – 8 duo also has the Lifepath filters of 1 and 8. Interesting isn't it, the perfection of numerical intricacies and how these three pairs of exact opposites all have the exact same Lifepath filters?

A. **7** Expression + 1 Lifepath (filter) = **8** PE
B. **8** Expression + 8 Lifepath (filter) = **7** PE
(8 + 8 = 16: 1 + 6 = 7)

In the 7-1-8 pattern the generally internal, shy and retiring individual will be forced through his 1 Lifepath of self, independence, identity and leadership to become involved in the external, social and interactive world of others, business and commerce. This said, no two numbers are more solo and solitary than the 1 and 7, so their 8 PE will not be a heavily social 8 but a reserved, analytical, reflective, thoughtful and internal 8.

In contrast, the 8-8-7 pattern is more social, based heavily in the 8's energy, and no number is more socially powerful than the 8. It is the highest octave of the 2-4-6-8 energies.

The internal structures of these two 7 – 8 pairings give rise to a noteworthy potential problem. The 7 is the most internal of all numbers, while the 8 is the most external of all numbers. Hence, there is a very powerful and intrinsic conflict in this pairing which is more challenging than those of the 1 – 2 and 4 – 5. Can we not all appreciate that when one's life is deeply internal but he's being pulled outward, there is strong discord? Likewise, when one's life is deeply external but he's being pulled inward, there is also discord? Although difficult, this 7 – 8 pairing gives the individual an opportunity to understand the characteristics of each number and demonstrate them, and in the process become involved with the most opposite of all opposites – the internal and external paths of life as reflected in the 7 and 8 respectively.

Mary & John's PEs

Now let's take a quick look at the PEs of Mary Jane Smith and John David Doey. Mary's Lifepath is a 7; her Expression is a 3. Therefore, her PE is a 1. John's Lifepath is 9; his Expression is a 1. Thus, his PE is a 1.

Mary Jane Smith – PE
3 Expression + 7 Lifepath = 1 PE (3 + 7 = 10: 1 + 0 = 1)

John David Doey – PE
1 Expression + 9 Lifepath = 1 PE (1 + 9 = 10: 1 + 0 = 1)

Descriptions of the PEs

As we've discussed, there is a close resemblance between the Expression (the person) and the Performance/Experience (the role in life). Therefore, in giving a narrative of each of the nine basic PEs, and without having to be redundant, it is best to read the descriptions of the Expressions in Chapter 4. Just remember to reference each description of the Expressions as the *role* of a person's life and not the person himself when reading the Performance/Experience components.

In lieu of having to read the extended narrative of each Expression, a short list of PE descriptions follows.

Performance/Experience (PE) – Descriptions

PE #1: The role of a person's life with a One PE will focus on the self, ego, independence, personal identity, leadership, direct action and taking charge of his life through self-responsibility and accountability.
Negative aspects: ego-mania, arrogance, abrasiveness, self-centered.
- Famous People with a One PE: *General Douglas MacArthur, Heidi Klum, Jackie Evancho, Muhammad Ali, Tiger Woods*

PE #2: The role of a person's life with a Two PE will focus on being the team player, partner, supporter, friend, diplomat, peace-maker.
Negative aspects: adversarial, detractor, deceiver, enemy, anger.
- Famous People with a Two PE: *Abraham Lincoln, Angelina Jolie, Charles Darwin, Elizabeth Taylor, George Foreman, John Wayne, Marilyn Monroe, Oprah Winfrey, Prince Charles, Prince William, Princess Diana, Shaun White, Steve Jobs*

PE #3: The role of a person's life with a Three PE will focus on self-expression, art, communication, words, image, beauty, health and well-being, children, joy, media, pleasure.
Negative aspects: unhappiness, non-fulfillment, illness, disease, dis-ease, caustic communication, verbal abuse.
- Famous People with a Three PE: *Michael Phelps, Mohandas Gandhi, Sam Walton, Serena Williams, Sylvester Stallone, Walter Cronkite*

PE #4: The role of a person's life with a Four PE will focus on work, service, security, stability, building, constructing, organizing, helping, planning, developing, reliability, dependability.

Negative aspects: extremely stubborn, hardness of personality, recalcitrant, selfish, miserly, extremely insecure, limited, unethical.

- Famous People with a Four PE: *Arnold Schwarzenegger, Charles Lindbergh, Dolly Parton, Ernest Hemingway, Howard Hughes, Phil Mickelson, Warren Buffett, Winston Churchill*

PE #5: The role of a person's life with a Five PE will focus on freedom, change, diversity, variety, detachment, experience, exploration, movement, motion, the senses, loss.

Negative aspects: over-indulgence, intemperance, non-controllability, wildness, excessive sensual appetite and pursuits, risk-taking.

- Famous People with a Five PE: *Albert Schweitzer, Danica Patrick, Edna St. Vincent Millay, General George Patton, Jack LaLanne, Michael Jackson, Napoleon Bonaparte, Sarah Palin, William Shakespeare*

PE #6: The role of a person's life with a Six PE will focus on the domestic environment – personal, community, national; matters of the heart, love, artistic expression, beauty and harmony.

Negative aspects: hate, envy, jealousy, resentment, anger, personal abuse, vindictiveness.

- Famous People with a Six PE: *Albert Einstein, Anna Nicole Smith, Bob Hope, Helen Keller, John F. Kennedy, Larry King, Martha Stewart*

PE #7: The role of a person's life with a Seven PE will focus on all things internal, mental, spiritual, religious, analytical, scientific, research oriented, examinatory, study, teaching, preaching, writing.
Negative aspects: anti-social behavior, ruthlessness, callousness, coldness, extreme critical nature, ignorance, foolishness.

- Famous People with a Seven PE: *Billy Graham, Frank Sinatra, Henry Wadsworth Longfellow, Marion Jones, Martin Luther King, Jr., Mother Teresa, Naomi Campbell, Queen Elizabeth II, Rudyard Kipling, Tom Brady, Whitney Houston*

PE #8: The role of a person's life with an Eight PE will focus on the flow of social involvement, orchestration, administration, execution, commerce, business, marketing, being in the social loop, doing.
Negative aspects: untoward manipulation, overbearing leadership, disconnective actions, abuse of power, impatience, poor management skills, procrastination.

- Famous People with an Eight PE: *Babe Ruth, Bob Dylan, Cameron Diaz, Dr. Phil McGraw, Edgar Cayce, George Washington, Jackie Robinson, Peter Jennings, Thomas Jefferson, Tommy Lee Jones, United States of America*

PE #9: The role of a person's life with a Nine PE will focus on universal principles, the public stage, artistic endeavors of all kinds, humanitarian fields of theater, education, music, health, travel, art, transportation, the media in all facets and philanthropy.
Negative aspects: malefic conduct, arrogance, disrespect for self and others, lack of compassion and understanding for others, haughtiness, abuse of power, corruption.

- Famous People with a Nine PE: *Amelia Earhart, Elvis Presley, Garth Brooks, George Armstrong Custer, J.K. Rowling, Patrick Swayze, Peyton Manning*

A child is a person who is going to carry on what you have started . . . The fate of humanity is in his hands.

~ Abraham Lincoln

7

Soul (Desire) Layers

Arguably the most important numbers in a numerology chart are the layers of the Natural Soul and Material Soul – the energies defining a person's inmost desires both on a primary and secondary level.

The energies in these Soul Layers reflect what our children want and desire in life. They do not signify something they will necessarily get in this life; nor do they describe our children's basic assets and liabilities. Too, the Soul Layer energies may be exactly opposite from those energies identified by the Expression, Lifepath and PE, commonly known as the *umbrella* in the King's Numerology™ system.

The most critical reason the Soul Layers are important is that unlike the umbrella energies they are hidden – totally internal, while being externally inoperative. The Soul Layer energies burn deeply within our children and are highly active in shaping their needs, wants, desires and motivations, whether they (the needs and wants) are ever realized or not, and whether we, as parents, are aware of them or not. This is why they are extremely critical – as parents, we can't see them and, therefore, we may never know what drives our children at the core of their very beings, that is unless we use the numerological microscope to access and assess them.

The Two Soul Layers

The Natural Soul (Soul for short) vibration is derived from the vowels in our children's full birth names using the Vowel Value Chart below. The Natural Soul describes our children's most primal desires, their deepest innermost needs and wants. By knowing our children's desires, we parents can guide, serve and support them better by generating more harmony and stability in their lives as well as helping them understand who they are at their core.

Vowel Value Chart					
Vowels	A	E	I	O	U	Y
Values	1	5	9	6	3	7

Computing the Natural Soul

Discovering the Natural Soul is simple. Simply associate the vowels in the natal name with their numerical equivalents, add the numbers together and reduce to a single digit.

What are the Natural Soul numbers of our friends Mary and John? The vowels associated with Mary Jane Smith's birth name are: A-Y-A-E-I. The vowels in John David Doey's full birth name are O-A-I-O-E-Y.

Natural Soul: Mary Jane Smith

M	A	R	Y	J	A	N	E	S	M	I	T	H
	1		7		1		5			9		

1 + 7 + 1 + 5 + 9 = 23: 2 + 3 = 5 Natural Soul

Mary's Natural Soul is a 5. What does this say about her that her parents would be benefited by knowing? This 5 Natural Soul says that Mary desires her freedom more than anything else. She loves to be on the go, discovering new things, having adventures, being diverse and exploring. She requires a variety of excitement and stimulation. She could even harbor a wild side and be a non-conformist.

Undeniably, Mary does not want to stand still, be trapped, enclosed, limited, denied, constrained or contained. She may need to be disciplined for her own safety and have rules imposed on her as a teenager in order to keep her focused. She should definitely be taught the hazards and dangers of what can happen when she acts without considering the consequences of her actions. Being free is a good thing, but she must learn to curb the desire to act beyond the limits of her well-being. To engage in activities that are dangerously excessive and stimulating for the sake of adventure may be fun but the risks may also be hazardous, if not lethal.

What Mary's parents should not do is constrain her to a point of rebellion. This does not mean she should not be disciplined or taught the importance of rules. All children need discipline, and rules are intrinsic to a healthy life. However, it does mean Mary should be given the opportunity to explore different avenues of healthy expression, to be allowed to move, try different things, explore, play different sports and be active. Trying to confine her to what is "normal" could prove problematic.

Natural Soul: John David Doey

J	O	H	N	D	A	V	I	D	D	O	E	Y
	6				1		9			6	5	7

6 + 1 + 9 + 6 + 5 + 7 = 34: 3 + 4 = 7 Natural Soul

With John's 7 Natural Soul, his parents would be wise to not attempt to make him into a social butterfly. They would also be wise to remember that the number 7 is the most inwardly-driven of all the nine basic numbers. Therefore, John will desire time alone and to be engaged in activities that resonate with his mind, thoughts, analytical abilities, creative juices and his spirit. He may be drawn to computer science, writing, engineering, mathematics, religion, figuring out problems, discovering the secrets of the universe. He may very well have a reclusive side that prefers not to be social or a party goer.

Because the 7 energy is inquisitive and analytical, John will want to know things. He will ask questions. He will want answers. He may like to stay in his room and play his guitar, violin or instrument rather than hang out with the guys. His parents should expect him to be a thinker more than a talker. His inner energies are more mental than physical. Therefore, he may seem distant, cool, even cold at times because of the need to be alone, but it would be a mistake to think he is superficial. 7 waters run deep, and 7 Soul children are potentially the deepest of all. They are sensitive and intuitive and more connected to the powers within than any other number.

What John's parents should guard against is trying to mold him into an extrovert. They must never criticize or shame him for being shy or for being an introvert. That's how 7 Soul people are. They don't fit into a social mold.

Natural Soul vs. Material Soul

The Material Soul (MS for short) is a secondary layer of desire energy. It can be seen as being the worldly desires of an individual, whereas the Natural Soul addresses the primal desires.

The difference between "worldly" and "primal" can be understood in this way: before a child is born into the world, i.e., into the material realm, he is alive in the womb. His primal desires are active as a result of the vowels in his name (assuming the parents have named him before his actual birth), but his worldly desires will not take affect until he is born, at which time he will receive a birth date – a *material* designation of entering the world officially, so to speak.

Computing the Material Soul (MS)

Calculating the Material Soul is very easy. Simply add the Natural Soul to the Lifepath.

Material Soul Calculation
Natural Soul + Lifepath = Material Soul

Mary Jane Smith's Natural Soul is a 5. Her Lifepath is a 7. Therefore, her Material Soul is a 3.

$$5 \text{ Soul} + 7 \text{ Lifepath} = 12: 1 + 2 = 3$$
Mary's Material Soul is a 3

John David Doey's Natural Soul is a 7. His Lifepath is a 9. Thus, his Material Soul is a 7.

$$7 \text{ Soul} + 9 \text{ Lifepath} = 16: 1 + 6 = 7$$
John's Material Soul is a 7

Soul Notes

Here are some helpful notes regarding the Natural Soul and the Material Soul.

1. When either of the Soul numbers match the Expression number, individuals will generally feel comfortable with themselves. This is because the Expression energy is what the Soul energies need, want and desire. For example, individuals with an 8 Expression and an 8 in either of their Soul Layers will find harmony between their inner and outer selves, the inner self being the Soul Layers and the outer self being the Expression. Only one, not both of the Soul Layer numbers needs to match the Expression to have harmony.

2. When either of the Soul Layer numbers match either the Lifepath or the Performance/Experience, there will also be a feeling of being comfortable in one's own skin because there will again be resonance between the inner energies of the Soul Layer(s) and the outer umbrella.

3. If the Soul is in direction opposition to the Lifepath, vis-à-vis one of the three pairs of opposites (1-2, 4-5, 7-8) there will be a possible conflict. For example, a child whose Soul is a 1 and whose Lifepath is a 2 may be frustrated because the 1 Soul's desire for self, independence, leadership and to be the star will be challenged in having to learn about the 2's energies regarding working with others, sharing, being a team player and partner. A child with 2 Soul and a 1 Lifepath may find himself having to take the lead and be the boss when he'd rather support or follow. A child with a 5 Soul and a 4 Lifepath will potentially feel restricted because his desire for freedom will find it hard to break free of the

roots and regimen the 4 Lifepath creates. A child with a 4 Soul and a 5 Lifepath may have his desire for stability challenged with the freedom, movement, change and uncertainty created by the 5. The 7 Soul child with an 8 Lifepath may find himself drawn away from the sanctuary of his solitude and thrust into the public arena, while an 8 Soul child with a 7 Lifepath may be kept from socializing and mixing with others while being forced to be alone.

4. If one or both of the Soul Layers are an even number (2-4-6-8) representing social energies, and the Lifepath houses an odd number (1-3-5-7) signifying more independent and creative energies, or vice-versa, there may be some discomfort because odd and even numbers have different characteristics due to their bi-polar conflict. Even numbers have a negative charge; odd numbers have a positive charge.

5. Sometimes the Natural Soul and Material Soul will harbor an internal opposition where the Natural Soul is a 1 and the Material Soul is a 2 (or vice-versa); where the Natural Soul is a 5 and the Material Soul is a 4 (or vice-versa), or where the Natural Soul is a 7 and the Material Soul is an 8 (or vice-versa). For example, the 1 Soul of independence and self will rub against the 2 Material Soul of dependence and others. The 5 Soul of being non-conventional will find a challenge with the 4 Material Soul of convention. The 7 Soul of reclusion will fight the 8 Material Soul of being social.

6. Perhaps the most important note is that for a child to be fulfilled and comfortable with himself, one of the Soul components needs to find its identical number either through its own umbrella (Expression, Lifepath or PE) or through its own life journey as revealed in the Life Matrix (the internal structure of the Lifepath

discussed in *The King's Book of Numerology II: Forecasting – Part 1*) or through a life partner or spouse. If both Soul numbers can find no release through one of these avenues, it will be challenging for the individual to feel a sense of fulfillment and happiness. This concept is also addressed in *Your Love Numbers – Discovering the Secrets of Your Life, Loves and Relationships*. (Both of the aforementioned books are available through www.RichardKing.net/books).

As parents, we would be wise to remember the critical part the Natural Soul and Material Soul play in the lives of our children. Their energies are the fire in the belly. They motivate the individual, driving him forward. We need to pay attention to them because they're not visible on the surface, and they're not externally active. Yet, their power is there and it is real. For our children to reach their highest potential, these inner desire components must find some release, avenue of expression or be addressed with parental understanding. By being aware of them, we parents can raise our children with wisdom and knowledge, allowing the children to manage their lives with grace.

Descriptions for the Natural Soul and Material Soul

Prenote:

As a reminder, the descriptions of the numbers will seem redundant, as discussed in the Author's Introduction. If you're comfortable with each number's characteristics, feel free to skip this section, but make note that the Soul Layers describe the needs, wants, desires and motivations of the child.

Soul Layer Energy: One (1)

A One [1] Soul cipher means that your child's primary motivations are in the realm of the self and its sense of independence, leadership, achievement, accomplishment, creativity, fulfillment and personal satisfaction. The number One is the masculine energy of the Life Polarity Matrix, the 'yang' of the ancient Tao. It is the vibration of personal drive, action, creativity, assertion, dominance, will, leadership, independence, self-reliance. One's go first and show the way. They like to be either in the lead or in the center of life's circumstances. They do not like to serve others or take a back seat to anyone or anything. Therefore, at heart your child is the lone wolf, the maverick, the one set apart.

Regardless of what your child's destiny may choose for him or her, your child will definitely desire not to be a hand-holder or a person dependent on others. The One Soul likes to go first, be the leader, the boss, the star, decision maker and center of attention.

One is a fire sign. Therefore, One Soul children are dynamically aglow, if not aflame. They are the supreme "doers" of the Alpha-Numeric Spectrum. They have vision. They also have a sense of pioneering, of doing what others cannot or will not do. They want to be active, not passive, igniting the flame of life in others. They definitely want to be themselves, and they will want their own way.

The One Soul may make them deeply creative, especially with words, causing them to create using language as their canvass. They may also have a strong desire to be the head of the family or a primary mover in the work environment. Depending on the root structure of the single cipher [see *The King's Book of Numerology, Volume I: Foundations & Fundamentals*], they may desire to be a leader in the business and commercial fields, an entrepreneur, their own boss, their own decision maker. Leading the way as a humanitarian is also probable. Regardless of exactly how the One will play itself out, One Soul children will definitely desire to be their own person and do things their way because their independent spirit knows it can get the job done and take responsibility for its actions.

The One Soul child must guard against being too self-absorbed, self-centered, self-consumed. There are other Ones, other people, in the world, and although they may not be driven to be as independent, leadership-oriented, creative, assertive and active as your One Soul child, nonetheless, they are deserving of respect and attention. It is the pure One who is one with all. Such a state of oneness demands the utmost humility and understanding.

- Famous People with a One Soul:, *Anna Nicole Smith, Condoleezza Rice, Edgar Cayce, Kenny Rogers, Matt Damon, Roseanne Barr*
- Famous People with a One Material Soul: *Carl Sagan, Arthur Wellesley (Duke of Wellington), Howard Hughes, Muhammad Ali, Prince Charles, Prince William, Sarah Palin, Serena Williams, Thomas Jefferson, Walter Cronkite*

Soul Layer Energy: Two (2)

With a Two in your children's Soul, their basic desires, wants and needs rest in the field of relationships and others. They are the ones who endeavor to harmonize situations, bringing peace, equilibrium and balance to the ever undulating, if not conflicting, ebbing and flowing of life's polarized energies. In simpler words, Two Soul children have great potential for being peace-makers, negotiators and diplomats.

Two Soul children are not generally aggressive but passive and responsive. They have a need to support and care for others. The number

Two represents the female principle of the universe, the 'yin' of the Life Polarity Matrix, so caring, helping and supporting are intrinsic to it.

A Two Soul child is generally more comfortable with following than leading because the Two energy is quiescent by nature, not openly active like the male One energy, at least on the surface. It is, however, very active underneath the surface, which is why women, ruled by the number Two, have often been referred to as *the power behind the throne*.

Two is a water sign. It flows. Its path is to go around things, not through them. As an expression of water, next to air (our most precious substance and nutrient), Two Soul children can be wonderful nurturers. Seeds, for example, may be active and grow to produce fruit-giving trees, but they need support, they need nutrition in order to grow and flourish. As part of their nutritional requirement, seeds obviously need water to grow, some less than more, but all life needs water to develop and survive. In this way, Two Soul children have a desire to be the water which nourishes others through love, caring, support, balance and equilibrium.

In another aspect, Two Soul children may be activated by a desire to be competitive and dominant. This is because the Two energy, operating in the realm of others, rules competition and adversarial conditions. Many great athletes, competitors and lawyers have Two dominant in their charts. They like one-on-one challenges to see who the best is when pitted against each other.

Because Two rules balance, there is also a strong desire for those with a Two Soul to be the diplomat or negotiator, the one who brings both sides of an issue or argument together to create harmony. Again, this speaks to the peace-making aspect of the Two. Yet, the opposite side of peace is war, and depending on other aspects in your children's chart, they may like to create confrontation, interference and problems for others. This would be most unwise because the seeds we plant always bear fruit that we are eventually forced to eat. *As we sow, so shall we reap*, is the eternal law of this creation, and it applies to everyone. No one escapes this law of compensation and adjustment.

Two is an extremely intuitive number. Therefore, we parents should encourage our Two Soul children to use their intuition to solve problems. And because Two rules female energy, they are also enjoined to express Yin characteristics. If your Two Soul child is a male, know that feminine does not equate to effeminate. Being in touch with the Two [feminine] energy means to be tender-hearted, supportive, helpful, encouraging, balancing, the team player and partner, the one who bends when he needs to bend, and who understands both sides of issues.

When positively aspected, Two Soul children have a great desire to help others, to be the supporter that others need, the follower to the leader, the volunteer who gives without expectation of recognition. They may not like to be the star, the one out front of the pack, or the one who makes the final decision, but they definitely desire to be involved in helping and seeing things through to their completion. The highest expression of the Two is balance. Thus, teaching our children that balance is primary will be of great service to them as well as to those with whom they interact.

The master number associated with the Two is the Eleven. It is referred to as the *Master Aspirant/Achiever* number in The King's Numerology^{tm}. Many famous people have the 11 dominant in their charts. It is the fire of the double 1s that creates the need to achieve (1) in the realm of others (2).

- Famous People with a Two Soul: *Dr. Phil McGraw, John F. Kennedy, Oprah Winfrey, Sylvester Stallone, Warren Buffett*

- Famous People with a Two Material Soul: *Angelina Jolie, Babe Ruth, Phil Mickelson, Winston Churchill, Whitney Houston*

Soul Layer Energy: Three (3)

Your children's Three Soul Layer energy is focused in the field of self-expression, communication, health, words, writing, singing, image, beauty. This need may manifest in a desire to be an actor, singer, writer, model, lawyer or artist of any genre. With this Three Soul, it is intrinsically natural for them to want to seek joy, pleasure, ease and good times and share these with those in their world. Three children enjoy their friends and often have a love of beauty.

A Three Soul often creates a desire and need to sing – the process of vocally combining the qualities of love with harmony, rhythm and words in an expressive capacity. It may also manifest in desires to be on the public stage and in the universal theater as an actor, actress, newscaster, journalist, reporter. Because Three governs beauty and image, individuals may desire to be a photographer or model. In fact, many world-class models have Three dominant in their charts, especially when accompanied by a Nine.

Three rules health and well-being. Therefore, to be involved in the health and wellness aspect of life may be an important part of their basic needs.

Three rules children. Having a need to positively influence the youth of the world may be a strong desire in Three Soul Layer children. After all, in all cultures children are its future, and the more whole children are, the greater the potential outcome in creating a society that is itself whole.

One of the considerations of the Three Soul is the difference in the pleasure it seeks. On an earthly level, the Three will seek, want, need and desire material and sensual comfort and human companionship. On a spiritual level, the Three will seek to express the divine beauty and perfection in all things of the Spirit. Three represents perfection and is the sign of the Trinity: Father-Son-Holy Ghost; Master-Disciple-Word; Man-Woman-Marriage; Father-Mother-Child. Three also integrates these three separate components into one, unified, spiritual whole.

On a cautionary note: because Three rules pleasure, it would be wise to monitor your children's pleasure-seeking side as they mature. Even a frank discussion may be in order as they come of age. Three can elevate people to wonderfully fulfilling heights, but be warned – no number has destroyed more people than the Three running out of control with reckless abandon, thoughtless of its well-being, its future and the joy and happiness of others.

Pleasures such as recreational drug use, alcohol consumption, illicit sex, partying too much and basically being blind to the fact that the opposite side of pleasure is pain can create a mountain range of problems, far more problems than the pleasure these activities are worth. Show business, as one example, has produced a tragic litany of actors, actresses, singers and celebrities who have over-indulged in the pleasures of the senses to their ultimate demise, not to mention their health. This should serve as a sobering warning, especially for those who seek a joyous life.

It's appropriate here to repeat the words of 20th Century Saint Charan Singh: "No matter how great the pleasures of the world may be, they are not only short lived but also have equally unpleasant reactions at some time or another." An equally powerful quote is from 15th/16th Century mystic, Saint Ravidas, who stated: "True happiness lies in realizing true holiness." Holiness speaks to purity of living. Thus, the purer the living, the greater the potential for true happiness – wise words to live by.

- Famous People with a Three Soul: *Charles Lindbergh, Elvis Presley, Mohandas Gandhi, Muhammad Ali*
- Famous People with a Three Material Soul: *Charles Lindbergh, Elvis Presley, Gisele Bündchen, Michael Jackson, Michael Phelps, Mohandas Gandhi, Naomi Campbell*

Soul Layer Energy: Four (4)

For Four Soul Layer children, their needs, wants and desires are centered in concepts and principles of stability, security, strength, roots, work, unchanging regularity, convention, tradition, construction and social movement. The Four, like all basic numbers, possesses different root forms which color its desires, giving it different sets of clothes so to speak. However, in a general sense, all people with a Four Soul love to be stable and secure. They do not want change to disrupt their lives and leave them feeling insecure – financially, emotionally, physically, psychologically, socially, structurally, domestically [for more on the root systems of numbers, see *The King's Book of Numerology, Volume I: Foundations & Fundamentals*].

Four Soul children love roots – the bigger, stronger and deeper the better. They like anchors too, and may even like being the anchor that weathers all storms. Fours are generally conventional, not choosing to wander out of the boundaries which give them the security they seek. In fact, they usually spend a great deal of energy creating boundaries and secure systems to give them the comfort they need. Many very wealthy people have Four Souls because money buys them the security and stability they desire.

A Four Soul individual generally wants to build and construct – anything from actual buildings and material structures to financial portfolios, works of art and integrated families. The Four also enjoys serving and doing for others, especially where the focus is on order and organization. Librarians often have Four in their charts and they are some of the most ardent servants in the public service environment. It's quite common to find Certified Public Accountants [CPAs] expressing Four energy. Sculptors, photographers and painters whose art involves working in the realm of form, often reflect Four ciphers in their charts. Body builders, carpenters, mechanics, secretaries, personal assistants and law enforcement personnel are some other types of people who often have Four energy in their charts. The common thread – order, security, service.

Four Soul people enjoy working and are not afraid to work. They also tend to "go with the flow," not wanting to upset the status quo. They are quite strong individuals, and seem to weather the storms of life better than any other number because of the anchoring quality of the Four.

One of the cautions of Four Soul individuals is to not allow stability to become rigidity. Roots are fine, but if those roots inordinately attach them to some idea, concept, opinion, place, person etc., they may find themselves too anchored to move and change when it's expedient to do so in order to survive. History is replete with people who have lost their lives stubbornly defending their property, for example, in the onslaught of a hurricane or other natural disaster when it would have been prudent for them to move to a safer place. One's life is more important than one's opinion, position or possessions. The moral of the story: if Four Soul Layer individuals cast an anchor into the seas of life, they need to make sure they can pull it up when they need to.

- Famous People with a Four Soul: *Amelia Earhart, Billy Graham, Dolly Parton, George Armstrong Custer, Helen Keller, Howard Hughes, Napoleon Bonaparte, Sarah Palin, Winston Churchill*

- Famous People with a Four Material Soul: *Albert Einstein, General George Patton, George W. Bush, Theodore Roosevelt*

Soul Layer Energy: Five (5)

Five Soul Layer children have their needs, desires, motivations and wants focused in principles and concepts of freedom, detachment, change, speed, fun, motion, movement, variety, diversity, people, experience, adventure, exploration, unconventionality, sex and the senses. Unlike the Four, they do not crave that which is conventional, traditional, stagnant, unmoving and arguably boring. They like and need excitement, change and freedom to make them content. This need will cause their minds to explore new things, to break the bonds of convention, or at least step outside them to experience what it is like outside the fences or walls of limitation, normal convention, custom, practice, procedure, fashion, routine and staid tradition. The Five Soul loves to be flamboyant and free.

As a Five Soul, children may dream of flying, of being free or helping others to be free in order to experience all they can in life. They do not like being tied down as a general rule, and if their life is fully replete with Four energy in their Lifepath or Performance, their life might seem very restrictive and confining, causing them stress, distress, angst and discomfort.

Five Soul Layer individuals must be cautious in understanding that true freedom is not license carte blanche – unrestrained action and behavior normally interpreted as freedom but which can become incarcerating and enslaving. All actions do have consequences. Acting on whims of adventure and irresponsibility without regard for their consequences can create dire, painful and sometimes life-long conditions of irreversible sorrow. Being free is not being careless and irresponsible.

Five Soul Layer children therefore need to think before they act; i.e., think of the consequences of every behavior before it is taken. There is no such thing as action without consequence. Wisdom demands forethought.

Five Soul individuals love good times and pleasure-seeking experiences with friends. If ever there were a party vibration, this is an excellent candidate. One must be careful here because unrestrained action can generate inextricable bondage. Yet, on the other side of the party energy is the restrained action of the monk, the preacher, the nun who understands that true spiritual freedom is based in temperance.

Discipline and true understanding are vital to maintaining balance, harmony and peace with the Five energy. Where there is little or no self-control, life becomes extremely problematic. How many people have died because some fun-loving, party-minded person got drunk, jumped in a car and killed people while he or she was under the influence of alcohol? How many people have been tragically hooked on drugs because they thought it would be fun to experiment with them? How many sexually transmitted diseases have negatively impacted people's lives due to a lack of discretion and self-control? How many unwanted babies have been born after an episode of fun and frolic? Life is hard enough if we do everything right. Taking risks, which the Five loves to do, has consequences, and not all consequences are good. Parents of Five Soul Layer children would be wise to instill them with a sound sense of common sense, discipline, restraint, temperance and control lest the Five energy run away with them.

Once under control, however, the Five Soul person is driven to enjoy a diverse life, full of fun, new adventures and experiences. No number expresses more diversity than the Five. It is the fulcrum of the *Avenue of Crowns* [the single numbers One through Nine]. When tamed, the Five is more free, fun, exciting and spontaneous than any other number. If not tamed, it's like being on a runaway horse, a speed boat without a rudder or a car that has lost its steering. Therefore, the Five must never forget that one side of the Five coin is total and complete freedom, but the other side is total and compete slavery. Wisdom demands wise choices.

- Famous People with a Five Soul: *Bob Dylan, Bob Hope, General George Patton, George Washington, Mother Teresa*
- Famous People with a Five Material Soul: *Abraham Lincoln, Billy Graham, Charles Darwin, Danica Patrick, Elizabeth Taylor, General Douglas MacArthur, George Foreman, Mother Teresa, United States of America*

Soul Layer Energy: Six (6)

The basic needs, wants and desires of Six Soul Layer children are centered in concepts and principles of love, nurturing, the home, domestic environment, relationships, romance, family, community, art, beauty, harmony, music, singing and personal compassion. Six rules the heart more than any other single vibration. As a Six Soul, therefore, there is a great need for these children to be personally loving and share their life experiences with others on a personal level, a level of home and community. Sixes love the family and desire to be domestically oriented or romantically involved. None of the other numbers is as home-oriented as the Six.

All things being equal, one with this Six Soul energy would be a likely candidate to be the loving mother, father, grandmother, grandfather, aunt, uncle, brother, sister, friend, companion, head of home, community, country. The Six is the one who offers a big hug, a warm knee to sit on or a kind ear to hear other's troubles. Cookies in the cookie jar and soft kisses for the little boo-boos of life are standard reflections of Six energy.

The Six energy is not uncommon to leaders of causes, communities and countries. George Washington, the Father of the United States, had a Six Material Soul. Martin Luther King, Jr. and Oprah Winfrey also have a Six Material Soul. These are examples of leaders who care deeply.

Six, like the Three and Nine, is an extremely artistic energy. It is not uncommon for the Six to be prevalent in the charts of singers, musicians, actors, beauticians, interior designers, landscapers, architects, community organizers and basically any occupation in which the home and community are involved. Because Six is personally compassionate, nurturing and tender-hearted, a desire to be a doctor, nurse, teacher, educator, counselor, or other occupation where the personal touch is important is also a viable option.

Sometimes, however, those who love can actually love too much, and if they're not cautious, can be used and taken advantage of by people who prey upon their nurturing instincts. Therefore, it's important that Six Soul Layer children value their own worth and not become a doormat for those whose callous mindsets abuse their personally loving gifts and gestures.

As the Six is double the Three energy of pleasure, the same caution remains in effect for the Six. Misuse of drugs, sex, alcohol and other intoxicants poses as a harbinger of potential problems. In consideration of such things, the words of Saint Dadu warrant wise counsel: "Hold pure, stay pure, say pure, take the pure, give the pure."

- Famous People with a Six Soul: *Calvin Coolidge, Elizabeth Taylor, General Douglas MacArthur, Michael Jackson*
- Famous People with a Six Material Soul: *Amelia Earhart, George Armstrong Custer, George Washington, Jackie Robinson, John Wayne, Marilyn Monroe, Martin Luther King, Jr., Oprah Winfrey*

Soul Layer Energy: Seven (7)

Seven Soul Layer children are placed at the threshold of the divine! This Soul vibration is like no other and is, in fact, so opposite to the ways of the world that these children might find themselves feeling very isolated, alone, separate and distant from others and the earthly status quo.

People do not often understand Seven Soul Layer individuals because they like to be alone, separate and apart, and this makes them appear cold and aloof. The irony is that they are neither cold nor aloof – maybe from the world and society, yes, but not from the deep and mystical core of all that is eternal, spiritual and divine. The desires of these children carry them deeply into feelings where others only touch them superficially, and while others exist on the surface of the water, Seven Soul children live deeply within the inner currents and tides of life, seeking causes, not effects, and asking questions regarding how, why, what, when and where, for their minds never stop asking, never stop inquiring, never stop seeking answers to that which is normally held to be unknown and unknowable. But it is axiomatic that unless we seek, we can never find, and so the Seven Soul is always on the proverbial treasure hunt.

It is not easy to be a Seven Soul because, of all the numbers in the Avenue of Crowns, it is the most internal, the most inward seeking, the most drawn to the world *within*. Contrarily, the world lives and thrives in the great *without* and could care less about the spiritual, inner side of life.

Seven is, at its zenith, consumed with mysticism, not money. It seeks knowledge, answers to life's questions, soul liberation and salvation, not worldly success or material accumulation. The Seven Soul is the key to the inner worlds of the spirit where energy, not matter, reigns supreme; where God awaits to embrace the weary and worldly lovelorn soul and take it Home to the supernal, ethereal realms of eternal peace, love, light and bliss.

As the indwelling Seven energy separates its individuals from the external show of the phenomenal world, there should exist no major concern. The world does not have the answers to creation. Such answers exist *within*, not *without*. The Seven Soul individual's desire for isolation, withdrawal and privacy are the keys which allow them the space to go within during critical times of the human experience and find the answers they seek. Therefore, Seven Soul individuals would be wise to embrace the isolation and loneliness they feel. It is designed to motivate them to move inward where life's greatest secrets lay in waiting.

This prior description of the Seven Soul may seem too focused on its spiritual aspects. For those who have Seven Souls and are not spiritually disposed, the potential still exists to tune in to the Seven's higher energies. If they are not desired, the more mundane characteristics of the Seven will focus on mental traits such as analysis, research, study, teaching, philosophy, material science, writing – activities requiring an inquiring and critical set of mental skills.

One of the important things for parents of Seven Soul Layer children to understand is that the Seven energy loves its privacy, solitude, separation. Depending on the amount of Seven energy in a chart, Sevens will need time alone – sometimes a lot of time or a little time, but still time to themselves. It is in silence and separation that the Seven recharges and renews itself, unlike the Eight that is reinvigorated by social gatherings and group activities. Sevens are true loners, more than any other single number. They tend to be reclusive, shy, detached, withdrawn, secretive. That doesn't mean they're weird. It just means they prefer to be alone and separate. To them, isolation is an integral aspect of their life. They need it, and will not be happy unless they get it. Therefore, the way to love Seven Soul children is to give them their space and distance from time to time and not pressure them to be something they are not, i.e., social butterflies. That distinction is left to the Eight.

- Famous People with a Seven Soul: *Albert Einstein, Albert Schweitzer, Babe Ruth, George W. Bush, Larry King*
- Famous People with a Seven Material Soul: *Albert Schweitzer, Bob Hope, Patrick Swayze, Princess Diana, William Shakespeare*

Soul Layer Energy: Eight (8)

The Eight Soul desires connection and integration. Eight, the highest expression of the social numbers 2-4-6-8, loves to be in the flow of all that is happening, for Eight is the vibration that connects polar opposites manifested in life as buyer and seller, idea and completion, producer and consumer, actor and audience, directives and their execution, and so forth. Eight brings things together, makes them efficient, coordinated, successful. Eight wants to be 'in the loop' of success in any field – business, athletics, theater, music, politics, art, education, management and administration.

The Eight Soul, unlike the Seven Soul, does not seek isolation or reclusion but external connection and social integration. Eight is an even number and therefore social by nature. It loves to mix and socialize unless affected by substantial Seven energy elsewhere in the chart. Therefore, Eight is a vibration common to all that is on the 'outside'. To be worldly successful is normal for this vibration.

The Eight Soul is, generally speaking, driven to seek success, wealth, fame, riches, material comfort, applause and power in the external world of society. The caution here is to not let the desire for such earthly and temporal success overshadow the spiritually obligatory directive for moral and ethical behavior. Eight, because it loves to connect, may seek to connect through dishonest and untoward means, thus causing it much heartache at some future time when the rebounding consequences of its original actions return to bless the giver with the gift – the gift of pleasure or pain, success or failure. Because of this connection-seeking quality, Eight can be an extremely manipulative vibration for better or for worse. The admonishment for Eight Layer individuals once again: be careful of violating the law of action and reaction, cause and consequence – a universal law which returns all things to its creator. . . all things – good or bad, and if it's *bad in*, it's *bad out*; if it's *good in*, then it's *good out*. This is the operational law of the universe.

It is very common to see executives, generals, admirals, presidents, prime ministers and other leaders with Eight dominant in their charts. Eight is a double Four. Four focuses on order, organization, rules, discipline, consistency. But Four doesn't manage. It serves as the helper. It is the Eight that takes the concept of order, rules, structure and organization and applies it to the integrative social loop as a manager and administrator where it brings people, ideas, concepts, buyers and sellers together to function smoothly in the world of business and commerce.

Eight Soul Layer children will definitely love to connect, integrate, manage, administrate, socialize and connect the dots of the social scene. They will most probably love to be 'in the loop' of all that's happening in their world. In fact, they're probably the ones who created the loop of their social network. The number ruling socialites more than any number is the Eight. Not only does it like to mix and mingle, but if it has the resources, it can be very charitable.

Eights love to coordinate and orchestrate too. They make excellent planners and organizers of functions such as business meetings, weddings, graduations, group parties, neighborhood functions – anything that needs a person in charge to make things run smoothly and efficiently.

Another avenue for release of the Eight Soul is through understanding varying systems of mechanics, electricity, plumbing, etc. Eight governs circulation, and therefore people with an Eight Soul often love to see how things fit together, work together, flow together. Regardless of the application, the general desire of the Eight Soul is to connect and create a smooth flow to all they touch. What they touch may be money and finances, organizational development, educational systems, athletics, mechanics, character depiction (as in the case of actors and actresses playing various roles), coaches, hospital administrators, etc. The key phrase is: Eights administrate, circulate, integrate, orchestrate, manipulate, interact, involve and connect.

- Famous People with an Eight Soul: *Arthur Wellesley (Duke of Wellington), Jackie Robinson, Marilyn Monroe, Phil Mickelson, Prince Charles, Theodore Roosevelt*
- Famous People with an Eight Material Soul: *Calvin Coolidge, Dolly Parton, Larry King, Sylvester Stallone*

Soul Layer Energy: Nine (9)

Nine Soul Layer individuals will seek the macrocosm, the universal stage of life, the international/global landscape, the public domain, the theater of *the many*, the fields of art, humanity, education, science, politics or philanthropy. Because Nine is the Grand Elemental, the Nine Soul often seeks power, rulership, dominion, completeness, completion, victory and triumph. Nine is intrinsically ambitious, powerful and generally wants to dominate. The caution is that it must not be overly dominating, arrogant or imperious in the process or it will make a mockery of its higher expression of regal rulership, generosity and magnanimity.

The Nine Soul often desires to live and breathe in the arena of humanity, serving as a teacher, doctor, counselor, nurse, lawyer, theologian, humanitarian, philanthropist, artist, thespian, musician, volunteer, etc. Nine is a very complete vibration, the most complete in fact, and wants to share itself and its talents with others, assisting and helping them in whatever way it can.

Because of its connection with the macrocosm, the Nine Soul can be very ambitious. The symbol for the Nine is the crown, and the Nine Soul wants to rule, without question; not necessarily lead, but rule. There's a difference. Nines love their thrones but not so much the barren frontier.

Because of its all-encompassing nature, the Nine Soul likes to be among the many, to be recognized, publically known and famous. It is very different from the Seven which seeks its solitude. The masses – this is what the Nine Soul loves, seeks, needs and desires.

The Six energy is the most personally loving of all the numbers. The Nine is the most impersonally loving of all the numbers, but still loving. It desires to be the compassionate humanitarian and philanthropist, the giver and benefactor of all – that is unless it is negatively aspected, in which case it seeks to be the malefic, evil ruler of its subjects. Nines love to rule. They may be the benevolent ruler or the malevolent dictator. Rulership is rulership. Kings are kings. Queens are queens. Titles confer no goodness or greatness on anyone, just position.

Besides becoming too overbearing and imperious, a main caution for the Nine Soul is to be judicious in choosing the company it keeps. We become known by the company with whom we associate, and because the Nine is the chameleon of the Alpha-Numeric Spectrum it can blend and mix equally well with the forces of light or darkness. Once again, rulership guarantees no inherent goodness. History teaches us that. How many powerful leaders were unwholesome leaders, to say the least?

The best advice and warning for Nine Soul individuals and their parents can be found in the following quotes. Thoughts for contemplation.

Power tends to corrupt, and absolute power corrupts absolutely. Great men are almost always bad men.
~ Lord Acton

No man is wise enough, nor good enough to be trusted with unlimited power.
~ Charles Caleb Colton

Power, like a desolating pestilence, pollutes whatever it touches.
~ Percy Shelley

- Famous People with a Nine Soul: *Abraham Lincoln, Carl Sagan, Charles Darwin, Garth Brooks, Patrick Swayze, Princess Diana, United States of America, William Shakespeare*
- Famous People with a Nine Material Soul: *Condoleezza Rice, Dr. Phil McGraw, Helen Keller, Henry Wadsworth Longfellow, John F. Kennedy*

Our children come through us but they do not belong to us.

~ Saint Charan Singh

8

Nature (Personality) Layers

As the Soul Layer energies are determined from the vowels in the name, the Nature Layer energies in Natural and Material forms are derived from the consonants. The Natural Nature (Nature for short) can be viewed as the personality, the quiet self, the quiescent self. Specific to the King's Numerology^{tm} is the Material Nature which adds a secondary or worldly energy to the personality.

The Nature Layers describe not just the personality but the way or manner in which the individual does things. For example, assume a person has a Two Expression, making him or her supportive and generally passive. Yet, assume this person with a Two Expression has a Nine Nature – a powerful personality vibration. One who has a Nine Nature could very well be a dominant figure, if not dominating. The way or manner such a person might behave with this combination Two Expression and Nine

Nature could possibly be anything but totally passive, sweet and harmonious. Nines like to rule, so this combination could make for a strong supporter or one who is powerfully divisive in relationships, perhaps even being contrary, interfering and argumentative. It could even manifest in being passive-aggressive.

If one were to consider the two aspects comprising the Expression (the Soul and the Nature) as a manifestation of the Yin and Yang polarities of the life spectrum, the Soul could be argued to be the passive feminine aspect, while the Nature would be the masculine active aspect for, certainly, the Nature is an active vibration addressing the manner or way in which the individual personality is manifested.

Computing the Natural Nature

To calculate the Natural Nature, simply associate the numerical value of the consonants with those in the natal name, add left to right and reduce to a single digit. We'll use our friends, Mary Jane Smith and John David Doey. For easy reference, here's the letter value chart:

	Simple Letter Value Chart								
The Letters	A	B	C	D	E	F	G	H	I
	J	K	L	M	N	O	P	Q	R
	S	T	U	V	W	X	Y	Z	
Number Value	1	2	3	4	5	6	7	8	9

Example #1: Mary Jane Smith: Natural Nature

M	A	R	Y	J	A	N	E	S	M	I	T	H		
4+		9+		1+		5+		1+	4+		2+	8	=	34
34: 3 + 4 = 7															
The Nature of Mary Jane Smith is a 7															

Mary's Nature is a 7. Here's a quick way to check our work. Since we already know from our previous study that Mary's Expression is a 3 [calculated from all the letters in her full birth name, both vowels and consonants] and her Soul is a 5 [calculated from the vowels], the remaining consonants must add up to a 7.

Quick Check Formula: Mary

Vowels	+	Consonants	=	Expression
Soul	+	Nature	=	Expression
5	+	?	=	3
5	+	7	=	12: 1+2 = 3

If we had wanted, we could have simply determined the Nature using this Quick Check Formula by filling in the missing number. When we know any two of the numbers in the formula, the third is easy to determine.

Example #2: John David Doey: Natural Nature

J	O	H	N	D	A	V	I	D	D	O	E	Y		
1+		8+	5+	4+		4+		4+	4				=	30
30: 3 + 0 = 3															
The Nature of John David Doey is a 3															

John's Expression is a 1. His Soul is a 7. Therefore, he would have to have a 3 Nature. Let's check our work.

Quick Check Formula: John

Vowels	+	Consonants	=	Expression
Soul	+	Nature	=	Expression
7	+	?	=	1
7	+	3	=	10: 1+0 = 0

What is the Natural Nature of your child or children? To compute it, add the consonants of the natal name and reduce to a single digit, or use the Quick Check Formula.

Vowels	+	Consonants	=	Expression
Soul	+	Nature	=	Expression
#____	+	?	=	#____
____	+	____	=	____

Vowels	+	Consonants	=	Expression
Soul	+	Nature	=	Expression
#____	+	?	=	#____
____	+	____	=	____

Vowels	+	Consonants	=	Expression
Soul	+	Nature	=	Expression
#____	+	?	=	#____
____	+	____	=	____

Computing the Material Nature [MN]

The Material Nature gives a second layer, if you will, or second way and manner in which the child's personality will be manifested. One way we can think of the Material Nature is that it reflects how the Natural Nature operates in the material world. Hence, it is not the primal personality. That label belongs to the Natural Nature. Rather, the Material Nature can be considered more of a worldly personality, just like the

Natural Soul is the primal vortex of one's desires, needs, wants and motivations, while the Material Soul represents the child's material or worldly aspirations – those energies created when the child in the womb is given birth into the world vis-à-vis its birth date.

Calculating the Material Nature is very easy. Simply add the Natural Nature to the Lifepath. Mary's Lifepath is a 7 and John's Lifepath is a 9. Let's see what their Material Natures are.

Material Nature Calculation
Nature + Lifepath = Material Nature (MN)

1. Mary Jane Smith: Nature is 7; LP is 7; Material Nature is 5.

Nature	+	Lifepath	=	Material Nature
7	+	7	=	14: 1 + 4 = 5
Mary Jane Smith's Material Nature is a 5					

2. John David Doey: Nature is 3; LP is 9; Material Nature is 3.

Nature	+	Lifepath	=	Material Nature
3	+	9	=	12: 1 + 2 = 3
John David Doey's Material Nature is a 3					

What is the Material Nature of your child or children?

Nature	+	Lifepath	=	Material Nature
	+		=	
Material Nature is a _____					

Nature	+	Lifepath	=	Material Nature
	+		=	
Material Nature is a _____					

Nature	+	Lifepath	=	Material Nature
	+		=	
Material Nature is a _____					

Following are the Nature Layer descriptions. One explanation will suffice for both. It may be helpful to review the Lifepath and Expression descriptions for each number to increase the meaning of each number.

Descriptions for the Natural Nature and Material Nature

The numerical descriptions of the Natural Nature and Material Nature will seem identical to those of the other components of the Basic Matrix. This is because the qualities, characteristics and attributes of the numbers do not change. What does change is *how* numbers *manifest* in a chart depending upon where they're located in the chart. Following is a simple guideline describing these differences based on chart placement.

Basic Matrix Guideline

Expression	The actor/actress with full potentials
Lifepath	Script of life; energy world; life lessons
Performance/Experience (PE)	Role in life; performance given
Soul	Primal desires
Material Soul (MS)	Secondary desires
Nature	Primary Personality
Material Nature (MN)	Secondary Personality
Voids	Missing numbers in the natal name

Nature Energy: One (1)

With One in the Nature or Material Nature position, the way or manner in which our children will do things is centered in the 'yang' aspect of life. This, of course, represents the male energy manifested as self, ego, will, action, initiation, creation, courage, independence, assertiveness, leadership. Therefore, they will be self-starters, will like to be in the lead or in the center of the action. They will be creative, assertive and love to do things their own way. They tend to be driven from within themselves, as opposed to being driven by others. They like to stand alone and be seen as their own person, replete with their own ideas, values and sense of being. They also tend to be logical and reasonable rather than illogical and emotional. They behave in a direct manner, not indirect, preferring face-to-face interaction rather than employing a third party to do their talking or bidding for them.

One is a fire sign, and when it is the substance of our children's Nature, they can heat things up – driving, pushing, leading, creating, manifesting, doing. As they become adults, they may well be seen not just as the leader, but as the mother or father figure, perhaps even the head of the household, community, organization.

One of the cautions of our One Nature children is the over-assertiveness of their ego and pride. Yellow flags here. Ones can become too self-centered, too self-absorbed, too ego-centric, too arrogant, too aggressive, oftentimes for their own good. Ones do not like to follow others. They like to go before others or be the center of attention where other ones focus on them. They do this because they know they can get the job done. Ones like to initiate and get things moving. They do not like to wait around for others to take action.

Owing to their strong will power, Ones also do not like to bend. They can be very rigid. Sometimes this can be very beneficial, especially when strong, decisive leadership is required. Sometimes, however, a softer approach may be the best solution. Kind words and honey go a long way in influencing others and motivating them, as opposed to iron wills and harsh hands. Leadership is all about balance and knowing when to apply the proper touch at the proper time. Sometimes a kind word is needed. Other times a pat on the back or an arm around the shoulder works magic.

Then again, like an alpha mare or a stallion, some strong discipline is the only viable solution.

When Ones understand their oneness with the universe and place themselves in the proper perspective as a solitary, short-lived, single bubble on the great cosmic ocean of life, they can become truly radiant and divine. We all need leaders and creators but ones which, like a branch hung heavy with fruit, bow low to the ground and share their wonderful gifts, substance and nourishment with others.

- Famous People with a One Nature: *Charles Lindbergh, General George Patton, Kenny Rogers, Martin Luther King, Jr., Prince Charles, Prince William*
- Famous People with a One Material Nature: *Babe Ruth, Bob Hope, Charles Lindbergh, Sarah Palin, Sylvester Stallone*

Nature Energy: Two (2)

With Two in the Nature or Material Nature position the way or manner in which our children do things is centered in the 'yin' or female aspect of life. Thus, as they work to the highest level of the Two energy, they will be warm, supportive, caring, congenial, cooperative, conciliatory, cordial, comprising, compassionate, diplomatic, pleasant, agreeable, friendly, gentle, kind-hearted, emotional, considerate, inspirational and partnership oriented.

Two children are prone to being a soft touch. Their gentle nature draws others to them as well as their tactful sense of dealing with situations and people. They like to help, support and assist others and prefer being more passive than overly assertive or aggressive. They are generally not seen as people who are self-centered, dominant or hungry for leadership, center stage or the spotlight. They are more comfortable in the background in a support role, preferring to be the "power behind the throne" rather than the one sitting on the throne; the one behind the camera, not in front of it. Rather than create turmoil or disturbance, which is possible when the Two is operating negatively, in their highest expression Two Nature children prefer to be peacemakers, friends, negotiators and healers. Equilibrium, balance and peace are important to them, as well as not being confrontational. Their gentle ways act as a salve, soothing the ills and heartaches of others.

However, as everything in the universe possesses a negative charge, especially numerical vibrations, the Two does have its dark side. One of the characteristics of the nether pole of the Two lies in its duality and duplicity. Two can be as openly discordant as it is concordant, as truculent and warlike as it is peaceful, as contentious as it is conciliatory, as interfering as it is supportive.

Of its ten binary roots (11-20-29-38-47-56-65-74-83-92), all but the number Twenty intrinsically carry an Eleven transition root (see *The King's Book of Numerology, Volume I: Foundations & Fundamentals*). As you will notice, except for the number 20, when the single numbers of each of the Two's binary roots are added together, an 11 emerges in the reduction process [29: 2 + 9 = 11; 38: 3 + 8 = 11, etc.] This 11 is called a transition root. All single numbers have a binary root structure.

Eleven (11) is a high intensity master number juxtaposing dual Ones, Ones which often exist in opposition to one another. These dual Ones can be seen as one person versus another person; one team versus another team; one system of ideals versus another system of ideals; one religious philosophy versus another religious philosophy; one culture versus another culture and so forth. This juxtaposition of ego-centered Ones often manifests as competition, contention, opposition, conflict, hostility, resistance and a general adversarial relationship between people, ideals, concepts, philosophies.

Because Two rules others and relationships as well as duality, this can create obvious problems. War is the polar opposite of peace. Since both war and peace constitute the polar apexes of the Two continuum, there is as much a possibility of one charge being manifested as the other. Thus, a Two Nature in its lowest level of expression can be extremely combative, aggressive, hostile and militant, creating disharmony, discord, disruption, contention, strife, competition, disputation, opposition and antagonism. Yet, the Eleven master number can also be extremely inspirational and encouraging, helping others realize their goals and dreams – when it is operating at its highest level.

The key for the Two Nature is to express its positive energy. Unlike the uncontrollable events and circumstances that will be part of our children's lives, the children do have the ability to choose how they act and react to life's events. Markedly, this is especially true for the Two because it is intrinsically dual by nature and, hence, is the vibration manifesting the true life test of balance and equilibrium. Therefore, as a Two Nature our children's challenge is to find the Golden Mean – the middle ground between polar opposites and manifest it. Parental wisdom dictates we help them see both sides, be diplomatic, balancing and. . . be at peace within themselves.

- Famous People with a Two Nature: *Albert Einstein, Billy Graham, Calvin Coolidge, George Washington, Jackie Robinson, Michael Jackson, Mother Teresa, Tommy Lee Jones, Winston Churchill*
- Famous People with a Two Material Nature: *Abraham Lincoln, Charles Darwin, Helen Keller, Martin Luther King, Jr., Matt Damon, Mother Teresa, Princess Diana, Teddy Roosevelt*

Nature Energy: Three (3)

Pleasant, expressive, communicative, artistic – these are major qualities of children with a Three Nature or Material Nature. As arguably the most amenable and friendliest of people, they smile a great deal, and people love to be around them. They are embracing and approachable. Too, it is harder for things to get them down than most of the other vibrations. This is a result of their positive attitude, which always finds them seeing or seeking the silver lining in every dark and foreboding cloud.

If there is a social butterfly among the Avenue of Crowns, it is the Three, especially if combined with Eight energy in the chart. No number is more fun, social, artistic, gregarious and genuinely happy than the Three, which sees just about everybody as a friend. This includes children, adults and animals alike. Their personality naturally exudes a pleasantness unlike anyone else.

The number Three rules communication. Unless the Three is negatively aspected in a chart as a *void* or being in a *Challenge* position, Three Nature children are very likely to be talkative and quite self-expressive. They may enjoy reading, writing, singing, acting, modeling, performing – any activity involving communication in some form.

Beauty is common to the Three, but the beauty we're talking about is not necessarily physical beauty, although that is highly possible with the Three, but internal beauty, the kind that emanates from the spirit and the heart. Having a religious or spiritual point of reference is also a strong potential in the Three's character makeup because of its trinity aspect.

The opposite side of the Three coin of ease, happiness, self-expression and perfection is one which reflects vanity, dis-ease, unhappiness, negative self-expression and a lack of confidence. Not having a sense of worthiness, a good self-image or too strong an image are possibilities. Therefore, parents can play a major role in either boosting their children's image or curbing its potential vanity. What parents should be careful of, however, is not contributing to their children's unworthiness and negative self-image by criticizing, ridiculing, denigrating or ignoring their children.

The Three energy rules beauty as we mentioned, and Three people are often quite physically beautiful, even stunning. Such beauty does draw attention, lots of it. If the individual is not anchored in a sense of humility, such attention can easily grow into vanity and arrogance, a glaring narcissism in which the personality is forever shouting, "Look at me! Look at me! Look at me! Aren't I beautiful, lovely, exquisite?" Ephemeral beauty can be a potential trap, however. As the mystic Rumi queried, "Don't you see how many beautiful faces are buried underneath the earth?" Therefore, parents of beautiful children should do their best to not let their children's beauty get out of control and morph into the ugliness of vanity.

Three loves pleasure, but it's best to seek pleasure of that which is pure and leads one to health and wholeness. Because of the pleasure-seeking quality of the Three, there is the risk of the Three saturating itself in material pleasures, which may ultimately lead to enormous pain and suffering. As Saint Dadu exclaims, "Hold pure, stay pure, say pure, take the pure, give the pure." Saint Ravidas states, "True happiness lies in realizing true holiness," and 19th Century Mystic, Swami Ji Maharaj, corroborates, "All worldly pleasures are a source of pain and eventually will betray their possessors."

- Famous People with a Three Nature: *Amelia Earhart, George Armstrong Custer, Howard Hughes, United States of America*

- Famous People with a Three Material Nature: *Billy Graham, Cameron Diaz, Danica Patrick, George Washington, Marilyn Monroe, Naomi Campbell, Prince Charles, Prince William*

Nature Energy: Four (4)

Four is the most structured of all the basic numbers. Unless voided or offset by a strong contingent of Five energy in the chart, Four Nature children resonant with events, conditions and circumstances that are ordered, stable, secure, strong, conventional and traditional. At its most positive point, the Four Nature is often manifested as the loyal, devoted, diligent worker, friend, associate, team player, partner and employee, steadfast in upholding the status quo and being reliable, dependable, strong and trustworthy.

Four is the vibration of roots, anchors and solid, immovable rocks. Four seldom budges. It sinks its teeth into its work and sticks right to the task. It is diligent, dogged, reliable and dependable.

Fours can go on forever without change. They like routine. Keeping things just the same is intrinsic to them. They generally do not like to move, adjust or be displaced. They love security and would much rather stay at home than explore the outer reaches of Never-Never Land. The Four Nature is strong, unbending, untiring, unwavering, service-oriented and relentless. Four is the vibration of discipline, control, persistence, perseverance and commonalty.

With a Four Nature, children are practical, pragmatic, orderly, sensible, systematic and service-oriented. They need to be these things to ensure their security, stability and safety. They are not risk-takers in general, nor are they very spontaneous. To get up and go on a moment's notice just on a lark and fly upon the wind to see where it will take them is not their preference. It's frankly too risky for them. Yet, they are excellent servants in the greatest sense of the word. Too, they can be excellent developers and builders of things, concepts and ideas.

The negative side of the Four Nature is that it can be too rigid for its own good. Fours can sometimes be so stubborn and unyielding they refuse to make sensible adjustments and critically positive changes. This rigidity can cause them to be blind to new, different and better ways of thinking, acting and doing. Progress, however, is based on change and the shedding of old skin, of old and outdated habits, ideals, patterns and entrenched ideas and concepts; in rounding out and softening the edges of the square of the Four's basic nature so it's not too abrasive to others.

Although being rock-solid and immovable can be virtuous, given the right set of circumstances, it can also be deadly. This is one critical aspect of the Four – it doesn't always move, adjust and change when, perhaps, it would be better served to do so.

As Four is the vibration of building and construction, it is also the vibration of destruction – its negative polarity, the other side of the Four coin. The universe expands and contracts. Just as there is life, there is death. Physical structures such as buildings and mountains, as well as social structures such as empires, rise and fall. Such is the nature of life. The Four Nature expresses both. How children choose to express it is germane to their well-being.

All in all, Four Nature children are the rock of the Avenue of Crowns, the salt of the earth, the anchor in the storm. Their beauty rests in their commitment to the ideals of strength, courage, devotion, control, service, security, dependability, fidelity, loyalty, hard work, persistence, discipline and undaunted determination. People trust them, a gift that should never be taken for granted, for it is trust that is the basis of all lasting relationships.

However, if the glass of trust is shattered, it can never be, like Humpty-Dumpty, put back together again, and the trust could be lost forever.

- Famous People with a Four Nature: *Bob Dylan, J.K. Rowling, Naomi Campbell, Princess Diana, Sarah Palin, Tiger Woods*
- Famous People with a Four Material Nature: *Calvin Coolidge, General Douglas MacArthur, George Foreman, John F. Kennedy*

Nature Energy: Five (5)

Children with a Five Nature or Material Nature enjoy being on the move, are freedom-loving and adventurous. Their mercurial energy keeps them exploring and seeking new experiences. It's very hard for them to be still, and they get bored if confined to one thing. They like variety and enjoy being non-conventional. However, if they have a Four Soul, Expression, Lifepath or Performance/Experience, they may experience an internal tug-o-war due to the Four's anchoring and stabilizing qualities, which could be beneficial in keeping the Five's movement energies from being too free.

The number Five is the *Number of Man*, so it's natural for Five Nature children to enjoy different kinds of people who can stimulate their need to explore and experience. Because Fives like to talk and converse, they would do well in situations where they are free to move about, explore and be spontaneous, unrestricted by the conventions which others find more security-esque, comfortable and traditional.

All Fives love freedom and this is where parents would be wise to help children control their mercurial nature. Freedom, true freedom, is the result of great discipline, restraint and self-control. True freedom is based solidly in the concept of detachment. Too often, freedom is defined as action without consequence, but the reality of life is that all actions produce consequences, and too much uninhibited action devoid of the consideration of consequence or an appropriate amount of critical thinking, can produce horrendously negative results.

Freedom, for example, does not equate to unlicensed, wanton sensual indulgence or promiscuity. And if any number has a reputation for being wild, indulgent, promiscuous and a party animal, it is the Five. Such unbridled actions can lead to incarcerating emotional, physical, financial, social and sexual confinement, disease, even death – hardly a condition of freedom. Life doesn't always give second chances, and a single, solitary act of miscalculation, lack of forethought, discipline and self-control can create a lifetime of sorrow and sadness.

Yet, when responsible action is undertaken as a result of clear thinking it can lead to real freedom, liberating freedom. Parents of Five Nature children would be wise, therefore, to consider this point of view. Children should be taught to enjoy their freedom but be careful of imbuing false concepts of freedom which may entrap them in the shackles of unrestrained behaviors.

Five energy loves speed. It's quite common to see this mercurial number in the charts of people who engage in motion sports or activities. Dancing, skiing, swimming, martial arts, sports car, boat and horse racing, etc., are all within the domain of the Five's love of motion and movement. Gambling is attractive too because it offers a chance for fast money, as well as the excitement Fives enjoy, even crave. Speed is addictive, and if there is any number that rules speed, it is definitely the Five. Yet, speed kills. Its momentum can create situations beyond the control of its owner, resulting in dangerous to lethal consequences. Yellow and red flags here.

As mentioned earlier, Five is the *Number of Man*. This is because all human beings have Five in common more than any other number: five fingers on each hand, five toes on each foot, five physical senses, thirty-two teeth; five rings on the Olympic flag. There are also 365 days in a year, a five in reduction. Too, Five is the fulcrum of the Alpha-Numeric Spectrum, the pivot point of all the basic numbers. Therefore, it can move from one end to the other with equal ease. No number moves more easily than the Five. This ability not only gives it its facility of movement but an excellent ability to communicate with all people. And since it is the fulcrum of the Avenue of Crowns it must, more than any other number, exude balance in all things.

The main lesson for Five Nature children is to learn the difference between freedom and slavery – the two sides of the Five energy. Freedom demands responsibility and self-control, and if these virtues are not respected and manifested, the potential result is slavery of all kinds – physical, emotional, financial, psychological, familial, sexual, spiritual. No one really wants to be a slave, and while Five is the apotheosis of freedom, it is also the greatest contender for becoming a slave . . . to itself.

- Famous People with a Five Nature: *Carl Sagan, Dolly Parton, General Douglas MacArthur, Edna St. Vincent Millay, Marilyn Monroe, Oprah Winfrey, Warren Buffett*
- Famous People with a Five Material Nature: *Amelia Earhart, Angelina Jolie, Elizabeth Taylor, George W. Bush, Jackie Evancho, Michael Phelps, Whitney Houston, William Shakespeare*

Nature Energy: Six (6)

Children with a Six in their Nature Layer are governed by their hearts. The home and domestic environment are important to them. Home is home, and that home may be a personal family unit, community or homeland.

These children have a genuine warmth, gentleness and softness about them that is very attractive and comforting to others. They are the nurturers who gently smooth the salve of love, compassion and concern on the wounds of people's lives. Potentially, they are excellent mothers, fathers, spouses, siblings, compassionate leaders and loving personal friends. They are loyal and responsible and in most cases would rather stay at or near home with the family than go gallivanting around the countryside like Five children would do.

The positive aspect of the Six is that at its zenith, it is pure love, personal compassion, harmony, beauty and art. At its nadir, it is degenerate lust, hatred, envy, jealousy, bitterness, resentment, inharmony and ugliness.

Six also has the indwelling condition of being the great nurturer or the great destroyer. Nothing hurts more than a wounded or broken heart. Contrarily, nothing is more radiant or joyful than a heart filled with pure love and compassion and, from a spiritual perspective, it is love, not passion, that creates joy, harmony and happiness which can lift the soul and psyche to wonderful levels of comfort, warmth and peace.

People with a Six Nature are quite comfortable in beautiful environments. Males often make excellent fathers, brothers, coaches, counselors, boy scout leaders and team players. Females under this energy can also make wonderful mothers, sisters, coaches, trainers, community leaders and organizers. Generally, Sixes love all things associated with family life from the kitchen to the baby's room to the garden and all points in between.

Six Nature children should be taught not to allow others to abuse their love and compassionate spirit, especially as they grow older. People may well take advantage of them if they're not careful.

Six Nature Layer individuals would be wise to becoming enablers. There is such a thing as tough love, i.e., making people own up to their own actions. As Six children become adults, they should be taught that being too soft at the wrong moment actually weakens and cripples children by teaching them there will always be someone to take care of them, which is not necessarily how real life works. Helping children learn to stand on their own two feet is critical to making them strong, responsible and mature adults who know the true meaning of love and compassion.

Six, of course, is two times Three – the cipher of self-expression and pleasure. Therefore, the negative side of the Six vibration can, like the Three, lead one down the path of excess, addiction, drug use, dangerous sexuality and hatred, especially if the master number Thirty-Three is present in the root system (for more on master numbers, read *The King's Book of Numerology, Volume I: Foundations & Fundamentals*).

- Famous People with a Six Nature: *Abraham Lincoln, Babe Ruth, Charles Darwin, Elizabeth Taylor, Elvis Presley, Helen Keller, John F. Kennedy*
- Famous People with a Six Material Nature: *Carl Sagan, Condoleezza Rice, Kenny Rogers, Elvis Presley*

Nature Energy: Seven (7)

Seven Nature children are governed by all things internal. They can be shy, reserved, reclusive, introverted, withdrawn, quiet, secret, private. As they grow, they will most probably make good students, for their energy is that of the thinker – the one who reflects, analyzes, ponders, cogitates, studies, examines. Because of their critical thinking skills, they will most probably choose activities in which they can use their minds. The sciences, mathematics, reading, writing, editing, accounting, teaching, religion, engineering and all occupations involving some aspect of mental and spiritual faculties are within their domain.

The Seven Nature is, potentially, the most spiritual vibration of its kind. Seven wends within. Therefore, these children are prone to being pensive, quiet, separate, even distant. To others they may seem odd, cold and strange because they don't necessarily like to mix with others in the outer world of social activity.

However, Seven children are not necessarily cold, distant or strange – maybe to the outer world, but certainly not to the inner world. These individuals are simply different, motivated by interests and desires unknown to those absorbed in the outer world of external phenomena, experiences and activity. Yes, they may like to be alone, but separation and isolation from the turmoil of day-to-day activity is important for them in order to recharge and refocus.

Being alone, withdrawn, reclusive and liking their own company is natural to the Seven Nature. To discover deeper truths and live at a deep level mandates time and space to ponder life and its critical questions. Living on the surface doesn't appeal to these children unless they also maintain a good amount of Two, Four, Six or Eight energy in other parts of their charts. As has been mentioned several times already, Seven is the most internal vibration in the Avenue of Crowns and it is not socially driven. It is internally driven, and therefore Seven individuals resonate with a solitary drumbeat that resounds within, not without.

The Seven Nature not only makes individuals spiritually, religiously, metaphysically and philosophically oriented, it also gives them a propensity to be poised, calm, quiet, reserved and elegant. Seven can be very stately, august and noble. It is regal and worthy of a crown – not a crown of arrogance, but one of majestic humility, peace and grace.

The Seven Nature, because it likes its privacy and reclusiveness, is often seen as shy. Unfortunately, those living in the outer world mistake shyness for weakness rather than a manner of being. There is no law in the universe that says one has to be popular, gregarious or socially gifted to be whole or acceptable. Sevens are fine just the way the are, as they are.

A couple cautions. First, because of its perfection-seeking, meticulous nature, the Seven can be too critical of others who don't share their degree of precision. Therefore, being patient, soft and forgiving will go a long way to softening the appearance of a cold and calculating exterior. Thus, in personal relations it would be wise for parents to teach their children to, as Saint Charan Singh states, "Be fault forgiving and defect concealing."

Second, Seven Souls can potentially be intrigued by secrecy, intrigue and the dark side of life. There may be at times a positive place for such interests, especially in security work. Yet, such activities do harbor concerns, the dangerous affects of which should not be overlooked.

Seven rules both saints and sinners – its opposing sides. The Light is pure and erases all shadows. The Dark is impure, adulterated and adulterates, hunting the precious life, destroying it and everything within its milieu. Obviously, it is always best to move children in the direction of the Light, constantly reinforcing its life-giving attributes.

Finally, Seven Nature children would be served well by having their parents teach them to love their sense of separation and isolation. Spiritual and mystic literature is replete with reassuring statements regarding the necessity of spending time alone. It is in one's "alone time" that the opportunity to go within and make deep connections with the indwelling Spirit resides because, ultimately, the Path of Light is found Within, not without.

- Famous People with a Seven Nature: *Albert Schweitzer, Condoleezza Rice, Henry Wadsworth Longfellow, Larry King, William Shakespeare*
- Famous People with a Seven Material Nature: *Albert Schweitzer, Edgar Cayce, Martha Stewart, Muhammad Ali, Walter Cronkite*

Nature Energy: Eight (8)

Eight rules social interaction, success, commerce, business and external power. Therefore, Eight Nature children will grow to be the ones who like to manage, lead, take charge and be in the center of all that flows. Generally speaking, these souls are quite social and enjoy mixing. Money, wealth, riches, material success, comfort, personal prestige, recognition and achievement are important to the Eight Nature because the Eight energy is the 'energy of the loop', of material success, leadership and management. Eight connects and disconnects. It sees what needs to be done and gets it done, usually by taking charge and managing others, administrating and coordinating all of the various tasks and duties essential to the efficient accomplishment and success of the project at hand.

Eight administrates. It also manipulates. Manipulation is not a bad word. Doctors and health care professionals, for example, manipulate people to better health as a course of their daily function. Generals, CEOs, presidents, executives and other leadership personnel are duty-bound to manipulate all of the components within the structural confines of their authority for the benefit of all who come within the boundaries of their jurisdiction.

Eight Nature individuals are the ones responsible for connecting the opposing polar charges – positive and negative, buyer and seller, concept and completion, etc. The main concern, however, is that because they have these skills, they must be taught to use them for the good of all, not just the good of themselves. Selfish manipulation for personal gain creates problems. Eventually, what goes around, comes around. It's a fact of life.

Eights have a natural propensity for being able to figure out how things work; how an idea, product, process, service or electrical current, etc., flows to create a continuous circuit. It's a wonderful trait. This is where the Eight shines – in knowing, or being able to figure out, how things work, whatever those things are. Because of this unique skill, people with Eight energy strongly dominant in their charts make excellent generals, admirals, administrators, presidents, CEOs, managers, mechanics, technicians, coaches, principals, doctors, engineers, police and fire captains, etc. – anything to do with solving problems through understanding *flow*.

Because Eight is the highest octave of the social numbers Two, Four, Six and Eight, it is the most socially gifted and astute. Therefore, Eights are usually found in the socialite section of the local newspaper. Such people love to connect, interact, move and mix, be in the loop and in the center of all that's social.

Eight Nature children should be taught to enjoy their social gifts, to be the organizers, managers, leaders, administrators, executives, mechanics, assistants, planners. They should be raised, however, to be careful with their abilities and to be patient with those who are not as gifted as they are. Knowing how to connect opposing polarities and make things function smoothly is a rare gift, a gift these children should be pleased to possess.

- Famous People with an 8 Nature: *Bob Hope, George W. Bush, Jack LaLanne, Jackie Evancho, Martha Stewart*

- Famous People with an 8 Material Nature: *Albert Einstein, John Wayne, Larry King, Michael Jackson, United States of America*

Nature Energy: Nine (9)

Nine Nature children are unique. They radiate a natural power and presence unmatched by the other basic numbers. Therefore, their way and manner of doing things are power-based and dominant. Their presence is always felt and is unmistakable. Because Nine is the Grand Elemental, its vibration encompasses all vibrations. These children therefore have a propensity of attraction, an inherent magnetism that is real but untouchable and somewhat inexplicable.

Nine Nature children often have charisma and charm. There seems to be a completeness about them that the other basic Natures lack. They are dynamic, and it is in their nature to rule, not be ruled. There is a strong possibility that, although they have a definite universal quality about them, they may tend to be more of a pubic figure and person than a private or personal one. Nine is not a personally loving vibration. It is a universally loving one. The energies of these individuals are intrinsically rooted in the ability to connect with all people.

As a Nine Nature, they do not do things in a small way. Their energy is too expansive and all-inclusive for that. They encompass everything, and there is a definite side to them that is dominant. The caution is that it should guard against becoming oppressively domineering.

The Nine energy brings an enormous test of power, responsibility, humility, restraint and gracious generosity, coupled with the refinement and bearing of a magnanimous monarch. It is this goal to which Nine children should be guided. In doing so they may avoid the pitfall of imperious, overbearing rulership and behavior.

Probably the greatest caution for the Nine Nature is in the use and misuse of power. The symbol for the Nine is the crown because Nines rule. Yet, rulership can be just as nefarious as it can be magnanimous. Power is power. It plays no favorites between the forces of light and darkness. In this regard, a quote from Shakespeare is germane: "Uneasy lies the head that wears a crown." [Henry The Fourth, Part 2, Act 3, scene 1, 26–31].

People with a Nine Nature would do very well in occupations and vocations set on the public stage such as doctors, nurses, dentists, lawyers, educators, actors, entertainers, writers, reporters, newscasters, authors, volunteers of all kinds, teachers, preachers, therapists, humanitarians – anything to do with the public stage and humanity in general. Nine is the energy belonging to everyone because it is everyone.

- Famous People with a Nine Nature: *Angelina Jolie, Danica Patrick, Michael Phelps, Mohandas Gandhi, Muhammad Ali, Queen Elizabeth II, Shaun White*
- Famous People with a Nine Material Nature: *Dolly Parton, Garth Brooks, General George Patton, Howard Hughes, Jackie Robinson, J.K. Rowling, Mohandas Gandhi, Oprah Winfrey, Patrick Swayze, Steve Jobs, Winston Churchill*

There can be no keener revelation of a society's soul than the way in which it treats its children.

~ Nelson Mandela

9

Voids

Voids are missing letters and their corresponding numbers in the full birth name. In the Simple Letter Value Chart, each of the single numbers 1 through 9 is associated with different letter groupings called *genera*. The number 1, for example, is associated with the A-J-S genera; the number 2 is related to the B-K-T genera; the number 3 corresponds to the letter genera of C-L-U and so forth. When any of these letter classes is absent in a natal name, there is a void – a numerical vacancy, an empty vibration.

Simple Letter Value Chart									
Voids are missing letters/numbers in the full birth name									
The Letters	A	B	C	D	E	F	G	H	I
	J	K	L	M	N	O	P	Q	R
	S	T	U	V	W	X	Y	Z	
Number Value	1	2	3	4	5	6	7	8	9

If a voided number is also absent in any component of the Basic Matrix, it is called a Grand Void. For example, an individual with a 3 void [no Cs, Ls or Us in the birth name], as well as no 3s in the Basic Matrix is said to have a 3 Grand Void.

Void Analogies

There are several ways we can look at voids. First, we can think of voids as a lack of construction tools. For example, if a carpenter were to begin building a house but had no saw to cut the wood needed to construct the dwelling, he would obviously have a void, not only in his tool chest (the missing saw) but a void in his ability to perform his job. If a writer wanted to create a book but had little or no understanding of words, he, too, would suffer a void, for words are the tools of the writer. If a parent lacked an understanding of structure, the importance of discipline and establishing foundations in a child's life – important tools in building solid, responsible and whole children – he or she, too, would suffer a void. Voids reflect absences of skill, substance and ability.

A second analogy is that of wiring in which each of the nine basic numbers 1-2-3-4-5-6-7-8-9 represents the composite "wiring" of the individual. Each number, as a wire, manifests specific characteristics and attributes across which flow specific energies allowing the individual to operate as a conscious living being. When an individual's full natal name houses all of the single numbers, his wiring is complete and his ability to operate as a balanced, harmonious and functionally integrated human being is enhanced. When a number or numbers are missing in the chart, however, the wiring is incomplete and the individual's chances to live a full, whole, balanced and effective life are compromised.

Think of an automobile and its structure. It is filled with all kinds of wires which send mechanical or electrical signals to its various parts, thus allowing the car to run smoothly and efficiently. If even one of the wires isn't connected, the entire functionality of the vehicle is put at risk.

Perhaps the ignition system is in tact but there are no break lines from the brake pedal to the wheels. The car will not be able to stop even if it gets moving. If there's no wiring from the steering column to the front end wheel assembly, the car may be able to start, it may be able to go, it may be able to stop but it won't be able to turn. Thus, it is obvious that an automobile's wiring system is critical to its health, integration and functionability. Without it, the automobile may not only be inefficient but dangerous . . . to itself and others.

A third analogy of voids is that they're just holes in the armor of an individual's being or, if one prefers, chinks in the armor of one's personal defenses. In the battle of life, we all need defenses to protect us from the aggressive attacks of predators, whether they're assaulting the physical, financial, professional, personal, emotional, psychological or spiritual components of our being. No one in their right mind would think of entering a nuclear reactor chamber with hole-ridden protective clothing, or spending extended time in the sun without adequate sunscreen, or working in a construction zone without a helmet, boots, gloves and the correct type of clothing.

Voids – whether we see them as an absence of tools, wiring, armor or protective clothing – are critical factors relating to our lives, especially to our relationships. In lieu of the nature of voids, it would be wise for parents to consider them and their effects as they apply to their children's lives.

Most of us have a void or voids in our chart. It's normal to have them, but the more voids we have, the more potential problems and challenges we may have in life. Having voids doesn't mean we are a bad person. Many great souls have had voids. General George Patton and Marilyn Monroe had a 3 void in their charts. Mother Teresa maintained a 4 void in her chart. Amelia Earhart, Charles Lindberg, Martin Luther King, Jr., Helen Keller and William Shakespeare all had a 6 void. Abraham Lincoln, Albert Schweitzer, Charles Darwin and Helen Keller had a 7 void. Isaac Newton, arguably the greatest scientist in history, had voids of 4-7-8. Albert Einstein, the greatest scientist of the Twentieth Century, had voids of 4-6-7-8. Having voids simply means we will potentially have issues at some time during our life in those areas associated with the voided number(s).

How Voids Manifest Themselves

How do voids manifest themselves? Usually in one of three ways:

1. <u>Ignoring the void</u>

The individual will totally ignore its energy and characteristics. The void's attributes and energies may simply hold no interest for him. For example, a person with a 2 void may have absolutely no concern or regard for others and their well-being or for close personal relationships. A person with a 6 void may have no interest in domestic matters or involvement with the home life.

2. <u>Filling the void</u>

The person will do everything he can to try and fill the void(s), even possibly over-compensate by totally involving himself in the conditions which the void represents. This would be an example of Nature filling a vacuum. For example, many people with a 6 void may spend their lives trying to find love and romance rather than displaying no interest in love. Certainly Isaac Newton and Albert Einstein, both with 4 and 7 voided in their charts, spent their lives searching and finding answers to many universal life questions, thereby filling their 7 void.

3. Displaying negatives

The person will display the negative aspects of the number involved. In the case of the number Six, the person may become a firestorm of hate, jealousy, animosity, anger or envy. An individual with a Seven (7) void may become secretly treacherous, foolish and ignoble with a cold and calculating approach to life and people.

Void Chart

The following Void Chart details the assortment of issues (noted by keywords) a person may have with a particular void.

Void Chart

Void	General Description - Issues Related to . . .
1 A-J-S	The self and its worth, independence, solo, the Yang aspect of life, male influence, fathers, brothers, uncles, bosses, leaders, managers, authority figures, action, leadership, creativity, ego, self-esteem, taking charge, standing up for one's self, being alone, drive, ambition, direction, will power
2 B-K-T	Others, relationships, the Yin aspect of life, female influence, mothers, sisters, aunts, following and being the follower,

		supporting and being the supporter, balance, receptivity, sensitivity, tolerance, caring, helping, sharing, diplomacy, deceit, duplicity, indirectness, intuition, close personal relationships
3	C-L-U	Self-expression, health, beauty, personal integration, marriage, children, speech, friends, words, happiness, joy, ease, disease, dis-ease, sickness, communication, harshness of expression, criticism, personal image, vanity, pleasure, entitlement
4	D-M-V	All things of structure, order, work, service, effort, control, roots, discipline, regimentation, details, clerical tasks, security, rules, regulations, duty, devotion, fidelity, honesty, trust, strength, safety, stability, stubbornness, endurance, rigidity, mechanics
5	E-N-W	Freedom, change, detachment, people in general, movement, motion, speed, experience, talents, variety, the senses, sex, crowds, activity, excitement, adventure, exploration, shifting, spontaneity, wildness, uncertainty, intemperance, absence or lack of restraint, being undisciplined, out of control, enslaved
6	F-O-X	Matters of the home, heart and hearth, domesticity, family, love, sex, romance, nurturing, compassion, balance, beauty, harmony, community, personal responsibility and accountability, honoring, adjustment, duties in the home environment
7	G-P-Y	Inner peace, spirituality, mysticism, religion, inquisition, insight, being alone, alienation, isolation, separation, solitude, privacy, reflection, poise, perfection, depth of being, thoughtfulness, concern, calm, chaos, confusion, nobility, ignobility,

	thoughtlessness, cold, cruel, ruthless, indifference, inconsiderate, withdrawing, receding, recession, secrecy, wisdom
8 **H-Q-Z**	Interaction, involvement, connection, disconnection, continuity, flow, business, commerce, worldly status, management, executive leadership, wealth, success, material power, riches, comfort, administration, manipulation, orchestration, marketing, usury, being in the loop, connecting the dots
9 **I-R**	Universality, compassion, strength, power, rulership, respect for others and the law, service, understanding of the 'all', the 'many', the macrocosm, impersonal love, comprehensive feeling, arrogance, dominance, being over-bearing, impudent, rude, imperious, malevolence, benevolence, broadcasting, recognition

Managing the Spectrum of Voids

Would you knowingly scream at a deaf child to make him move? Of course not. Would you find fault with a blind child who didn't understand the concept of colors? Of course not. Would you criticize a child who didn't have the capacity to speak for not being able to sing? Of course not. In all such cases sensitive and caring individuals would exercise patience and understanding in how they interact with children.

In much the same way, it is best to be understanding of children and people with voids. Most of us have voids, and we are usually challenged in the area of the void's attributes and characteristics. If, for example, we have the number 8 dominant in our charts and it is not voided, we should exercise patience with those people who have an 8 void and correspondingly who do not have the same ability we have to manage, execute and orchestrate the flow of life's events.

Getting angry or hostile with people and their voids is not an efficient management strategy. We need to assess the void situation correctly and act accordingly, exercising patience, tolerance, kindness, understanding and most of all, wisdom. Please remember, we don't see things the way they are; we see things the way our numbers are, and if the amalgam of our "numbers" includes a void or voids, we will see things accordingly. Most importantly, if our children have a void or voids in their name, we definitely need to be informed of the void and what it represents and then act in positive ways commensurate with helping our children grow to be confident and whole individuals. How many children have a void or voids in their full birth name and the parents are unaware of the challenges their children face because of such voids? What are your voids? Your children's voids? Parents? Spouse? Partner? Friends? Business associates?

Naming Children

To prevent having to deal with the potential problems generated by voids, one important consideration involves creating children's names that have no voids. Having no voids in a child's name would create a more balanced name (and child) and mitigate any major issues and their subsequent problems if there were a void or voids in the birth name. Of course many parents may not know of this parenting strategy, and their children may have names with voids. In this case, exercising knowledge and understanding of how to manage voids will be beneficial.

To create a name without voids, simply make sure there is at least one letter of each genera (letter grouping) in the full birth name using the Simple Letter Value Chart. Having at least one letter from each of the genera would insure the full name contains every single number 1 through 9 and, therefore, the name would have no voids. It may be repetitive, but let's review this process again.

Simple Letter Value Chart									
The Letters	A	B	C	D	E	F	G	H	I
	J	K	L	M	N	O	P	Q	R
	S	T	U	V	W	X	Y	Z	
Number Value	**1**	**2**	**3**	**4**	**5**	**6**	**7**	**8**	**9**

For example, the letters A-J-S have a numeric value of 1. Therefore, the child's name should have an A, J or S in the full birth name. Having all three of the letters is not necessary. If there were not an A-J or S in the full birth name, the child would have a 1 void. Simply follow the same procedure for the other numbers and their genera, i.e., having a B, K or T for the number 2; a C, L or U for the number 3 and so forth.

For example, in the fictitious name *Clive Thomas Gentry* below there is at least one letter of each genera and its corresponding number represented. In other words, all of the single numbers (1-2-3-4-5-6-7-8-9) exist in the name *Clive Thomas Gentry* which, therefore, has no voids.

C	L	I	V	E	T	H	O	M	A	S	G	E	N	T	R	Y
3	3	9	4	5	2	8	6	4	1	1	7	5	5	2	9	7

Parenting Wisdom in Managing Voids

If you have a child or children with a void or voids, which is more likely than not, following are some ideas to not only help your children in managing their lives but to also help you with your parenting management skills and strategies. As a note, in the following lists of famous people with a certain void, the void is from their full birth name, not their more common public, professional or stage name.

One (1) Void

If our children have a One void, they will need to concentrate on, and work toward, being whole and independent without being egocentric, arrogant or self-absorbed. A One voided child would be well-served in being patient with authority figures but not allowing others to dominate him or her or do for them unnecessarily. A One void demands children learn to do things for themselves, stand on their own two feet, as well as standing up and being counted, being strong and courageous. It also means they must learn to be direct and forthright in their dealings with others, as well as being able to look at their faults, failings and shortcomings and not point the finger of blame toward others.

A One void can make a person very empty but dangerous. People lacking self worth often attempt to cut others down to build themselves up – a tactic that only further impacts them negatively. The One rules male energy and therefore male issues, and males in general will be associated with a One void. Ego, self and yang issues will be exacerbated when the One occupies a Challenge position [1st E-P-C Triad]. Incidentally, when One is in any Challenge timeline, whether it is voided or not, problems with the ego or males and their accompanying issues loom large, so one is cautioned to be ever vigilant if possible in keeping yang attributes in check.

- Famous People with a One Void: *Ted Bundy* (born: *Theodore Robert Cowell*) who was more infamous than famous. Note: There are three numbers that rarely appear as a void in the charts of famous people – the numbers 1, 5 and 9. This is because famous people have strong identities (1), move among men (5), and play their destinies out on the universal life stage (9). Plus, the two numbers signifying the masses more than any two numbers are the 5 and 9.

Two (2) Void

A child with a Two void must learn to be the helper, team player and supporter, paying close attention to the feelings of others. Having a Two void can often make a person very indifferent, even rude, to other people.

Females, or individuals with strong Two energy, may well be a challenge. This would include mothers, mothers-in-law, grandmothers, sisters, aunts, female friends and associates. A Two void could be difficult for a person with a large amount of One energy because the One focuses on himself, not others. A Two voided child must be cautious of ignoring others or even violating their right to life and happiness. A Two void often causes conflict and stress in close personal relationships.

To overcome the negative effects of such a void in their children, parents can help by teaching them balance in all things, being sensitive to others and seeing life from the other person's point of view. Caring, being compassionate, friendly, supportive, the team player and responsive partner are all positive strategies. Stressing to children the importance of manners is good, as well as learning to share with others and having respect for all people.

- Famous People with a Two Void: *Arnold Schwarzenegger, Edgar Cayce, Elvis Presley, George Foreman, Jack LaLanne, J.K. Rowling, Larry King, Marion Jones, Michael Phelps, Muhammad Ali, Oprah Winfrey, Phil McGraw, Princess Diana*

Three (3) Void

Children with a Three void need to focus on being positive, happy, healthy and avoid habits and activities that interfere with or destroy health or well-being – their own or other people's.

Oftentimes, a Three void can equate to harshness and meanness in words, communication and actions. People with a Three void can be plagued with unhappiness, as is well-documented in the life of Marilyn Monroe [born Norma Jeane Mortenson], a soul who was constantly in search of finding contentment and joy in her life.

General George Patton Jr. is an excellent example of a person who worked to fill the void of the Three, sort of. He was a voracious reader, loved words, and often gave powerful, inspiring speeches to his men. Yet, his inappropriate use of language also got him into trouble more than once in his career.

Because Three rules beauty, one of the dangers is vanity and an overexaggeration with one's self-image or in some cases, no image. History has proven that both Monroe and Patton had image issues that bordered on, or translated into, vanity. Marilyn Monroe and George Patton are two of twelve famous people represented in *Destinies of the Rich & Famous: The Secret Numbers of Extraordinary Lives* available at RichardKing.net.

Three also rules children, and it's not uncommon for women with a Three void or voided Challenge to be barren or have no desire whatsoever to have children, even like them. A Three voided person needs to concentrate on being positive and grateful for everything . . . even if "everything" is not what the person wants. This will allow the individual to avoid the great sin of ingratitude, which may well be why the person was given the void in the first place – to learn to be grateful for everything in life in spite of what life dishes out to him or her.

Concentrating on health and well-being is very important for children with a Three void. Parents should note that attention should also be paid to insuring their children's self-image, which is an integral aspect to being healthy. It is common that a Three void often generates issues of unworthiness or a poor self-image, and if parents are aware of this they can help their children greatly by focusing on the positive attributes their children manifest naturally in order to strengthen what they lack. Find that which is good and build on it. Parents must be very wary of overly criticizing, finding fault with or ridiculing children with a Three void because no void reflects negatively on children's self-esteem more than the Three void.

- Famous People with a Three Void: *General George Patton, George Foreman, George Washington, John Wayne, Marilyn Monroe*

Four (4) Void

When Four is void there exist potential problems in areas relating to order, security and stability. When Four is a Voided Challenge or a Grand Voided Challenge [see *The King's Book of Numerology II: Forecasting - Part I*], the issues become intense. Faithlessness, non-accountability, infidelity and dishonesty potentially loom large, as does a person's personal security and safety. It's difficult to be organized with no organizational skills, no discipline, no self-control. Four in a Challenge position can also make one feel as though he is imprisoned. This is because of the Four's propensity to confine, constrict, restrict and limit.

Other scenarios exist for this structure-oriented cipher. For example, a person with a Four void may well have no code of morals or ethics to live by. Departures from the truth are certainly possible. Because Four rules matter and the material body, when it is void there may be issues of bodily strength, immune system deficiencies, personal security and wholeness.

Another caution for the Four void is to avoid being too resistant, stubborn and recalcitrant. Being strong is one thing, but being unruly and antagonistic may create a dangerous and unhealthy rigidity with people clinging too hard to the security they lack.

The parental wisdom with a Four void is to teach discipline, control, judgment, accountability, responsibility, reliability, duty, honor, trust, and personal ethics right from the get go. If these virtues are not established when children are young, their absence could prove highly problematic as the children mature.

- Famous People with a Four Void: *Albert Einstein, Albert Schweitzer, Bob Hope, Frank Sinatra, Garth Brooks, George W. Bush, Mother Teresa, Oprah Winfrey, Prince Charles*

Five (5) Void

It is very rare to have a Five void because "E" is the most used letter in the English language and "N" is also very common. Having no Five's would affect a person's sense of movement, freedom and ability to change. If Five is voided or challenged, drastic change, uncertainty and loss are quite possible. This is because one of the binary roots of the Five is the 14, the cipher of loss and detachment. Five not only rules freedom but also slavery, the opposite side of its coin. Coupled with Four energy, a person could easily find himself stuck in a rut, a ship anchored securely in place with no compunction to move, explore or be free.

A lack of Five energy may over-stimulate a person to experience a wide array of sensations, involvement in deleterious substances such as drugs and alcohol and seek a profligate, promiscuous lifestyle. The Five rules curiosity, and remember what curiosity did to the cat . . . it killed it.

Five also rules speed, so one must be careful not to move too fast, lest one lose total control of himself. Speed kills – in more ways than one. A Five voided child would be well-advised to be temperate, controlled and use discretion in all things. Acting without thinking first is a recipe for disaster.

- Famous People with a Five Void: *General Douglas MacArthur, Garth Brooks*

<u>Six (6) Void</u>

Six voids herald problems and issues with domestic matters, love, nurturing, family, heart, home and romance. It's not uncommon for famous people to have a 6 void. Einstein, Schweitzer, Shakespeare, Earhart, Lindbergh, Helen Keller and Martin Luther King, Jr. all possessed this missing cipher in their birth names. Yet, they were extremely successful in their fields of endeavor, leading one to surmise that perhaps if God wants a soul to dedicate itself to some line of work and not be anchored to the home, He gives it a Six void, thus limiting its involvement in a home life and allowing for more time and devotion to other endeavors.

It is a fact, however, that if a Six is in a Grand Voided Challenge position [no Fs, Os or Xs in the Expression or Basic Matrix but appearing in a Challenge position in the Life Matrix], especially if this void condition is prevalent in the early life of a child [1st E-P-C Triad], there will be major difficulties in the home life and in the heart. A lack of love, nurturing, harmony and peace within the domicile are viable possibilities. Such a lack can also turn into discord, arguments, parental fights, drug usage and other negative behaviors. Adjustments to these issues could be quite challenging.

The Six Voided Challenge is all about love and/or the lack of it. The Six void also carries the potential concentration of its polar aspects – hate, envy, jealousy, bitterness, resentment. It could also be manifested in a person who has responsibility for the home as a caretaker, gardener, butler, maid, servant, attending spouse for a sick or ailing partner or family member.

Regardless of the degree, a Six void will engage the individual in some facet of the love life, heart, domestic environment or community habitat. The solution to the heartache is to be loving, not angry for not having love; to be nurturing, caring, sympathetic and loyal so as not to plant negative seeds that will eventually grow to fruition at some future time, thus creating even more heartache or familial frustration.

If children do have a Six void in their charts appearing in their formative years [1st E-P-C Triad], parents would be wise to check their own behaviors and the environment they've created in their home for the family. This is because when children with an active Six void in their early life experience a lack of love, nurturing and affection, it can only be naturally associated with the parents or guardians.

- Famous People with a Six Void: *Albert Einstein, Albert Schweitzer, Amelia Earhart, Charles Lindbergh, Helen Keller, Larry King, Martin Luther King, Jr., Muhammad Ali, William Shakespeare*

Seven (7) Void

The main problem with the Seven void is depth of thought, or rather the lack of it. This Seven void can make one inconsiderate, indifferent, cold, distant, detached, disconnected, even ruthless. Seven rules all things internal, especially those things dealing with the mind and spirit. When

Seven is voided, there exists little to no deep thinking or wisdom, at least on one side of the Seven coin.

The irony is that, as we've discussed, one way voids are managed is that the person tries to fill them with the exact energy of the void. For example, Abraham Lincoln was, arguably, the greatest president in United States history and an extremely deep thinker. Yet, he maintained a Seven void, as did Helen Keller, Albert Einstein, Albert Schweitzer and Charles Darwin, although many of these people did have Seven's in other areas of their numerology charts. It's as if the lack of Seven energy drove them to think, reflect, ponder, examine, research and study, thus filling up the void.

Another issue with the Seven void is the ability to be still and calm since Seven rules peace and quiet. We know Lincoln had suffered from depression and despondency from time to time. Was this breakdown a manifestation of his Seven void? Helen Keller also had stillness issues, especially when she was young. The moral of this story, as it is with all voids, is to recognize that the polar differences within each number can and do manifest themselves in completely opposite ways. Parents, therefore, would be wise to teach their children the positive attributes of the Seven (or any number) to nullify its negative characteristics and thus bring balance into the life of their child or children.

Seven voids in the early life signal disturbances, often with the parents. It also carries a red flag as to the misuse or abuse of alcohol. To have a Seven void in the early years of a child's life is not a good indicator of peace and happiness in the home. Quite the contrary. Like the Six void, parents should take a close look at their own situation, habits, behaviors and conduct. Once again, a baby or little child is too young to create the disturbance caused by a Seven void. Therefore, any negativity appearing in the chart of a child during the formative years must be generated by the parents, family members or caretakers.

- Famous People with a Seven Void: *Albert Einstein, Albert Schweitzer, Charles Darwin, Helen Keller, Isaac Newton, Jackie Robinson, Marilyn Monroe, Marion Jones, Ted Bundy, Walter Cronkite*

<u>Eight (8) Void</u>

When Eight is void, there is no flow, no connection, no conduit. Hence, things do not go smoothly or run efficiently. To have, for example, a person in a management or administrative position with an Eight void and no Eights in the Basic Matrix, let alone having the Eight possibly be situated as a Challenge or Voided Challenge in the chart, is to court financial difficulties.

In order for things to flow properly, one must be able to connect idea to manifestation, concept to completion, product to sale, buyer to seller. It is the Eight that allows this to happen. Worldly success has often been associated with the Eight, and the reason for this is the Eight's inherent capacity to connect the dots and get things done. Without an Eight in the mix, things don't get done efficiently because the energy's not there to make things happen.

A person with no Eights simply has a hard time understanding how to connect or integrate, how to go from point A to point B. Eight is the great administrator and coordinator. Eight is also the great manipulator (remember, every number has a positive <u>and</u> negative aspect). Eight is equally applauded by crooks and gods alike. With Eights present in a chart, probabilities of success exist; without Eights, the outlook is slim to none that success will be a reality.

Two problems of which to be aware with the Eight void are non-responsiveness and procrastination. Eight is the highest and most powerful social vibration. When it's void, children tend to have issues with being responsive to others. They can also procrastinate when they should be being about the task at hand. Therefore, Eight void children must concentrate on being responsive and efficient.

Being non-responsive tends to make people indifferent to others, especially on a personal level. Few things destroy or kill a relationship faster or more efficiently than indifference. When Eight is void, there is no connection, no support. A total absence of feelings, sympathy, empathy or involvement in and for the lives of other individuals often occurs. People just don't care about others on a deep level when the connective vibratory tissue of the Eight is absent. Such people may be popular based on other energies in the chart such as a Three or Nine, but on an intimately personal level, there's little concern or endearment for others.

An Eight void is often present in the charts of criminals and predators, who may be superficially charismatic in order to lure their victims, but who have absolutely no regard for their prey. If they cared for others, they wouldn't be predators in the first place.

Two extremely infamous characters are notorious mass-murderer Charles Manson [birth name: "No Name Maddox"] and master fraud schemer, Bernie Madoff [birth name: "Bernard Lawrence Madoff"]. Neither of these souls had any concern for the people whose lives they destroyed. Too, in conjunction with their Eight voids, they both had a Seven void in their charts. The "7 void/8 void" combination is arguably the worst and most nefariously problematic ciphered compound there is. It's potentially ice cold and heartless.

Let's be clear: not all people with an Eight void are evil. There are many factors in a chart to consider when making assessments, but one would be wise to take note of such potentials and not ignore them.

- Famous People with an Eight Void: *Albert Einstein, Edna St. Vincent Millay, Elvis Presley, George Armstrong Custer, Isaac Newton, Jackie Robinson, Marilyn Monroe, Muhammad Ali, Naomi Campbell, Peyton Manning, Steve Jobs, Warren Buffett*

Nine (9) Void

The Nine void may cause people to seek the limelight or work with humanity in some manner, especially in a volunteer capacity. Nine in a Pinnacle or Challenge position [see *The King's Book of Numerology II: Forecasting - Part I*] will most likely generate travel on some level – physically, psychologically, spiritually, vicariously. Without a Nine present in a chart, an individual will have a difficult time connecting with the masses, that is unless he tries to fill his life with them.

With a Nine void it's not uncommon for a person to be involved with the public in some capacity, even to be anti-public. To what degree and in what aspect [positive or negative] depends on other numbers and factors in the chart.

A Nine void often manifests by the person not having a full grasp of the big picture or having little to no respect for others and their lives and pursuits. It can also cause one to perform untoward actions in order to gain public recognition or acceptance. If a person craves acknowledgement beyond the norm and is denied such recognition, then negative circumstances can arise. To be acknowledged, it is important to acknowledge, so the solution for a lack of acknowledgment is to acknowledge and recognize others first, be generally happy for them and their success. This will plant good seed which, by natural law, must one day grow to fruition and bless the sower with an abundant harvest.

- Famous People with a Nine Void: *Steve Jobs, Tommy Lee Jones*

A Positive Note Regarding Voids

Voids can be highly problematic in a chart. Of this there is no doubt. However, if a voided number appears in the Soul or Material Soul of the individual, the negative effects of the void may be mitigated, if not totally erased. The reason for this is that the Soul Layers govern the desires of an individual and such desires would not ignore the voided energy but seek it. Therefore, the void would have little negative effect in the life.

If a void is present in the Basic Matrix, this is also an indication that the negative effects of the void will not be as severe as they might otherwise be. In fact, it's not uncommon to find a void(s) occupying a Basic Matrix component(s). A person with an 8 Nature, for example, will demonstrate the attributes of the 8 more than ignore them. The same is true for all the numbers. Voids only become highly problematic when they do not appear in the Basic Matrix but do appear in the Life Matrix or in the PE position of the Name or Letter Matrices. More on these timelines can be found in *The King's Book of Numerology II: Forecasting – Part 1*.

Mary & John: Voids

Let's now take a look at the charts of Mary Jane Smith and John David Doey to determine if they have any voids in their charts.

Mary Jane Smith: Voids 3 & 6

M	A	R	Y	J	A	N	E	S	M	I	T	H
4	1	9	7	1	1	5	5	1	4	9	2	8

No 3s (C-L-U) or 6s (F-O-X)

The Voids of Mary Jane Smith are: 3 & 6

By assessing the numbers associated with each of the letters in Mary's natal name, we see she has no Cs, Ls or Us representing the 3 energy; nor does she have any Fs, Os or Xs, the energy of the 6. All the other numbers between 1 and 9 are accounted for. Therefore, Mary's voids are 3 & 6.

The 3 void indicates Mary will potentially have challenges, issues, concerns or problems with her self-expression, image, words, communication skills, health, pleasure. This should not be too severe, however, because her 3 Expression makes her the epitome of the 3 energy itself. Too, her Material Soul of 3 gives her a desire to seek and give pleasure, happiness, joy to others, as well as being a good communicator.

Mary's 6 void is, in fact, a 6 Grand Void because she has no 6s in her Basic Matrix. Mary will definitely experience issues relating to love, romance, the home, heart and hearth, nurturing, supporting and being domestically oriented. Thus, we can surmise that love, in some capacity, will be an issue for Mary throughout her life. Given this reality of the 6 Grand Void, she may totally neglect the 6 energy, perhaps giving time to a professional career, finding happiness and fulfillment in her work rather than in a family environment. She may try to fill the 6 void with multiple love affairs, or she may exhibit anger as an outpouring of frustration. By analyzing her *Life Matrix* we could easily assess the extent to which the 6 would or would not be problematic in her life.

John David Doey: Voids 2 & 3

John's natal name has no Bs, Ks or Ts, thus creating a 2 void. He also has no Cs, Ls or Us, giving him an additional void of 3. His Basic Matrix does have 3s, a good thing. Yet, he is absent a 2 in his Basic Matrix, making John's 2 a Grand Void. Thus, John will have issues, challenges, concerns and potential problems with close personal relationships, others, female energy, finding balance in his life, being a team player, supporter and partner.

J	O	H	N	D	A	V	I	D	D	O	E	Y
1	6	8	5	4	1	4	9	4	4	6	5	7

No 2s (B-K-T)   or   3s (C-L-U)

The Voids of John David Doey are: 2 & 3

Void Summary

Voids play a major role in our lives. They need to be assessed and addressed. They are not to be feared; they are to be managed, and they can be problematic. However, having voids can be a positive thing. They may force us to concentrate on an energy our soul needs for its growth and well-being, or perhaps avoid such energy so we can be released from its conditions and attributes to pursue other directions in life.

Remember the people we mentioned earlier who had a void or voids in their charts: General George Patton, Princess Diana, Marilyn Monroe, Mother Teresa, Amelia Earhart, Charles Lindberg, Martin Luther King, Jr., William Shakespeare, Abraham Lincoln, Albert Einstein, Albert Schweitzer, Charles Darwin and Helen Keller? These were distinguished souls who did great things, so having voids does not preclude us from being of service or exuding a substantive life. Almost every one of us has a void or voids in our name.

This said, it is a fact that voids can create problems, especially if they're located in the Challenge position of the Life Matrix. What voids are calling us to do as individuals, or as parents teaching our children, is to concentrate on the positive attributes and characteristics the voids represent. This is key. If the characteristics of the voids are totally ignored, then problems can occur, from slight to severe. Consult the keywords chart and focus on the positive characteristics of each number in order to gain an understanding of how to manage a void or voids.

Children are great imitators. So give them something great to imitate.

~ Anonymous

10

Names & Letters

Names and their letters are powerful components of one's destiny. Although we parents think our children's names come from us, in reality they come *through* us from a higher power. Life is not always as it seems. There is a divine essence at work in our lives that transcends human understanding.

Names are Living Energy

Names are living energy. Every time a name is spoken or written, its energy, attributes and characteristics are generated. For example, our friend Mary Jane Smith's first name *Mary* carries a crown of 3.

$$M + A + R + Y$$
$$4 + 1 + 9 + 7 = 21: 2 + 1 = 3 \text{ crown}$$

Therefore, when the name *Mary* is spoken or written, the attributes of the 3 are given life. These include, but are not limited to, ease, joy, self-expression, happiness, words, communication, artistry, health, beauty, children, a positive disposition, art. All people with the name *Mary* will possess these traits to some degree.

Another example is from our other friend, John David Doey. His first name *John* carries a 2 crown. When his name is spoken or written, the traits brought into focus are those of relationship, others, teamwork, partnership, support, advocacy, diplomacy, interference, competition, contention, division, balance, peace and war – all attributes of the 2 in both its positive and negative aspects.

$$J + O + H + N$$
$$1 + 6 + 8 + 5 = 20: 2 + 0 = 2 \text{ crown}$$

Names Have Timelines

Not only do names have attributes, they have timelines – periods of time during the life in which the name is specifically active. For example, the name *Mary* (and its attributes) will be specifically active for 21 years, the 21 being the sum of the single letters/numbers of her name. The name *John* (and its attributes) will be specifically active for 20 years, the 20 being the sum of its single letters/numbers.

If *Mary* is the first name for anyone, it will be active from birth through the 21st year. If *John* is the first name of anyone, it will be active from birth through the 20th year.

These timelines are important to know because they offer a picture of the destiny as it applies to the specific name in question and the time period in which that name is active.

Name Timeline PEs

As we have already studied, when the Expression is added to the Lifepath, a PE or outcome is created. The same is true for each of the separate names of the full birth name. This creates an IR set (Influence/Reality pattern) of each particular name, thus creating yet another layer of the child's destiny.

Any Name + Lifepath = Name Timeline PE for that Name

For example, Mary Jane Smith's first name of *Mary* carries a 3 crown and is active for 21 years. When this 3 is added to her 7 Lifepath, the result is a 1 PE (3 + 7 = 10: 1 + 0 = 1). Thus, a Name Timeline (NTL) of 3/1 is created for Mary Jane Smith's first name of *Mary*. The more exact ciphering is 3/(7)/1 where the 3 is the *influencing* energy of the name, the 7 is the *filter* energy of the Lifepath and the 1 is the *outcome* PE energy.

This 3/(7)/1 IR set gives us powerful information regarding Mary's first 21 years which will manifest energies that are self-expressive (3), individual and self-oriented (1), internalized and solitary (7). Mary may well like being by herself. In fact, she may prefer it. She will most likely like to read, write, act, draw. The key is that the energies of the 3 will focus on herself, the 1. Because the 3 filters through the internalized energy of the 7, the 1 will have a solitary, mental, spiritual, analytical, reflective, withdrawing, recessive aspect to it.

The same process can be applied to the life of John David Doey who has a 9 Lifepath. His first name of *John* will last for 20 years. The IR set for this early time period of his life will be a 2/2. The full *Influence/Reality* set is written as 2/(9)/2 (2 + 9 = 11: 1 + 1 = 2).

In this 2/2 IR set, it is important to note that because of the 9 Lifepath filter, the *influencing* number (in this case the 2) will always be the same as the *reality* or outcome number, also a 2. It's the same for every IR set with a 9 filter. If the name were a 3, the IR set would be 3/3. If the name were a 4, the IR set would be 4/4 and so forth. This is because of the 9's Grand Elemental property of generating the exact single number which is added to it.

As far as John's 2/2 NTL is concerned, his early life will feature a major thread of relationship and others. Female energy is the dominant vibration in this set, so his mother will be a major aspect to his early life. Other females could be prominent, such as grandmothers, aunts, sisters.

This could also be a time of John's life in which competitive athletics will be featured because the number 2 rules adversity – one person versus another person, one team versus another team. What is certain is that the first twenty years of John's life, as far as his first name NTL is concerned, will neither be solitary nor solo. It will definitely feature female energy, others and relationship.

After John's early life has passed, marked by his twenty year 2/(9)/2 Name Timeline period of *John*, he will move into his Name Timeline of *David*, which will begin at age 21. It houses an IR set ciphered as 4/(9)/4; the short version is 4/4.

```
D     A     V     I     D
4  +  1  +  4  +  9  +  4   =   22: 2 + 2 = 4 crown
```

This time period of John's middle name of *David* will be a time of structure, strength, order, duty, work, service, stability, regularity, building, construction, developing, dependability, reliability, tradition.

As parents, therefore, when we know the energy fields associated with each of the names of our children's full birth names we can guide them more wisely. How could we not? Parenting wisdom dictates that we, as responsible parents concerned with the highest and best good of our children, use every bit of knowledge we can to help further their success and well-being in life.

If you are skeptical of this process, that's okay. Such initial feelings are quite normal, especially given the fact that this is a new science – the science of destiny. Ultimately, however, this is not about belief. It's about the reality of numbers and their application to life. If you don't believe it, test it for yourself. Do your numbers. Do your children's numbers. Relate your numbers to your life's experiences and your children's numbers to their life experiences. The proof is always in the pudding, and the reality is always in the factuality. Life is numbers. A little due diligence will prove this extraordinary truth.

Letters Have Timelines

The individual letters, like each name, add yet another layer to the puzzle of a child's destiny. Letters create the Letter Timeline (LTL), which can be considered an internal aspect or sub-layer of the Name Timeline.

Any Letter + Lifepath = Letter Timeline PE for that Letter

Like each separate name, each letter houses its own timeline, attributes and characteristics. The length of time each letter is active is determined by the single number associated with it, as the following chart describes.

Time Periods of Letters with General Keywords

Letters	Time	General Issues (short list)
A-J-S	1 year	self, solo, identity, males, independence, starts
B-K-T	2 years	others, relationship, females, dependence, yin
C-L-U	3 years	self-expression, health, joy, image, friends
D-M-V	4 years	work, service, stability, security, duty, rules
E-N-W	5 years	change, freedom, detachment, loss, senses
F-O-X	6 years	love, home, family, community, nurturing, art
G-P-Y	7 years	internalization, thought, study, seclusion
H-Q-Z	8 years	externalization, socialization, involvement
I and R	9 years	universality, expansion, endings, public

For example, in Mary's Letter Timeline – which is contained within her 3/(7)/1 Name Timeline of 21 years – the M is active for four years, the A for one year, the R for nine years, and the Y for seven years. The letters break down this way:

    M – a four year period of structure, stability, order

    A – a one year period of new beginnings, the self, ego

    R – a nine year period of universality, public stage, endings

    Y – a seven year period of introspection, recession, study

John's Letter Timeline – which is contained within his 2/(9)/2 Name Timeline of 20 years – is as follows: the J is active for one year, the O for six years, the H for eight years, and the N for five years.

    J – a one year period of beginnings, action, male energy

    O – a six year period of love, family and nurturing issues

    H – an eight year period of social involvement and interaction

    N – a five year period of change, loss and detachment

Letter Timeline PEs

Like each individual name and timeline, each individual letter has its own timeline whose IR set is generated by simply adding the letter (the *influencing* energy) to the Lifepath (the filtering energy) to create the outcome PE (the *reality* energy), as noted earlier. Each individual letter IR set gives us more specific information regarding the destiny.

Mary Jane Smith's Letter Timeline IR sets for *Mary* would break down this way:

M: 4/(7)/2 – a four year period relating to the stability and structure (4) of relationships, most likely involving her mother or females (2), but which contain potential stresses and problems (the 7 filter). Note: because the 7 Lifepath is the filter, all of the outcome Name and Letter PEs will be colored to some degree by the 7's attributes.

A: 1/(7)/8 – a one year period of new beginnings (1) creating an outcome involving some kind of social involvement, interaction, connection or disconnection (8). Because this 1/8 pattern is an entrepreneurial energy and will be active when Mary is five years old, perhaps she'll have her own lemonade stand, oppressive governmental regulations permitting. Because of the 7 LP filter, this fifth year of her life could be the harbinger of the subsequent nine year period of challenges destined for her in her 'R' timeline.

R: 9/(7)/7 – a nine year period involving expansion, travel, the public environment, education and potential endings (9) creating outcome experiences involving study, concentration, anxiety, turmoil, stress and possible parental discord or unhappiness (7).

This 9/(7)/7 IR set is one of the most challenging and potentially difficult periods in a person's life. There may well be personal issues, potential discomfort, testing, possible alcoholism, addiction or divorce in the family. Thus, the focus here must be on spiritually pure conduct and wisdom. There is a possibility of some type of ending or long-distance suffering. It could also translate into a powerful time of study for Mary in which she could excel in school. Because the 7 rules all things internal, Mary could reveal a mystical side to her personality, becoming very intuitive and deep in her perceptions of life. In fact, all of the above options could be rolled up into one package – family issues and conflicts causing her to recede into herself, giving greater time to her studies, intuitive or mystical experiences. Her parents would be wise to especially look after her emotional needs during this time.

<u>Y:</u> 7/(7)/5 – a seven year period of potential study (7) in a wide variety of subjects (5). There could also be internal stress and concern (7) creating loss and change (5). Having this 7/(7)/5 LTL follow a 9/(7)/7 LTL raises a yellow flag of potential turmoil. This is an opportunity for study, but familial turmoil is a possibility. Mary's parents need to be sensitive to her and their other children (if there are any) during these times, making sure that if the conflicts are with the parents, the children remain loved and nurtured.

Because John David Doey's Lifepath is a 9, his Letter Timeline will have the same type of IR set format as his Name Timeline – the first number in the IR pattern will be the same as the final outcome number. Therefore, the Letter Timeline for *John* would break down in the following manner:

J: 1/(9)/1 – this first year of his life brings a focus of male energy (1) filtering through the 9 energy of either travel or endings to create a new beginning. For example, John's father could get a new job, the family could travel, even move to a new location or John could become the center (1) of attention in his world.

O: 6/(9)/6 – a six year period in which the family life will definitely be the dominant issue and outcome. The 6 rules personal love; the 9 rules impersonal love and the public stage. There could be turmoil in the family because of the 6's dark side of anger, resentment, envy, jealousy. If the parents are both very loving, this could be a wonderful six year period in John's early life filled with nurturing, warmth, compassion and attention. Music could also be involved because both the 6 and 9 contain musical potentials. Regardless of the specifics, the general energy is all about love and the family.

H: 8/(9)/8 – this is an eight year period of social interaction and involvement. John could be very popular in school. When this IR set becomes active, he will be eight years old, and since this pattern lasts for eight years, John could be quite active in school life in some capacity. This 8/(9)/8 pattern is a powerfully social energy. It is also a pattern of success and recognition. No two numbers are more socially and publically dominant than the 8 and 9 in tandem.

N: 5/(9)/5 – there will be changes and losses of some kind during this period when John is sixteen to twenty. The 5 brings change, and the N brings more change and detachment than either the E or W, both of which are also 5s. With a 9 filter (his Lifepath), the result will also be a 5. No two numbers in concert bring more changes, losses, detachments and endings than the 5 and 9. John will need to be prepared for this by his parents helping him understand that change and loss are part of life's natural process. Change can also be a good thing. It depends on circumstances and one's attitude. Nothing lasts forever in this life. Change is the only true constant. Therefore, the concept of balance being a primary ingredient of happiness and success in life is critical.

Summary

The Name Timeline (NTL) and the Letter Timeline (LTL) are very powerful components of one's destiny. Through their Influence/Reality sets, parents can glean valuable knowledge to assist their children in reaching their highest potential.

When we know, we can never not know. Furthermore, we can never get blind-sided. Being intimate with our children's Name and Letter Timelines is like having a network of weather satellites giving us forecasts and, when appropriate, warnings of storms or inclement weather.

First names are particularly important to know because their timelines compose an integral part of the foundation of a child's formative years, years which can set the psychological and emotional framework for the remainder of the child's life.

It's no secret that many adults carry the burdens of their childhood with them for their entire lives. If parents were aware of their children's numbers from the very outset of their lives, the pain, suffering, torment and problems a child could develop and carry with him into adulthood because of his early life's negative experiences could possibly be avoided. In this manner, the child's highest and best good would have been served, and what is more beautiful than a child growing into a healthy, balanced and wisdom-filled adult, a potential parent who could, in turn, create healthy, whole children of his or her own? Thus, parenting wisdom is vital, and some meaningful time spent in understanding our children's destinies based on their numbers will be time extremely well spent.

For more information regarding the Name and Letter Timelines, read *The King's Book of Numerology, Volume II: Forecasting – Part 1* available at RichardKing.net.

If we are to teach real peace in this world, and if we are to carry on a real war against war, we shall have to begin with the children.

~ Mohandas Gandhi

11

The 1st E-P-C Triad

The Lifepath is the script of our life. The internal superstructure of the Lifepath is the *Life Matrix* – an amalgam of acts and scenes, each replete with their separate lessons, events, issues, problems, circumstances, situations, challenges, dramas and timelines.

The Life Matrix is comprised of the three main components of the birth date – day, month and year (Epochs) – and the components derived from them, the Pinnacles and Challenges. As we will discuss, the first Epoch, Pinnacle and Challenge components of the Life Matrix are identified as the 1st E-P-C Triad or simply, the *1st Triad*. Their importance to the beginning years of a child will become apparent as this chapter unfolds.

As a script, the play of the Lifepath begins with the raising of the curtain in Act I, Scene 1, Line 1 (the moment of birth) and moves through the entire drama of the play, concluding in the final line of the final scene of Act III when the curtain falls (the moment of death). The acts and scenes are the substance of the Life Matrix.

How powerful and priceless a tool can it be for parents to know the scripts their children will follow during their lives, especially during their formative years when their future lives are being formed and their foundations set? If we're concerned with helping our children attain the highest level of their highest good, such knowledge is priceless.

Epochs

Using the metaphor of the Lifepath being the script of our life and the Life Matrix being its superstructure, the day of birth is Act I, the month of birth is Act II, and the year of birth is Act III. In numerology these three components of the Lifepath Matrix are called Epochs. Epochs generally have a timeline of twenty-seven years each and comprise a major thread of the destiny tapestry.

Epochs give valuable information about the early part of our children's lives and destinies. These Epochs possess *influencing* energies describing the issues, concerns and themes associated with each of their timelines, as well as the general *outcome* fields indicating how our children will respond, react or manage the *influencing* energies.

<u>Mary Jane Smith's Epochs</u>

Our friend Mary Jane Smith was born on 8 January 1960. Therefore, her 1st Epoch (Act I of her Lifepath Matrix script) is an 8. Her 2nd Epoch, January (Act II), is a 1, and her 3rd Epoch (Act III) is a 7 (year of birth, 1960, reduced to a single digit).

Epochs for Birthdate of Mary Jane Smith Date of Birth: 8 January 1960		
1st Epoch (Act I)	2nd Epoch (Act II)	3rd Epoch (Act III)
8	January	1960
8	1	7

Epochs, like Names and Letters, have their own timeline PEs. The Epoch IR Sets are created by simply adding the Epoch to the Expression and reducing to a single digit.

Epoch Performance/Experience (PE) Calculation
Epoch + Expression = Epoch PE

Mary's Expression is a 3. Adding each of the single Epoch numbers to her 3 Expression generates each of her three Epoch IR sets – the three main Acts of her life's play.

Influence/Reality (IR) Sets for Mary Jane Smith's Epochs 3 Expression		
1st Epoch (Act I)	2nd Epoch (Act II)	3rd Epoch (Act III)
8	January	1960
8 + 3 = 11 = 2 PE	1 + 3 = 4 PE	7 + 3 = 10 = 1 PE
IR Set: 8/(3)/2 (full)	IR Set: 1/(3)/4 (full)	IR Set: 7/(3)/1 (full)
IR Set: 8/2 (simple)	**IR Set: 1/4** (simple)	**IR Set: 7/1** (simple)

With her 1st Epoch (Act I) IR Set being an 8/2, Mary's life from birth through age 27 will be governed by influencing energies of social interaction, involvement, continuity, being in-the-loop (8) and playing themselves out in the arena of relationships, others and female energy (2).

Mary's 2nd Epoch (Act II) IR Set is a 1/4. This brings into focus influences and lessons of the self, ego, independence, identity, leadership and male energy (1) being activated in the arena of work, the house, employment, stability, security, organization, building, regimentation (4).

The 3rd Epoch (Act III) for Mary and its IR Set is a 7/1. This will be a time of reflection, solitude, examination, analysis and research (7) in the area of her self, her independence, identity, male energy, being solo and perhaps having to deal with authority figures. This 7/1 IR set speaks to a major thread of anyone's destiny that is solitary and solo. It is an excellent time for self-assessment, study, solitary work, projects requiring isolation, spiritual achievement, prayer and meditation. It is a time when the person has the opportunity of reflecting upon and assessing life and its meaning. Any 7/1 period will not be a time of socializing but internalizing.

In many ways the 1st Epoch and its IR set is the most important of the three Epochs because it is during the 1st Epoch when any child's life begins and traverses the formative years into adulthood. In essence, what happens within this first act of the play will have a direct bearing on the rest of the play. Act I of any play always sets the stage for what is to come.

John David Doey's Epochs

John David Doey was born on 14 August 1985. Therefore, the single number associated with his 1st Epoch is a 5; his 2nd Epoch is an 8, and his 3rd Epoch is a 5 (1985 reduced to a single digit).

Epochs for Birthdate of John David Doey Date of Birth: 14 August 1985		
1st Epoch (Act I)	2nd Epoch (Act II)	3rd Epoch (Act III)
14	August	1985
5	8	5

John's Expression is a 1. The IR Sets of his Epochs are:

Influence/Reality (IR) Sets for John David Doey's Epochs 1 Expression		
1st Epoch (Act I)	2nd Epoch (Act II)	3rd Epoch (Act III)
14	August	1985
14 + 1 = 15	8 + 1 = 9 PE	5 + 1 = 6 PE
1 + 5 = 6 PE	8 + 1 = 9 PE	5 + 1 = 6 PE
IR Set: 5/(1)/6 (full)	IR Set: 8/(1)/9 (full)	IR Set: 5/(1)/6 (full)
IR Set: 5/6 (simple)	**IR Set: 8/9** (simple)	**IR Set: 5/6** (simple)

The thing of note about John's Epoch IR Sets is that his 1st and 3rd Epoch patterns are the same, a 5/6. This 5/6 pattern signifies influences and issues of change, freedom, movement, motion, detachment and potential loss (5) in the family, domestic environment and love life (6).

This 5/6 pattern has the potential of creating uncertainty and/or instability in the family because of the mercurial nature of the 5. Because the filter/funnel of the 5/6 IR simple set is a 1, the *outcome* 6 energies will be colored with hues of the self, ego, will, independence, identity, action, male or authority issues.

John's 2nd Epoch IR Set is an 8/9. This is a powerful energy pattern of social power and involvement. Therefore, for the middle part of his life, John will be involved with the public in some capacity (9), most likely in a managerial, administrative, orchestrative or business context (8).

Again, regarding parenting wisdom, the 1st Epoch IR Set is the one of importance because of the developmental aspects for John and his life. What changes, movement or freedom in the home or heart will be going on in his early life? What part will the parents be playing in the changes?

How will the parents manage John's changing life circumstances? How can John use the experiences of the first part of his life in Act I to prepare for Act III? Will there be negative feelings that John harbors for his entire life as a result of his 1st Epoch's 5/6 experiences, or will he, during his life, gain wisdom and knowledge to assist him in managing the recurring 5/6 IR set energies in his latter years? Having this forecasting knowledge at his disposal will certainly give John the ability to create a life of balance, centeredness and maturity.

Pinnacles and Challenges

Epochs are not the only substantive component of the Life Matrix. There are two others: Pinnacles and Challenges. There are four sets of Pinnacles and Challenges (noted as PC Couplets) in a numerology chart. The Pinnacle and Challenge in each set act in tandem with each other and occupy their own separate timeline, which is separate from the Epoch timeline. (Note: for a full treatise on Epochs, Pinnacles and Challenges, read *The King's Book of Numerology II: Forecasting – Part 1*).

Pinnacles are derived from *addition* of the Epochs. They represent activities, events, conditions, themes and subjects which are generally known or viewable to the outside world and which pull the individual forward. If Epochs were described as the surface of the earth, the Pinnacles would be described as that which is visible above its surface.

The First Pinnacle, and its sibling Challenge, are very powerful aspects to any of our lives because they depict the major issues, themes and challenges confronting a person from birth to a period of time between ages twenty-seven and thirty-six. Coupled with the 1st Epoch, the Pinnacle and Challenge form the 1st E-P-C Triad (*1st Triad* as previously noted).

Challenges are derived from *subtraction* of the Epochs. They reveal personal areas of focus, friction and toil which are not generally known to the outside world of an individual's life. They are more personal issues. As the Pinnacles are those things visible above the surface of the earth (Epochs), the Challenges lie underneath the surface, invisible to the general public but quite active.

Challenges are exactly that, challenges. They are the issues, problems, events, conditions, situations, people and circumstances that confront us and force us to pay attention to them, work with them, manage them, deal with them. They can be very demanding. They also signal potential problems. In some ways, Challenges, which we all have in our charts, are the emery boards of our lives, the crosses we have to bear. We cannot avoid them.

There are silver linings to our Challenges, energies which hone our character and spirit. Challenges play their part in making us better people, more whole, capable, confident. By working with them, we strengthen our weak links and improve our lives.

Parenting wisdom requires us parents to know the Challenges in our children's charts, pay close attention to them and the effects they have on our children. If there is any one component in the numerology chart of our children that is more critical to address than any other component, it is Challenges. If not addressed, their energies can have a marked negative impact on our children for their entire lives. However, if addressed, they can strengthen our children so the children grow to become confident, capable, whole, fulfilled and mature adults.

1st Pinnacle/Challenge Couplet Timelines

The length of time for each PC couplet is based on the single number of the Lifepath and is different from every other Lifepath.

1st Pinnacle/Challenge Timelines

1 Lifepath	birth through age 35
2 Lifepath	birth through age 34
3 Lifepath	birth through age 33
4 Lifepath	birth through age 32
5 Lifepath	birth through age 31
6 Lifepath	birth through age 30
7 Lifepath	birth through age 29
8 Lifepath	birth through age 28
9 Lifepath	birth through age 27

Mary Jane Smith – 1st Epoch-Pinnacle-Challenge Triad

Let's now apply this knowledge to Mary Jane Smith's destiny. As we recall, her date of birth is 8 January 1960 and her Expression is a 3. For simplicity purposes, we'll use the simple ciphers of the birth date data to construct her 1st E-P-C Triad. We'll also use a simple IR set format.

1st E-P-C Triad
Mary Jane Smith
DOB: 8 January 1960 = 7 Lifepath
Expression: 3

1st Pinnacle
(Birth to age 29)
9/3

1st Epoch
(Birth to age 27)
8/2

2nd Epoch
(28 to 54)
1/4

1st Challenge
(Birth to age 29)
7/1

Mary – 1st E-P-C Triad: Notes

We've already discussed Mary's 1st Epoch. Her 1st Pinnacle is a 9/3. It will last from birth through age 29. This 9/3 IR set shows *influencing* issues and themes of a universal, expansive, artistic and public nature (9). The *reality outcome* is in the field of the 3 – words, communication, health, beauty, image, joy, friends, children.

With this 9/3 IR 1st Pinnacle, Mary will definitely be drawn to an expansive life as she grows. She'll have many friends. She will also be attracted to art, education, theater. She could like writing. She may well like being in school plays, and because the 9 and 3 in tandem represent beauty and the public stage, as well as being often found in the charts of models, Mary may be drawn to modeling, cosmetics, hair and beautician work. Parental wisdom would encourage her to be artistic, to express herself and learn to be comfortable with lots of people and the public.

In stark contrast to her 9/3 Pinnacle, her 7/1 IR Challenge warrants yellow flags. The 7 in a Challenge position references the potential of worry, concern, stress, secrecy, sadness, turmoil, trouble, tumult, tears, heartache, heartbreak and isolation playing themselves out in the field of male energy and the self. This could manifest as problems with a father, grandfather, stepfather, brother, uncle or males in general. It could also manifest as a troubled (7) self (1). Because the number 7 is commonly associated with alcoholism and addiction, this is a possibility, especially with the father because of the 1 in the outcome position. Another scenario is that this 7/1 pattern could be separation from the father or feelings of concern and worry for or about him or even because of him.

The positive side of the 7 reflects spirituality, purity, nobility, study, privacy, shyness and introspection. Therefore, this 7/1 combination could also reference a very shy, studious, reserved period of life in which Mary will be forced, by her destiny, to feel alone and separated, if not physically, then emotionally or psychologically. In some capacity Mary is definitely going to be alone or feel alone and isolated. She may also have identity and confidence issues.

Parental wisdom dictates that her parents take close note of this 7/1 IR set in Mary's 1st Challenge position. It would also be wise, should occasion permit, for any counselors, teachers, psychologists or other concerned adults to take note. The 7/1 IR set can be potentially troubling. The number 7 does have a dark side, and when the outcome energy is in the self (1) after passing through the filter of the 3, which rules personal image and well-being, the possibility of Mary having internal negative issues exists. Furthermore, with the 1 in the outcome position, there could be parental abuse related to a male or males.

Generally, the 1 represents the male. However, the 1 could reference a mother with dominant 1 energy in her chart or an authority figure of some variety. The bottom line is that this 7/1 IR set should not be ignored by the parents or concerned adults. It must be addressed for the sake of the child's well-being. If not addressed, Mary could easily be scarred for life in areas related to men, authority figures or her own self image, confidence and personal identity.

John David Doey – 1st Epoch-Pinnacle-Challenge Triad

Let's now look at John's 1st E-P-C Triad.

1st E-P-C Triad
John David Doey
DOB: 14 August 1985 = 9 Lifepath
Expression: 1

1st Pinnacle
(Birth to age 27)
4/5

1st Epoch	2nd Epoch
(Birth to age 27)	(28 to 54)
5/6	8/9

1st Challenge
(Birth to age 27)
3/4 & 6/7

John – 1st E-P-C Triad: Notes

As with Mary, we've already discussed John's 1st Epoch 5/6 IR set so we'll move on to his 1st Pinnacle, a 4/5, which will last from birth through age 27, matching his Epoch timeline period. This 4/5 IR set is one that reflects *influences* of the house, security, stability, routines, regimes, work, service and all things related to structure (4). Yet, the *reality outcome* is the 5 of change, movement, variety, diversity, detachment, loss.

Therefore, there is a possibility of John experiencing a variety of housing structures when he is young. Perhaps his family will be moving often, especially since his 1st Epoch is a 5/6, which would strengthen the possibility of changes in the family life. As he grows into early adulthood, he may hold a variety of jobs or have a job in which he is free to move about, not restricted by the confines of the 4's structures.

One of the noteworthy aspects of John's 1st E-P-C Triad are his two Challenges – the 3/4 and the 6/7. The 3 Influence of the 3/4 IR set was generated by subtracting the 5 (the single number from his day of birth, the 14th) from the 8 (month of August). The 6 was generated by subtracting the 8 from the specific day of birth, the 14th (14 minus 8 = 6). This second IR set of 6/7 encompasses a deeper understanding of IR sets which can be studied in *The King's Book of Numerology II: Forecasting – Part 1*).

These dual IR Challenge sets of 3/4 and 6/7 tell us that John's happiness, well-being and self-image (3) could possibly be subject to limitation, restriction or problems in the house (4). He may feel very stifled and trapped. The 6/7 IR set speaks to turmoil, problems, concern and trouble (7) as a result of issues in the family and love life. Because the 7 is an energy of recession and isolation, John will most likely feel distance from his parents or a lack of love in the home. Growing up will very likely be an uncomfortable time of his life, at least as far as his family life is concerned. There is also the possibility of alcoholism, drug addiction, divorce or discord in his parents' relationship. Given the 4/5 Pinnacle and the 5/6 Epoch, these Challenge IR sets of 3/4 and 6/7 only add fuel to the potential of a difficult upbringing and early life for John.

The positive thing about knowing all of this, of course, is that having foreknowledge of John's destiny, any problematic issues or concerns related to his formative years could be potentially mitigated by his parents by having them concentrate on the positive attributes of the numbers appearing in his chart at this time of his life. In this way any negative experiences John would potentially encounter could be diluted by his parents. If his parents could not accomplish this, then perhaps other loving, concerned and responsible adults could, such as grandparents, uncles and aunts, other family members, teachers, professionals, health workers and so forth.

Celebrity Case Studies - 1st Epoch-Pinnacle-Challenge Triads

Studying the charts of known individuals who have a verifiable history is an excellent way to learn numerology. Because celebrities are known to the world, they make excellent resources to corroborate the science of numbers.

Following are the 1st Epoch-Pinnacle-Challenge Triads of five famous individuals: Elvis Presley, Marilyn Monroe, Princess Diana, Oprah Winfrey and Michael Jackson. These 1st E-P-C Triads are very briefly discussed here to corroborate the truth of numerology.

As with all famous individuals, there are many numbers, number patterns and numerical combinations in their numerology charts validating their extraordinary lives. In fact, a book could be written about everyone's life, not just the lives of celebrities, based on their numbers.

Often, the beginnings of a person's fame and fortune are clearly indicated in their 1st Epoch-Pinnacle-Challenge Triad, which is why this brief catalogue of historical icons is offered – to show the relationship between their extraordinary destinies and their numbers and thereby validate the fact that the reality of destiny is exactly that, reality, and the reality of anyone's destiny can be known through his or her personal numbers – those associated with the full birth name and birth date.

In the numerical patterns illustrating the 1st E-P-C Triads of our featured icons, the "v" behind a number indicates the number is void. (For further reading and deeper knowledge regarding the lives of these famous individuals, read *Destinies of the Rich & Famous: The Secret Numbers of Extraordinary Lives* available through RichardKing.net).

Elvis Presley

Elvis Presley was a giant among giants in the entertainment world, a global sensation by the time he was twenty-one years of age. His influence in the music industry caused John Lennon of The Beatles to comment: "Before Elvis, there was nothing." Rod Stewart corroborated Lennon's quote by noting: "Elvis was the king. No doubt about it." And world renowned conductor, composer, author and pianist Leonard Bernstein eloquently stated: "Elvis is the greatest cultural force in the Twentieth Century."

The question is, of course, what numbers in Elvis Presley's chart reflect such extraordinary power, fame and celebrity? His 1st E-P-C Triad doesn't tell the whole story of his life, as no E-P-C Triad can, but it certainly reflects his early life.

1st E-P-C Triad
Elvis Aaron Presley
DOB: 8 January 1935 – Lifepath 9
Expression: 9 Voids: 2 & 8

1st Pinnacle
(Birth to age 27)
9/9

1st Epoch
(Birth to age 27)
8v/8v

2nd Epoch
(28 to 54)
1/1

1st Challenge
(Birth to age 27)
7/7

Based on what we've covered so far, let's see if you can match the IR sets of Presley's early life with the following brief accounts.

First, it's important to note that Elvis Presley's Lifepath, Expression and PE are all 9s. This is the first key to consider before even assessing the numbers in his Life Matrix.

Presley's early childhood was difficult. His journey at birth began with a disconnect when his twin brother died at birth, a stillborn. The family often had to rely on relatives and government food assistance. Presley's father was often out of work and occasionally had problems with the law. Elvis was quite shy and reserved in his early childhood.

Presley was often told in his early years he could not sing. Yet, his destiny of fame kept pulling him forward. His big break came with the recording and release of *That's All Right* on the Sun Music label in July of 1954 when he was only nineteen. His fame began to swell. In addition to his music, Presley also began a movie career, becoming a massive superstar in his twenties.

Elvis was inducted into the army in 1958 when he was twenty-three. His mother, Gladys, with whom he was exceptionally close, died a few months later – a devastatingly disconnective moment for him. Yet, he survived and continued into his life journey of super stardom.

So which number pattern reveals Elvis Presley's massive success in his 1st E-P-C Triad? If you said both the 8v/8v Epoch and 9/9 Pinnacle, you're correct. And what about the tearful turmoil with his brother's stillborn death, his mother's death and his father's problems? The answer is both the 8v/8v Epoch of disconnects and the 7/7 Challenge of turmoil. Of course these number pattern assessments are extremely brief but they do give us a glimpse of the major energies manifesting in his early life.

Marilyn Monroe

Marilyn Monroe died at thirty-six years of age on 5 August 1962. Yet, in her short life span she became a cinematic institution, still remembered today as a powerful female force of her time.

Monroe's Lifepath is a 7. As we see in the following chart, her first Pinnacle (from birth through age 29) is also a 7. This creates *stacking* – the simultaneous occurrence of the same number or number pattern or patterns in a chart. Stacking creates intensity. Monroe also has a 7 void in her name, so from the get-go Marilyn's life would be problematic, as history has proven.

1st E-P-C Triad
Born: Norma Jeane Mortenson
DOB: 1 June 1926 – Lifepath 7
Expression: 4 Voids: 3-7-8

1st Pinnacle
(Birth to age 29)
7v/2

1st Epoch	2nd Epoch
(Birth to age 27)	(28 to 54)
1/5	6/1

1st Challenge
(Birth to age 29)
5/9

Marilyn Monroe's mother was psychologically distressed to the point of being committed to a health care facility. Interestingly, Monroe's mother's first name was Gladys, like Elvis Presley's mother, although Presley's mother was not beset with mental health issues.

Marilyn's mother issue is clearly indicated in her 7v/2 1st Pinnacle. As we've discussed, the number 7 is often a harbinger of concern, stress, discomfort, trouble and turmoil. The 7, which is void and stacked in Marilyn's 1st Pinnacle, moves through her 4 Expression (representing the house) to generate a 2 outcome – the energy representing females. Therefore, the full IR set for Marilyn's 1st Pinnacle is a 7v/(4)/2. This is a clear indication of trouble with the mother (or female) in the home. This 7v/2 pattern would also be indicative of the stress and concern she would have regarding her various foster homes and foster parents.

Marilyn's father abandoned her early on. Basically, he just detached and left his baby girl with her mother. This abandonment by the father (1) is indicated in her 1/5 1st Epoch. The number 5 is the energy of detachment and loss, so "loss of the father" is a fitting phrase for this 1/5 IR set.

Too, the 1/5 pattern also indicates a variety of male energy. Marilyn was married three times, twice within the time period of her 1st Epoch. She also was reputed to have had many relationships with powerful men in her life, among whom were John F. Kennedy and his brother Bobby Kennedy. This "changing (5) of males (1)" is also a workable phrase for the 1/5 IR set.

Marilyn's 5/9 1st Challenge indicates her fame. No two numbers together involve the public more than the 5 (*Number of Man*) and the 9 (*Number of Mankind*). It is the 5/9 IR Challenge that placed her within the center mass of public energy. No doubt she loved it because as she stated, "I want to be a big star more than anything. It's something precious." Interestingly, the 5/9 pattern is even more dominant in the chart of Princess Diana of Wales.

This 5/9 IR Set also indicates changes (5) and travel (9). This would act in concert with her 1/5 IR Set. All of this 1, 5 and 9 energy references constant changes and new beginnings during Monroe's 1st E-P-C Triad.

Princess Diana

Princess Diana's life is very similar to that of Marilyn Monroe. Both women were born on the first day of the month – Monroe on 1 June and Diana on 1 July. Both had 7 Lifepaths, 4 Expressions and 2 PEs. Both had an 8 void. Both had the 1/5, 4/8v, 5/9, 6/1, 7/2, 8v/3 and 9/4 IR Sets dominant throughout their Life Matrices. Both died at thirty-six under suspicious circumstances – Marilyn's death has been shrouded in a mystery of possible murder; Diana's death shrouded in a bizarre auto chase and lethal crash. Their tragic lives and destinies are about as close to one another as any two destinies could be. But then again, the numbers ruling their lives are very similar, so it makes logical sense that their destinies would be similar as well. Again, this is another validation of numerology as a science. *Like numbers produce like destinies.*

1st E-P-C Triad
Diana Frances Spencer
DOB: 1 July 1961 – Lifepath 7
Expression: 4 Voids: 2 & 8

1st Pinnacle
(Birth to age 29)
8v/3

1st Epoch
(Birth to age 27)
1/5

2nd Epoch
(28 to 54)
7/2

1st Challenge
(Birth to age 29)
6/1

Like Marilyn, Princess Diana has a 1/5 1st Epoch indicating abandonment of male energy. It was during this timeline she experienced a fairytale marriage to Prince Charles, but a marriage which ultimately turned into a nightmare, the beginning of the end occurring during this 1/5 IR Set. It was also during this time that her two sons, William and Harry were born.

Diana's 1st Challenge was a 6/1. This would indicate a feeling of being alone and solo as a result of influences in the home and domestic environment. A 6 Challenge also references issues of not being or feeling loved and nurtured and therefore desiring love.

Diana's parents divorced in 1969 with her father gaining custody of the children (reflected in her 6/1 Challenge), an event that left her with emotional scars. As a young girl, Diana tried to care for her younger brother, Charles, who was also hurt deeply by the divorce (another 6/1 manifestation). As Andrew Morton stated in *Diana, Her New Life*, "It is a memory indelibly engraved upon her soul." He also references Diana's own words regarding her parent's divorce, saying, "I never want to be divorced."

Princess Diana's 8v/3 1st Pinnacle shows a clear disconnection in the joy and well-being of her life, as well as her own self-image and fulfillment. Because the number 3 rules children, this 8v/3 IR Set would indicate a disconnect of all the children in her family – her two older sisters and her brother.

The combination of her 8v/3 and 6/1 IR Sets is revealed in one of Diana's most telling quotes. When she was born her parents lamented the fact that she was not a boy, which they deeply wanted. As she grew, she was quite aware of this fact, which she never forgot. As she painfully recalled many times in her life, "I was the girl who was supposed to be a boy."

[For a complete study of the life of Princess Diana in numbers, read *Blueprint of a Princess: Diana Frances Spencer – Queen of Hearts* available through RichardKing.net].

Oprah Winfrey

There is no doubt Oprah Winfrey's professional life deserves the title *Queen of Media*. Oprah's destiny has led her down a path of being one of the most successful entrepreneurs in American history. She can legitimately claim the titles of actress, producer, philanthropist and, during her media reign, arguably the most influential woman in the world.

What numbers have driven the destiny of Oprah Gail Winfrey? Certainly there are many powerful numbers and numerical combinations in her chart contributing to her enormous success that do not appear in her 1st Epoch-Pinnacle-Challenge Triad, but her early life numbers do portend what she was to be and has become.

1st E-P-C Triad
Oprah Gail Winfrey
DOB: 29 January 1954 – Lifepath 4
Expression: 7 Voids: 2 & 4

1st Pinnacle
(Birth to age 32)
3/1

1st Epoch
(Birth to age 27)
2v/9

2nd Epoch
(28 to 54)
1/8

1st Challenge
(Birth to age 32)
1/8

Oprah has been very open about her early life challenges involving being molested by her cousin, her uncle and a family friend beginning when she was nine years old. Is this abuse visible in her chart? Yes. Take a look at her first Challenge IR Set. We have discussed the probability of the number 1 in a Challenge position as referencing male energy. In Oprah's 1/8 IR Set the 1 is clearly dominant. Besides the molestation issues, Oprah became pregnant at age fourteen and gave birth to a boy who died shortly after birth. Eventually, she came to live with her father, Vernon, whose strict discipline set her on a path to success. Hence, we can deduce that males in one form or another would most likely create a challenge for her in her early life, which is depicted in her 1/8 IR 1st Challenge.

However, there is also a positive aspect to this 1/8 IR Set and that is the entrepreneurial spirit that has come to define her. What is unique regarding Oprah's chart is that this 1/8 IR Set creates *life linkage*. In other words, this 1/8 pattern exists continuously throughout her life from birth to death. This has driven her (1) to achieve success in business (8).

Oprah's 3/1 1st Pinnacle reflects her interest in communication, beauty and acting. In high school she was voted the Most Popular Girl, joined the speech team and won an oratory contest. In college she majored in communication. Her 3/1 energy is also reflected in her winning the Miss Black Tennessee beauty pageant. Her interest in media continued after college, eventually leading her to create the empire that is Oprah Winfrey.

Oprah's 2v/9 1st Epoch reflects the challenges she had with females and relationships in her early life. She lived with her grandmother, Hattie Mae Lee, for the first six years of her life. It was Hattie who taught Oprah how to read. Oprah was also passed back and forth between her mother, Vernita Lee, and her father. Eventually, she was given to Vernon and under his guidance and discipline, Oprah began to flourish and, as the saying goes, the rest is history.

Michael Jackson

Self-proclaimed or not, Michael Jackson was the *King of Pop*. A massive musical talent, Jackson's life was filled with genius, eccentricity, fame, family and child-related issues. His destiny is so clear that his life serves as an excellent example of study for students of numerology.

Jackson's 1st E-P-C Triad reveals the power of his fame. This is obvious in his 1/9 Pinnacle – an energetic combination moving the individual (1) through the 8 filter of social connectivity (Jackson's Expression) to generate the 9's reality of the public stage, universal appeal, and mass recognition. The complete set would be 1/(8)/9. No combination is more individually powerful and dominant than the 1 and 9 together.

1st E-P-C Triad
Michael Joseph Jackson
DOB: 29 August 1958 – Lifepath 6
Expression: 8 Voids: none

1st Pinnacle
(Birth to age 30)
1/9

1st Epoch
(Birth to age 27)
2/1

2nd Epoch
(28 to 54)
8/7

1st Challenge
(Birth to age 30)
3/2 & 6/5

What is not visually depicted in the diagram above is that the 1st Pinnacle PE of 9 actually maintains a 99 master number root, making the 9 massively powerful. This dynamic energy was active from the moment of Jackson's birth, as revealed in his early performance group, The Jackson 5, with his brothers. It is also a reference to his solo career.

Another powerful aspect to Jackson's fame and success is his 2/1 1st Epoch IR Set. What is unique is that the 1 PE of this 2/1 pattern, like the 1/9 pattern, also houses a master number in its root structure, the 55, thus expanding the 2/1 pattern to a much more powerful 2/55-1 IR Set. No number expresses more originality, independence and uniqueness than the 55-1. In Jackson's case, it is the reality of the 2 (the primal energy of music, rhythm and dance) moving through his 8 Expression filter/funnel of coordination and orchestration to generate the extremely active, versatile, movement-oriented, fire-dominated 55-1 cipher of originality. Combined with Jackson's 1/99-9 1st Pinnacle, this 2/55-1 1st Epoch energy creates a powerhouse duo.

Jackson's family problems are well-documented. The father was quite hard on his children, and Jackson always lamented that he really didn't have a childhood. This condition is expressed in his 6/5 Challenge where the 6 governs family love and the 5 governs its loss and detachment.

Michael Jackson's problems with childhood issues were a major negative in his life. This is reflected in his 3/2 IR set where the 3 governs children and the 2 indicates relationship. In its full schematic, this 3/2 set is 3/(8)/11-2 where the 11 indicates tensions. Arrested on charges of alleged child molestation, charges subsequently dropped, Jackson's life was forever marred.

What is highly rare in Jackson's chart is that the 3/2 and 6/5 Challenge in its early position, continues as life linkage in every other

Challenge component in his chart. Having one IR Set as life linkage is rare, but two is exceptional.

Another aspect of the 3/2 life linkage Challenge is its focus on one's vanity and personal image. Jackson's many plastic surgeries and facial reconstructions to totally change his appearance during his life are a direct result of this 3/2 energy.

1st Epoch-Pinnacle-Challenge Summary

This chapter focusing on the 1st E-P-C Triad of a person's life has attempted to show the connection between people's numbers and their destinies. The Epoch, the Pinnacle and the Challenge components of the Life Matrix all play a major role in manifesting one's path in life. Parental wisdom suggests parents pay close attention to them because they serve as an excellent guide to helping raise their children.

The final section of celebrity case studies was used to reveal the numeric connections in the lives of famous people, individuals whose lives are all publically knowable. If someone approaches this knowledge with a clear, unbiased and analytical mind, it will be impossible to dismiss the interrelationship between a person's birth data and his or her course in life. Thus, a divine reality begins to emerge, a reality transcending the median level of human understanding.

Train up a child in the way he should go and when he is old, he will not depart from it.

~ Bible – Proverbs 22:6

12

The Teen Years

Arguably, there is no time period in the life of a human being more difficult or trying than the teenage years. Oh my, the exasperation of it all! These years and their intrinsic energies affect not only the teenager but all of those people attached to and existing within the teenager's environment. During these years, teens are often filled with confusion, defiance, insensitivity, egomania and a whole host of other behaviors all too common to parents, teachers and other adults.

Certainly, the normal biological cycle of life development can be regarded as a major scientific cause of the difficulties teenagers face. Puberty, of course, sets in around twelve or thirteen, bringing a whole host of physical and emotional changes in the life of the maturing person. But are there any other avenues we can pursue to find answers and explanations as to why the teen years are so pressing, challenging and difficult? Can numerology shed any light on this subject? The answer is 'yes.' Numerology gives a clear reason and explanation for the often turbulent teen years.

If we look at the following chart, we begin to see an obvious pattern explaining this teenage challenge. Can you see what it is?

$$10 \quad 11 \quad 12 \quad 13 \quad 14 \quad 15 \quad 16 \quad 17 \quad 18 \quad 19$$

If you surmised the recurrence of the number 1 as the reason, you were right. During the teen years, every human being passes through a ten year period where the 1 energy is extremely active. At no other time in life is this ten year energy pattern repeated, unless of course someone were to live from 110 to 119 years of age. To place this in further perspective, we could format the previous chart in the following manner, a manner more accurately depicting the dilemma and difficulty of the teenage time period.

Teen Years & the Number 1

10 **1**1 **1**2 **1**3 **1**4 **1**5 **1**6 **1**7 **1**8 **1**9

One is a fire sign – active, dynamic, aflame with heat and ego. It embraces itself, its independence and identity.

Notice the intent and intensity of the 1 vibration now? Fairly obvious, isn't it? But what is it that makes the recurrence of the number 1 significant? In numerology, 1 is the energy of the *self,* the *ego, action, independence, assertiveness (aggression* if extreme*), dominance, stubbornness, uniqueness.*

The 1 is the energy of the *sun*, the *yang* of the Chinese Tao, the *male* energy, a *fire* sign. During the teen years, every year for ten years is dominated by great fiery intensity as well as an energy of *emergence*, *initial growth* and *survival of individual being* and *identity*. Furthermore, the 1 energy can easily slip into its unfortunate and non-positive aspects (its negative polarity) of being overly *self-centered, self-absorbed, self-motivating, self-proclaiming, self-aggrandizing* and sometimes *self-defeating*. Negative 1 energy regards only itself to the exclusion of all others. Such self-centeredness is, of course, deleterious to positive socialization and future success in life. Please notice the emphasis on the word 'self,' for 1 is the vibration of the self.

Additionally, as we look at the Teen Years chart, we see that every year for the emerging teenage soul is confronted with, and attached to, a different energy (a different numerical cipher 0 to 9) and therefore a whole new set of annual circumstances, issues, conditions, situations, lessons, challenges and problems for the emerging child to manage as represented by each of the ciphers co-existing with the 1. In other words, not only are the teen years saturated with ego-filled and ego-driven energies, they are juxtaposed every year beginning on the child's birthday with new and challenging issues.

In the beginning of the Teen Years starting at age 10, the 1 is juxtaposed with '0'. When the zero cipher is attached on the backside of any number it represents the *core number* in gestation, i.e., in the womb. The binary numbers 10, 20, 30, 40, 50, 60, 70, 80 and 90 are the *womb years* for each of the *core numbers* attached to them.

The *womb years* (gestation years) are powerful because in any womb year the *addcap* and *subcap* match the core number. For example, in the binary number 10 the addcap is a 1 (1 plus 0 = 1), and the subcap is also a number 1 (1 minus 0 = 1). Thus, there is a dominance of only a single energy in a womb year – the core number. This is as it should be because the core number is in gestation and will be born when the core number is given birth, which will be in the first year (the 1 year) following the womb year. This is seen in the years 11, 21, 31, 41, 51, 61, 71, 81 and 91.

The year following the tenth year is, of course, the eleventh year – the birth of the 1 energy. At age 11, the teen is confronted with itself and other 1s, other individuals, egos and selves, creating potential tensions of the number 11 which focuses on others and relationships as seen in its addcap, which is a 2 (1 + 1 = 2). Notice, however, there is no subcap in the number 11 (1 minus 1 = 0). Any binary number devoid of a subcap is a master number. The binary masters are: 11-22-33-44-55-66-77-88-99. Master numbers are powerful energies. They are the expression of eleven times their core number manifesting in the energy field of their addcaps or *crowns*.

Master Numbers and Their Addcaps

Addcap Crowns	2	4	6	8	1	3	5	7	9
Master Numbers	11	22	33	44	55	66	77	88	99
Subcap Crowns	0	0	0	0	0	0	0	0	0

After age 11, the 1 combines itself with the reality of others (the 2) at age 12, which brings the concept of friendship and good times into focus because of its 3 addcap [1 + 2 = 3]. The subcap challenge of the 12 is the 1 (2 minus 1 = 1). Therefore, there is more energy of self (1) in the 12 than meets the eye. Except for age 10 (the gestation period or womb year), no other teen binary has a 1 subcap challenge.

Teen Years, Addcaps and Subcaps

Addcap Crowns	1	2	3	4	5	6	7	8	9	1
Teen Years	10	11	12	13	14	15	16	17	18	19
Subcap Crowns	1	0	1	2	3	4	5	6	7	8

Age 13 brings a powerful transformation of the individual, as naturally occurs in puberty. The self (1) focuses on its image (3) to create a new structure for itself, the 4 (1 + 3 = 4). The subcap is the 2, thus bringing relationships into focus as a challenge.

At age 14, individuals begin to seek their freedom (5 addcap) by confronting the structures, rules and regimentation of their lives (4) as their image and well-being are challenged (3 subcap).

Sexual instincts expand at age 15. The self (1), having a taste of freedom at age 14, now fully embraces the senses, adventure, experiences, freedom, and liberation (5). The addcap crown is a 6 – the number of personal love, romance, the heart, home. The subcap crown is the 4, bringing a challenge to the structures, rules, order and regimentation of life. Age 15 can be dangerous because of the conjunction of the self and its action (1) with the five senses and experimentation with them (5). The 4 subcap shows that matter and materialism are challenged. This can lead to material substance usage and abuse, i.e., drugs, alcohol (also a drug) and sex. Negative issues such as jealousy, anger, resentment and envy can also manifest themselves.

Life doesn't always give second chances, and if children exceed the safe boundaries of a balanced life and its concomitant rules and natural order, they run the risk (5) of experiencing the dark side of the number 6 – lust and craving for material substances, their sensual appeal and, ultimately, their degrading and destructive power.

Age 16 is, arguably, the most challenging of the Teen Years. Emerging from the freedom and sensual testing during age 15, individuals and their actions (1) focus on love, devotion, family and close personal interaction (6) while continuing to test the boundaries of freedom and exploration (5 subcap). At this time children are also confronted with the internalizing energy of the 7 (addcap), potentially leading to confusion, secrecy and untoward behaviors.

During this period, parents would be wise to engage their children with the idea of ethical behavior, thinking through their actions to potential consequences and being wise in their choices, all the time respecting their children's privacy.

At age 17 we find the self (1) focused on the mind and its processes (7) as it moves into the fullness of socialization (8 addcap) accompanied by a sense of familial responsibilities (6 subcap). The 7 energy always brings a sense of introspection, analysis, reflection, isolation, recession and examination into the life. By this time, the Teen Years are nearly over, and the reality of life after teendom begins to emerge.

Of course by age 17 children have pretty much established their life's foundation, but adult conversation (seventeen year olds are still teenagers) never hurts, especially when it is instructional, not judgmental. Too, it will be helpful to remember that the 7 versus 8 conjunction (which age 17 has between its 7 focus and 8 addcap) is difficult because the 7 is an inwardly moving energy while the 8 is an externally moving energy. Thus, there is a natural antagonism in this 17 binary.

At age 18 the teen experience begins to end its cycle in more sobering thought, interaction and expanding awareness as the energy of the self (1) integrates (8) to reach an understanding (7 subcap) of the whole (9 addcap).

Finally, at 19 the process concludes as the individual (1) reaches the end of the Teen Years (9) which generates new beginnings (1 addcap) and an expanded sense of socialization (8 subcap). The child has now passed through every single number of the basic nine numbers, preparing for its emergence into the realm of relationships and others – the 20s decade.

Not all teens, of course, go through the same degree or type of experiences during their teen years. Loving, positive and disciplining parenting skills can allay much of the difficulties and challenges inherent during these formative and often challenging times, especially if the parents are wise enough to foresee and prepare their offspring for the challenging 1 energy, which will unfailingly befall and encompass them. However, the troubles enveloping teens are difficult to say the least, especially in this day in age where basic values of respect, discipline, self-control, patience, courtesy, morals, ethics and virtue are taking a back seat to worldly achievement, material indulgence, instant gratification, power expansion and greed – traditional plagues of mankind.

Obviously, the teen years and their energies create an extremely difficult time for everyone. The challenge during this time is to not allow the 1 energy to become self-centered but rather divinely centered. Helping children understand that the world does not revolve around them will be helpful. As Copernicus proved, our world is not geocentrically based but heliocentrically based. In other words, the earth is not the center of our solar system, the sun is. By the same token, teens are not the center of the universe, although at times they may think so. Helping children understand the actual structure of life as divine, not worldly, will help them become better adjusted, aware, mature and whole as they move into adulthood.

If a child is given love,

he becomes loving.

~ Dr. Joyce Brothers

13

Parenting Wisdom & Beyond

Wisdom is the judicious application of knowledge. *Parenting Wisdom* is the judicious application of knowledge in order to raise children and provide for their highest and best good. *Parenting Wisdom for the 21st Century* is using the most up-to-date and forward-thinking knowledge to advance the raising of children for the love of children.

This work has proposed a revolutionary concept – that of raising children by their *numbers*, numbers associated with their full birth name and birth date. Although this concept may seem unrealistic, if not ridiculous to some, it is the author's experience and professional conclusion that numerology (the science of numbers) as applied to the upbringing and raising of children is a valid strategy for helping to raise and guide children during their formative years. Accompanying this conclusion is the hope that this knowledge will become commonplace with future generations of parents who, in turn, will pass the parenting wisdom of numbers to their offspring, ultimately leading to a society of individuals with an expanded consciousness of the divine nature of life and destiny.

It is natural that the incipient stages of this concept of raising children by their numbers be met with skepticism. Yet, the statement of truth by German philosopher Arthur Schopenhauer warrants consideration.

> *All truth goes through three stages:*
> *First it is ridiculed. Then it is violently opposed.*
> *Finally it is accepted as self-evident.*

To this author and numerologist, using the ancient science of numbers to not only raise children but to understand one's destiny, is irrefutably self-evident, but in all fairness such a conclusion has been the product of decades of research, study, application and corroboration by clients and students of The King's Numerology™ system. As the general public studies and applies the knowledge offered in this text, it will come to also realize the same truth – that the science of numerology is real, and its application to our lives has great merit, especially in the raising and guiding of children.

Numerology is not a new science. It may be new to the consciousness of mainstream humanity, but, arguably, there is no older communication system than numbers. Furthermore, numbers are more than mere arithmetic ciphers. Numbers are labels for energy fields and their relationship to life, and destiny is a reality of life. The use of numbers in the process of defining destiny and raising children may be new to this age, but it is not new in and of itself. It is certainly the hope of this work that numbers become one strategy parents can use for raising their children in the 21st Century and beyond, granting children the opportunity to rise to their highest possible potential.

Recalling the words of famous scientists Pythagoras, Isaac Newton and Albert Einstein will help us in understanding the reality of numbers as they apply to destiny, allowing us to utilize their power in our parenting wisdom efforts.

> *Numbers rule the universe; everything is arranged according to number and mathematical shape.*
> ~ Pythagoras

> *God created everything by number, weight and measure. It is the perfection of God's works that they are all done with the greatest simplicity. He is the God of order and not of confusion.*
> ~ Sir Isaac Newton

> *Everything is determined, the beginning as well as the end by forces over which we have no control. It is determined for the insect as well as for the star. Human beings, vegetables or cosmic dust – we all dance to a mysterious tune, intoned in the distance by an invisible piper.*
> ~ Dr. Albert Einstein

If these three esteemed scientists have averred the power of numbers and the reality of destiny each in their own way, should we not then open our minds to the same realities, the same truths? Until this knowledge becomes an intrinsic fabric of the warp and woof of life, it will take aware, forward-thinking, open-minded and courageous individuals to advance and promote it until it becomes, as all truth eventually becomes, self-evident.

Parents, however, are not the only individuals that would be wise to avail themselves of this knowledge. Grandparents, teachers, siblings, legal guardians, psychologists – anyone who has a direct influence in promoting the highest and best good of children should consider its merits.

As Pythagoras noted, numbers are life because they are labels of life, just as birthdates and birth names are labels for our destinies. Numbers transcend race, religion, culture, custom, language, gender and galaxies. Indeed, numbers *are* life. Raising our children by their numbers is simply to employ their natural and wise use.

The Numeric Picture Puzzle of Life

The knowledge this work has shared regarding the raising of children by their numbers can be likened to a numeric picture puzzle, a puzzle formed by the following numerology pieces:

- The Lifepath
- The Expression
- The Performance/Experience
- Soul (Desire) Layers
- Nature (Personality) Layers
- Voids
- Name & Letter Timelines
- The 1st E-P-C Triad
- The Teen Years

Each of these pieces plays its own part in ultimately creating the picture of a child's life and destiny. No one part can be considered the smoking gun of destiny. A puzzle is made of many parts. Likewise, our destinies, as revealed through our numbers, are also made of many parts. It is when all of the parts are pieced together that the full picture puzzle can be seen and interpreted.

What all of this is to say is that parents must consider all of the pieces of the puzzle of their children's destiny, not simply one or two. Every piece has its place, just as every character in a play has his or her part to play in the drama. When all of the numeric puzzle pieces are put into place, the entire picture will unfold, and when the picture is clear, the parents will be able to see their children's destiny and therefore be able to raise and guide them more appropriately and efficiently.

The Tree Trunk

All trees have trunks. Trunks, and their root systems, are the early formative foundation of the tree. If the trunk is weak, the tree cannot grow strong. If the trunk is strong, the tree can grow strong and live a valuable, substantive and fulfilling life.

Our children's lives, like trees, have trunks – the early, formative, foundational years of their lives. If those trunks are strong, our children's lives will have a strong foundation from which to grow and develop beautifully. However, if the trunk of the tree is not strong, or if it is damaged in some way, the possibility of the tree growing beautifully, healthy and whole is compromised.

How many adults have negative issues, burdensome baggage, psychological problems or emotional challenges relating to their childhood – the trunk of their life's tree? How many of these issues haunt them for their entire lives? Yet, how many of these problems could perhaps have been avoided if their parents had some knowledge of their children's destinies, especially an intimate knowledge of the trunk of their numerical tree of life, and applied that knowledge to raising their children?

Having a fundamental understanding of the numerical energies in the early life of a child affords parents a powerful and unique opportunity to raise their child or children with extraordinary wisdom, giving the children a huge head start in developing their highest potential. It can also give parents deep insight as to what challenges and potential problems their children will encounter in their developing years, the issues that will confront them, and the things they will go through. If managed properly, children will not have to grow into adulthood burdened by the problems associated with growing up, or at least such problems can be mitigated. Parents can have wonderful relationships with their children for their entire lives, as opposed to the often told tale of parent/child conflicts extending for the life of the child.

Too, and this is just as valuable, by understanding the numbers and number patterns dominating the early life of their children, parents may have the opportunity of seeing problems in their own lives and within themselves which could affect their children negatively. By addressing these issues within themselves, parents will gain another advantage to raising balanced, confident and mature children.

Numbers are far more than arithmetic ciphers. Numbers not only represent events, conditions, circumstances, challenges and situations, they also reference people. In fact, if the numbers identifying the parents – such as the Expression, Lifepath, PE and so forth – appear in a negative position in the child's chart, especially in the early formative years, the problem(s) for the child may reference one of the parents themselves or the parents' own negative issues (individually or collectively). Therefore, having an understanding of their children's charts may not only be of help to the parents in raising their children, it may also be of help in parents understanding themselves. Regardless, parents and children are both benefited, and thus wisdom, especially parenting wisdom, wins the day.

Summary

Children are not only precious, they are priceless and . . . they are the future of mankind. The worth of any society, nation, culture or civilization is directly proportional to the wisdom and consciousness of its people, and such societal value begins with its children and the parents who raise them, hopefully with wisdom.

The Greek admonition to *Know Thyself* applies not just to individuals, but also to the individual entities of societies, nations, cultures and civilizations. The more wise the amalgam of individuals comprising these entities, the wiser the entities as a whole become. Therefore, the more wisdom infused into the raising of children is critical to more than just the parents and children of separate families. It is critical to the earth as a whole and to its future.

Using numerology as one tool in the process of raising children by helping them to *know themselves* and their destinies will help establish a foundation for the evolution of mankind by creating an awareness of the divine nature of life and creation. Numerology and its use in everyday life might be new to some people, but it is not meritless. Quite the contrary. Numerology is an ancient science that serves all for the greater good, especially in the realm of raising children for one simple purpose – for the love of children . . . and their children . . . and their children during the 21st Century and beyond.

Appendix – Keywords

EXPANDED KEYWORDS/KEY PHRASE CHART

<u>Note 1</u>: every number maintains a positive and negative side (polarity), just as every coin has two sides. Furthermore, we cannot hold a coin without holding both sides simultaneously. The same is true for numbers and our lives reflect both the positive and negative aspects of each vibration to some degree. In other words, no number is perfect, no chart is perfect, no human being is perfect. We all have assets and liabilities, good karmas and bad karmas.

<u>Note 2</u>: every single number has ten binary or two-digit numbers attached to it and which, when added together, reduce to form that specific single number.

<u>Note 3</u>: it would be impossible to list every word in the English language which is attached to each of the nine basic numbers. After all, there are only nine basic numbers and hundreds of thousands of words. Therefore, a complete keyword list would be impossible to generate. Below, however, are more words and phrases than simply those used in the basic keyword chart.

<u>Note 4</u>: if a number is void in a chart, especially if a voided challenge occurs, the influences can be quite negative, reflecting the dark side of a number.

ONE - 1
(Fire) (Symbols: Sun, Staff)

10	19	28	37	46	55	64	73	82	91

The Primal Force, first cause, yang, fire, vitality, action, man, male, masculine, father, self, identity, creativity, ego, skill, individual, self-confidence, boss, leader, director, doer, initiator, creator, authority figure, pioneer, star, center of attention, willpower, self-control, independence, self-sufficiency, determination, activates, initiates, creates, dominates, leads, attains, driving, strong, courageous, powerful, dynamic, decisive, unbending, steadfast, dominant, linear, single-minded, unique, original, starts, new beginnings, creation, genesis, assertive, aggressive, overbearing, self-indulgent, ego-maniacal, selfish, self-obsessed, tom-boy, rational, reasonable, logical, unemotional, radiating, initiating, purpose, direction. TIME FRAME: a time of initiation, initiating, action, seed planting, new beginnings, starts; a period of the self and its attainments; being accountable and responsible; being the leader or bread-winner; issues of identity, self-worth, males and all things Yang; moving ahead; getting new direction; planting flags; solo excursions; tests of courage and standing alone against all people and all odds. Ones make things happen.

TWO - 2
(Water) (Symbols: Moon, Scales, Twin Towers)

| 11 | 20 | 29 | 38 | 47 | 56 | 65 | 74 | 83 | 92 |

Yin, water, woman, female, feminine, mother, others, relationships, especially those that are close, personal and intimate; 2s take sides, support, separate, helper, assistant, adversary, adversity, adversarial, assistance, follower, dependent, diplomatic, cooperative, cooperation, collaboration, consideration, teamwork, passive, patient, non-obtrusive, intuitive, receptive, responsive, agreeable, amenable, affable, kind, warm, devoted, sweet, gentle-hearted, peacemaking, harmonizing, equalizing, submissive, rhythmic, equalizing, equilibrium, competition, rivalry, contention, confliction, duality, duplicity, deceit, indecisive, division, the great divide, 'us vs. them,' intuitive, behind the scenes, bending, yielding, non-assertive, together, taking sides, opposition, vacillation, irrational, illogical, unreasonable, emotional, reflecting (as in the Moon reflecting light, water reflecting an image) and absorbing (vs. radiating of the 1), acquiescing.
TIME FRAME: a period of others, serving them, being helpful and supportive; being the helper, partner, team player, opponent, adversary, inhibitor, diplomat, judge, arbitrator, go-between; lessons of tolerance and intolerance; a time of all things Yin; period of competition, stress, adversarial conditions, tensions, tug-o-wars; learning to get along; being balanced; finding the middle path; being deceptive or dealing with deception and/or the interference or inhibition of others and either their helpfulness or hindering; a time of high energy and friction.

THREE - 3
(Air) (Symbols: Triangle, Trident)

| 12 | 21 | 30 | 39 | 48 | 57 | 66 | 75 | 84 | 93 |

Trinity, triads, air, the triangle (Ancient symbol of Perfection), The Golden Mean of Aristotle, Yin and Yang in perfect balance (the symbol of the Tao), art, artistry, artistic, image (moving or still), fashion, words, communication, expression, personal integration, fulfillment, complete approach to health, happiness, wholeness, holiness, holistic, well-being, marriage, joy, enjoyment, pleasure, parties, friends, good times, talkative, verbal, gregarious, approachable, gossip, social, outgoing, fun-loving, entertaining, light-hearted, vibrant, alive, creative, imaginative, happy, optimistic, cheerful, charming, health, beauty, vanity, writing, acting, performing, glamorous, ease, disease, dis-ease, hostility, poisonous words, harsh, critical, stern, harsh, vain, egotistical; often found in charts of politicians.
TIME FRAME: a time of self-expression and fulfillment, being creative, using words, being involved with health, beauty, disease, dis-ease, acting, writing, painting, modeling, sculpting; a time of children and seeking perfection and balance; a time of happiness (if positively aspected) and unhappiness and harshness (if negatively aspected); can give a sense of entitlement or ease of life

coming toward the self; issues of purity, holiness, unholiness, pure pleasure or debauchery, harshness and communication which is either uplifting or destructive. It is a time of integration and self-realization, a time where the goodness or meanness of life will reveal itself; a time of happiness and/or sadness; pleasure and/or pain.

FOUR - 4
(Earth) (Symbols: Square, Roots, Anchors, Chains)

| 13 | 22 | 31 | 40 | 49 | 58 | 67 | 76 | 85 | 94 |

Earth, order, structure, framework, form, foundation, boundaries, rules, regulations, guidelines, routine, status quo, concrete, confines, confinements, proprieties, mechanics, work, service, servant, matter, materialism, transformation, transmutation, security, stability, effort, hard, stubborn, recalcitrant, resistance, resistant, confinement, toil, physical strength, solid power, steadfast, sturdy, the rock, anchor, roots, chains, obstacles, tradition, convention, duty, loyalty, dependability, discipline, control, commitment, construction, prudent, clerical, industrious, down to earth, frugal, practical, organizing, house, beams, foundations, constancy, regimentation, classification, organization, organized, systemize, non-adventurous, predictable, obstinate, boring, routine, patterns, status quo, plodding along, unchanging, the order of things, events, situations, circumstances and relationships; if voided or challenged can be unstable, unfaithful, dishonest, weak, insecure, faithless. TIME FRAME: a time of work, effort, restriction (especially in conjunction with 5 energy), limitation, grinding it out, being consistent, not changing, conforming, nuts & bolts; a time when the focus is on the structures of life - financial, moral, ethical, routines, regimes, order, discipline; it is a time of learning about boundaries and borders, rules and regulations, service and work, faithfulness and devotion, sacrifice and surrender.

FIVE - 5
(Fire) (Symbols: Wings, Wheels, Needles, Broken Chains)

| 14 | 23 | 32 | 41 | 50 | 59 | 68 | 77 | 86 | 95 |

Free, freedom, fire, change, movement, detachment, detaching, shifting, wild, wayward, careless, adventure, adventurous, roam, roaming, liberation, liberate, unrestrained, undisciplined, unsettled, non-restriction, nonrestrictive, shifts, slavery mercurial, spontaneous, excitement, experience, experiential, variety, talent, versatility, people, senses, sexuality, sensations, stimulation, motion, energy, mercurial, multi-faceted, many sided, assortment, exuberant, enthusiastic, exciting, spontaneous, foot-loose, flamboyant, dashing, energetic, exploring, exposure, exhibitionist, adventurous, travel, unpredictable, unconventional, uncertain, unstable, instability, the crowd, diverse, diversity, letting go, free-spirited, rebellious, liberation, liberating, stimulating, stimulants, non-complacent, temptation, temperance, restraint, indulgence, animated, exuberant, flamboyant, volatile. TIME FRAME: a time of freedom, change, shifting, movement, uncertainty, detachment, letting go, releasing, wiping out the old, exploring, investigating, experimenting, sexuality, sensual gratification; temperance and fidelity challenged; not a time to cling, but a time to let go, detach, release and move on; also a time testing our true understanding of freedom which is not action devoid of consequence but action taken in consideration of consequence, action taken in pursuit of sensual pleasures, sense gratification and wild sorties into the realms of indulgence create slavery and bondage and all the suffering, woes and wailings associated with such incarceration, action of freedom taken in consideration of consequence by following the inner voice of conscience, temperance and restraint, the end result will be true freedom and liberation from sensual enslavement. The key note during a Five period is to be wise; look ahead to the results of your actions; exercise moderation and fidelity and do not step into the regions of material indulgence.

SIX - 6
(Water) (Symbol: Heart)

| 15 | 24 | 33 | 42 | 51 | 60 | 69 | 78 | 87 | 96 |

Love, hate, home, water, hearth, matters of the heart, romance, domesticity, adjustability, responsibility, accountability, personal love, art, artistic, beauty, community, harmonious, caring, warm, nurturing, understanding, soft, comfortable, dependable, conscientious, kind, responsive, protective, protecting, music, sex, singing, harmonizing, hatred, cruelty, family discord, family issues and concerns, addiction, jealousy, envy, resentment. TIME FRAME: a time of matters of the heart, love issues, domestic (individual, personal, community, national, global) energies, concerns, responsibilities, possible addictions, romance, lust, sexuality.

SEVEN - 7
(Air) (Symbols: Hurricane, Thinker, Cross)

| 16 | 25 | 34 | 43 | 52 | 61 | 70 | 79 | 88 | 97 |

Spirit, spiritual, mystical, meticulous, air, bliss, chaos, thought, the thinker, introspection, perception, investigation, inquisition, intuition, reflection, examination, judgment, recession, repose, receding, distancing, counseling, alienation, study, testing, reflecting, evaluating, reviewing, learning, processing, isolation, isolated, solitary, solitude, separate, separation, seclusion, secrecy, privacy, analysis, religion, rest, quiet, calm, peace, tranquility, inwardness, the 'within', perfection, poise, wisdom, saints/sinners, light/dark, curious, distant, cool, cold, removed, withdrawn, shy, reclusive, alone, lonely, loneliness, refined, non-social, purification, stressed, distressed, troubled, turmoil, torment, tumult, trauma, unworldly, considerate, inconsiderate, cold, cruel, calculating, harsh, ruthless, brutal thoughtful, thoughtless, private, secret, secretive, stealthy, hide, hidden, investigative, trouble, problems, worry, concern, anxiety, anxious, scandal, scandalous, misery, miserable, grief, deep, despair, anguish, chaos, chaotic, distressful, soul-searching, cynical, cynicism. TIME FRAME: a time for the building of inner strength and developing the inner self and all things spiritual; a time of being alone; a time of testing; a time of reflecting, analyzing, studying, teaching, pondering, going within and searching, asking questions and seeking answers, becoming mature through the fires of the heart and emotions, being brought to our knees in humble supplication of the power of God, Source, Spirit, the Lord; the time of the hurricane; choices of fidelity or adultery; peace or chaos; a time of purification by fire; a time to float across to the other side on a river of your own tears; the time to find and cling to God.

EIGHT - 8
(Earth) (Symbol: Lemniscate)

| 17 | 26 | 35 | 44 | 53 | 62 | 71 | 80 | 89 | 98 |

Earth sign, interaction, involvement, connection, disconnection, orchestration, coordination, manipulation, administration, circulation, association, associating, continuation, continuity, opportunity, responsive, (non-responsive if void), mixing, karmic conduit, circuits, circulate, systems, worldly success-power-wealth, opportunist, materialism, material comfort, management, marketing, promotion, commerce, business, flow, efficiency of motion-movement-management, being in the loop, administrator, executive, coordinating, socialization, socializing, external power, leadership, organization, involve, engage, usury, social importance and power, externalization, the 'without,' can also reference a lack of understanding of 'give and take' and 'cause and consequence.' TIME FRAME: a time of connection/disconnection, interaction, management, procrastination (if negatively afflicted), marketing, making business contacts, socializing, organizing and administrating, executing as one who is an executive; a time of association, administration, manipulation, orchestration, circulation, coordination; a time of bringing things together and making it happen; a time to be careful of using others to our advantage; a time of success or failure where all things work together harmoniously (for success) or fall apart to create failure.

NINE - 9
(Grand Elemental - All Elements) (Symbol: Crown)

| 18 | 27 | 36 | 45 | 54 | 63 | 72 | 81 | 90 | 99 |

Universality, timeless, macrocosm, endings, conclusions, completions, climaxes, chameleon, volunteer, inclusions, humanitarian, humanitarianism, teacher, impersonal love, broadcast, broadcaster, broadcasting, public exposure, pushy, magnanimous, regal, royal, philanthropic, philosophical, all encompassing, understanding, generous, tolerant, broad-minded, global, worldly, strong, dominant, domineering, controlling, artistic, intense emotion, acting, theatrical, charismatic, travel, the 'many,' healer, healing, the universal giver, expansion, the world, represents the universal languages of music, art, love. TIME FRAME: a time of conclusions, endings, resolutions, terminations, finalizations, volunteering, being public and being in the public eye and spotlight; moving within the macrocosm and life stage, moving among the masses, being famous or infamous; a time of travel - mentally or physically; a time of higher education and the advancement of thought and philosophy; a time to be universal and far-reaching; a time to be the great communicator, the powerful ruler, the icon of a culture; a time to serve humanity and expand one's thought beyond the finite boundaries of the self; a time to act, expand and be known. It is life stage for theater, medicine, sport and war; strong, even dominant personality and persona, possibly including or bordering on being over-bearing, domineering, imperious.

Glossary

1st E-P-C Timeline	1st Epoch-Pinnacle-Challenge Timeline in the Life Matrix; active from birth to ages 27 or 36; aka 1st E-P-C Triad
The 1st Epoch-Pinnacle-Challenge Timeline	The 1st Epoch-Pinnacle-Challenge Timeline in the Life Matrix; active from birth to ages 27 or 36; aka 1st E-P-C Triad
Abraham Lincoln	16th President of the United States of America
Addcap	A number derived through the vertical addition of numbers in a group
Albert Einstein	19th/20th Century German-born theoretical physicist; regarded as the father of modern physics
Albert Schweitzer	19th/20th Century German theologian, philosopher, doctor, organist, philanthropist, humanitarian
Alpha-Numeric Spectrum	The scale representing the single numbers One through Nine
Amelia Earhart	20th Century American aviatrix
Angelina Jolie	American actress
Anna Nicole Smith	American actress and model
Arnold Schwarzenegger	Austrian born American actor, body builder, politician and businessman
Aristotle	Greek philosopher, 384 BC to 322 BC
Arthur Schopenhauer	19th Century German philosopher
Artistic Triad	The combination of the numbers 3, 6 and 9
Avenue of Crowns	see Alpha-Numeric Spectrum
Babe Ruth	20th Century American baseball player
Basic Matrix	A general numeric profile of a person and his destiny comprised of eight components, each component identified by a number or numbers
Bernie Madoff	Infamous investment advisor imprisoned for fraud

Bible	Holy book of the Christian religion
Bill Gates	American businessman and co-founder of Microsoft
Bill Clinton	42nd President of the United States of America
Billy Graham	20th Century Christian evangelist
Binary	Any two digit number; can also serve as the root structure of single numbers, aka, *crowns*
Binary Masters	Double digit numbers of the same number. The nine binary masters are: 11-22-33-44-55-66-77-88-99
Biset	Numerical combination of two single numbers, number combinations or number patterns
Bishop Mandell Creighton	British historian and a bishop of the Church of England
Bistack	Simultaneous numerical combination of two numbers, number combinations or number patterns
Bob Dylan	American singer, songwriter, entertainer
Bob Hope	20th Century American comedian and actor
Book of Revelation	The final book of the Bible's New Testament, apocalyptic in scope
Buddha	Indian spiritual teacher; life approx. 400-500 BCE
Calvin Coolidge	30th President of the United States of America
Cameron Diaz	20th Century American actress and model
Capstone	The crown or single number of an addcap or subcap
Carl Sagan	American astronomer, astrophysicist, cosmologist, author
Challenge # 1	The Life Matrix number derived by subtraction of the day and month of birth
Challenge # 2	The Life Matrix number derived by subtraction of the month and year of birth
Challenge # 3	The Life Matrix number derived by subtraction of Challenges 1 & 2; known as the Grand Challenge; it is one-half of the core/center of a person's life; the other half is the Grand Pinnacle
Challenge # 4	The Life Matrix number derived by subtraction of the day and year of birth

Challenges	The four parts of the Life Matrix derived by subtraction; denotes challenges, difficulties, and places in one's life demanding focus
Charan Singh	20th Century Saint and Mystic, 1916 to 1990
Charles Caleb Colton	18th/19th Century English writer, cleric, collector, eccentric
Charles Darwin	19th Century English naturalist
Charles Lindbergh	20th Century American aviator
Charles Manson	American serial killer and leader of the murderous Manson Family cult
Christopher Columbus	Genoan explorer and navigator, 1451 to 1506
Condoleezza Rice	66th United States Secretary of State
Copernicus, Nicolaus	Renaissance astronomer and mathematician, 1473 to 1543
Core Numbers	The single numbers 1-9 attached to a zero cipher as in the *womb year* binaries
Crown	Single number identifying a series of numbers by virtue of the addition or subtraction process
Danica Patrick	American race car driver, model, spokeswoman
Destiny	A predetermined course of events; same as fate
Dolly Parton	American singer, songwriter, actress, entertainer
Dr. Phil McGraw	American psychologist, author and television personality
Duke of Wellington	19th Century British military and political leader [born: Arthur Wellesley]
Dyad	A number composed of two digits
Edgar Cayce	Famous American psychic of the 20th Century
Edna St. Vincent Millay	20th Century American playwright, poet, feminist
Elizabeth Taylor	20th Century American actress
Elvis Presley	20th Century singer and performer; known as the King of Rock and Roll

Epochs	The three parts of a birth date. The 1st Epoch is the day, the 2nd Epoch is the month and the 3rd Epoch is the year
Ernest Hemingway	20th Century American author and journalist
Expression (Exp)	That part of the Basic Matrix derived through addition of the numbers associated with the letters of a person's full name at birth; it is the personal profile of an individual describing his assets and liabilities
Exuded Qualities	Inherent characteristics associated with a person
Fate	A predetermined course of events; same as destiny
Filter	Also known as "funnel." The number (often not shown) through which the Influence number must pass to create the Reality number in an IR set; known also as a funnel
Frank Sinatra	(Francis Sinatra). 20th Century American singer, actor, entertainer
Garth Brooks	American singer, songwriter, entertainer
Genera	Letter groupings associated with the simple numbers 1 through 9
General Douglas MacArthur	19th/20th Century American military officer
General George Patton	19th/20th Century American military officer
George Armstrong Custer	19th Century American military officer
George Foreman	American Heavyweight Boxing Champion and entrepreneur
George Washington	First President of the United States of America, as well as a dominant military and political leader
George W. Bush	43rd President of the United States of America
Gisele Bündchen	Brazilian international supermodel
Grand Elemental	The number 9
Grand Pinnacle/Challenge Couplet	the 3rd Pinnacle and Challenge pair; also known as the Grand PC Couplet
Grand Void	A void that is absent in any component of the Basic Matrix
Grand Voided Challenge	A Grand Void appearing in a Challenge position in the Life Matrix

Heidi Klum	German-American model, actress, television personality and businesswoman
Helen Keller	19th/20th Century American author, political activist, and lecturer
Henry Wadsworth Longfellow	19th Century American poet and Harvard professor
Howard Hughes	20th Century American entrepreneur, industrialist, aviator and movie producer
IR Set - Full Influence/Reality Set (IR)	A numerical pattern or dyad showing the Influence energy (I) passing through a filter energy to create an Outcome or Reality energy (R), where the filter is either the Lifepath or the Expression depending on the placement of the IR Set in the chart
IR Set - Simple Influence/Reality Set (IR)	A numerical pattern or dyad showing the Influence energy (I) and its resulting Outcome or Reality energy (R)
Isaac Newton, Sir	English physicist, mathematician, astronomer, natural philosopher, alchemist, and theologian; 1642 to 1727
Jack LaLanne	20th/21st Century American fitness expert and motivational speaker
Jackie Evancho	20th Century American singer who gained fame at a young age with the voice of a mature classical singer
Jackie Robinson	1st Black American Major League Baseball player of the modern era
Jerry Rice	Professional National Football League player
Jesus	The center of the Christian religion, venerated as the Son of God incarnate
J.K. Rowling	British novelist, best known as the author of the *Harry Potter* fantasy series
John David Doey	Fictitious name used as an example in this work
John Donne	16th/17th Century English poet, satirist, lawyer and priest
John F. Kennedy	35th President of the United States of America
John Muir	Scottish-born American naturalist

John Wayne	20th Century film star
Kenny Rogers	American singer/songwriter, actor, entertainer
King's Numerology^{tm}	Eponymous numerology system created by Richard Andrew King
Larry King	20th Century American television and radio host
Learned Qualities	Characteristics learned in the living of life versus those that are naturally inherent in a person (*exuded qualities*)
Letter Groupings	see *genera*
Letter Timeline (LTL)	The length of time given to the numerical value of each letter in a person's full birth name
Life Linkage	Numeric linkage existing from birth to death; see *linkage*
Life Matrix	The internal framework of the Lifepath denoting time periods of a person's life and their fields of actions and outcomes
Lifepath (LP)	That part of the Basic Matrix derived through addition of a person's day, month and year of birth; describes the path of a person's life, its lessons and general field of activity; can also be seen as the script of a person's life or an energy world; designated as LP
Lifepath Analogies	Metaphors for describing the Lifepath which include but are limited to: 1. Path/Roadmap 2. Script 3. Automated Theme Ride 4. Energy World 5. Hand of Cards
Linkage	The continuous or repetitive occurrence of the same number, numbers, or number patterns in a chart; creates continuity
Lord Acton	John Emerich Edward Dalberg-Acton, 1st Baron Acton, English Catholic historian, politician, and writer
Mariah Carey	American pop singer
Marilyn Monroe	20th Century American actress
Marion Jones	American athlete forced to forfeit her Olympic medals for lying to a grand jury regarding the usage of performance enhancing drugs
Martha Stewart	American business woman, author, magazine publisher and television personality

Martin Luther King, Jr.	American clergyman, activist, and prominent leader in the African-American Civil Rights Movement
Mary Jane Smith	Fictitious name used as an example in this work
Master Artistic Triad	The combination of master numbers 33, 66 and 99
Master number	A multiple digit number of the same single number or cipher such as 11, 333, or 7777
Master number 11	The *Master Aspirant/Achiever* number
Master number 22	The *Master Builder/Partner* number
Master number 33	The *Master Imaginator/Communicator* number
Master number 44	The *Master Worker/Leader* number; also known as the generalship number
Master number 55	The *Master Explorer/Creator* number
Master number 66	The *Master Lover/Artisan* number
Master number 77	The *Master Thinker/Revolutionary* number
Master number 88	The *Master Interactor/Spiritual master* number
Master number 99	The *Master Performer/Master's master* number
Material Nature (MN)	That part of the Basic Matrix describing a secondary layer of an individual's personality; derived by addition of the Nature and Lifepath
Material Soul (MS)	That part of the Basic Matrix describing a second level of needs, wants, desires and motivations; derived by addition of the Soul and Lifepath
Matt Damon	American actor
Michael Jackson	20th Century American singer and entertainer
Michael Phelps	American Gold Medal swimmer
Mohandas Gandhi	19th/20th Century leader of Indian nationalism against British-ruled India
Moses	Liberator of the Hebrew people who received the Ten Commandments on Mt. Sinai
Mother Teresa	20th Century Catholic nun and humanitarian
Mount Sinai	The mountain where Moses received the Ten Commandments; location-Sinai Peninsula, Egypt

Muhammad Ali	20th Century American Heavyweight Boxing Champion
Name Timeline (NTL)	A person's full name subdivided into the separate names comprising the full name and designating a specific period of time based on the numerical value of each name
Naomi Campbell	Famous British supermodel
Napoleon Bonaparte	18th/19th Century French military and political leader during the latter stages of the French Revolution
Natal data	Birth information including the full birth name and birth date
Nature	That part of the Basic Matrix describing a person's personality and nature of doing things; derived by addition of the consonants in the full birth name
Nature Layers	The Nature and Material Nature
Number 1	Rules the self, ego, identity, action, independence, logic and masculine energy
Number 2	Rules others, relationship, support, dependence, reaction, emotion and feminine energy
Number 3	Rules self-expression, image, health, words, children, sex, pleasure, communication
Number 4	Rules order, work, service, security, stability, roots, routines, convention and tradition
Number 5	Rules freedom and slavery, detachment, movement, motion, diversity, variety and the five senses; known as the Number of Man
Number 6	Rules personal love, the home, family, community, nurturing, romance and devotion
Number 7	Rules all things internal, study, thought, reclusion, introspection, secrecy, privacy, wisdom and folly
Number 8	Rules all things external, connection, disconnection, interaction, management, orchestration, manipulation
Number 9	Rules universality, philanthropy, education, theater, power, public stage; the Number of Mankind

Number of Man	The number 5
Number of Mankind	The number 9; also known as the Grand Elemental
Numeric Houses	The numbers 1 through 9 associated with their particular letters (See *The King's Book of Numerology, Volume 1*)
Numerology	The ancient science and art of numbers, encompassing their interpretation, relationship and significance to life, wherein letters and numbers, derived from the full birth name and birth date, serve as divine codes and ciphers defining and describing our lives and destinies
Oprah Winfrey	American entrepreneur, philanthropist, television host, actress, producer
Parenting Wisdom	The judicious application of knowledge in order to raise children and insure their highest and best good
Parenting Wisdom for the 21st Century	the most up-to-date and forward-thinking knowledge to advance the raising of children for the love of children
Percy Bysshe Shelley	19th Century English Romantic poet
Patrick Swayze	20th Century American actor, singer, songwriter
PC Couplet	A Pinnacle and Challenge sharing the same timeline; also known as Pinnacle/Challenge Couplet
PE	see Performance/Experience
Performance/Experience (PE)	That part of the Basic Matrix describing the role a person will play in life; derived by addition of the Lifepath and Expression; designated as PE
Peter Jennings	American newscaster
Peyton Manning	American National Football League player
Phil Mickelson	Professional American golfer
Pinnacle # 1	The Life Matrix number derived by addition of the day and month of birth
Pinnacle # 2	The Life Matrix number derived by addition of the month and year of birth
Pinnacle # 3	The Life Matrix number derived by addition of Pinnacles 1 & 2; known as the Grand Pinnacle; it is one-half of the core/center of a person's life; the other half is the Grand Challenge

Pinnacle # 4	The Life Matrix number derived by addition of the day and year of birth; known as the Crown Pinnacle
Pinnacle/Challenge Couplet	A Pinnacle and Challenge sharing the same timeline; also known as Pinnacle/Challenge Couplet
Pinnacles	The four parts of the Life Matrix derived by addition; denotes activities that pull the person forward
Prince Charles	Charles Philip Arthur George; 20th Century royal and member of the House of Windsor
Prince William	Elder son of Prince William and Princess Diana; 21st Century royal and member of the House of Windsor
Princess Diana	Diana Frances Spencer, Princess of Wales; international personality; mother of Prince William and Prince Harry; first wife of Prince Charles
Pythagoras	Greek philosopher, mathematician; approximately 570 to 495 BC
Quadset	Numerical combination of four single numbers, number combinations or number patterns
Quadstack	Simultaneous numerical combination of four numbers, number combinations or number patterns
Quaternary	A number composed of four digits
Queen Elizabeth II	(born Elizabeth Alexandra Mary); Queen of England and of the House of Windsor
Quick Check Formula	Method of computing the missing ingredient in the Expression formula by knowing at least two of the three elements: Vowels + Consonants = Expression and determining the third
Richard Lovelace	17th Century English Romantic poet
Rodin's - The Thinker	A bronze and marble sculpture by Auguste Rodin, a 19th/20th French sculptor
Roseanne Barr	American comedian and actress
Rudyard Kipling	19th/20th Century English poet, short-story writer and novelist
Sarah Brightman	English classical crossover soprano, actress, songwriter and dancer

Saint Charan Singh	20th Century Saint and Mystic
Saint Dadu	16th Century Saint and Mystic
Saint Jagat Singh	20th Century Saint and Mystic
Saint Sawan Singh	19th/20th Century Saint and Mystic
Sam Walton	American businessman and Founder of Walmart
Sarah Palin	20th Century American politician, commentator and author; former Governor of Alaska; first Republican woman nominated for the vice-presidency of the United States
Serena Williams	American professional tennis player
Shaun White	American professional snowboarder; skateboarder
Simple Letter Value Chart	A graphic representation showing the simple value of each letter in the English alphabet
Sir Isaac Newton	17th/18th Century English physicist, mathematician, astronomer, natural philosopher, alchemist, and theologian
Sir Winston Churchill	19th/20th Century British Prime Minister and leader
Socrates	Greek Athenian philosopher, 469 BC – 399 BC
Soul	That part of the Basic Matrix derived from the numerical value of the vowels (A-E-I-O-U-Y) in the full birth name; describes needs, wants, desires and motivations
Specific Letter Value Chart	A graphic representation or form showing the specific numerical value of each letter in the English alphabet
Stacking	The simultaneous occurrence of the same number, numbers, or number patterns in a chart; creates intensity
Steve Jobs	American businessman, designer and inventor, best known as the co-founder, chairman, and chief executive officer of Apple Inc.
Subcap	A number derived by subtraction of numbers in a group
Sylvester Stallone	American actor
Tao (Taoism)	Chinese philosophical system evolved by Lao-tzu and Chuang-tzu
Ted Bundy	Notorious serial killer of the 20th Century

Teen Years	The age timeline from age 10 through age 19
The Kings Numerology™	A system of numeric analysis describing and defining the relationship between a person's natal data (full birth name and birth date) focused on the divine nature of numbers where God is King
Theodore Roosevelt	26th President of the United States of America
Thomas Jefferson	3rd President of the United States of America, principal author of the *Declaration of Independence* and an American Founding Father
The 1st Triad	The 1st Epoch-Pinnacle-Challenge Triad (the 1st Triad)
Tiger Woods	American professional golfer
Timeline	A period of time indicating a start and stop point
Tom Brady	American National Football League player
Tommy Lee Jones	American actor
Triad	A number composed of three digits
Triset	Numerical combination of three single numbers, number combinations or number patterns
Tristack	Simultaneous numerical combination of three numbers, number combinations or number patterns
Voids	missing numbers in the full birth name of the individual; designated in a chart as "v"
Walter Cronkite	20th Century American broadcast journalist
Warren Buffett	American businessman, philanthropist and famous investor
Whitney Houston	American singer and actress
Womb Years	Those ages marked by a zero. The binary womb years are: 10-20-30-40-50-60-70-80-90
William Shakespeare	16th/17th Century British poet and playwright
Winston Churchill	20th Century British Prime Minister and leader
Yang	Chinese word referencing male, masculine energy
Yin	Chinese word referencing female, feminine energy

Index

Topic	Pages
1st Epoch-Pinnacle-Challenge Timeline [1st E-P-C Triad]	7, 23, 24, 218, 223, 224, 245, 250, 252, 253, 255, 256, 257, 259, 260, 261, 262, 263, 265, 267, 269, 293
Abraham Lincoln	76, 124, 126, 151, 154, 173, 181, 192, 201, 212, 225, 231, 293
Addcap	93, 273, 274, 275, 276, 293, 294
Albert Einstein	9, 25, 81, 139, 152, 171, 177, 192, 206, 212, 213, 222, 225, 226, 228, 231, 281, 293, 324
Albert Schweitzer	92, 122, 152, 177, 204, 212, 224, 225, 231, 293
Alpha-Numeric Spectrum	37, 45, 83, 106, 125, 127, 136, 163, 180, 199, 293
Amelia Earhart	62, 126, 130, 131, 154, 170, 174, 194, 199, 212, 225, 231, 293, 325
Angelina Jolie	76, 126, 151, 167, 199, 207, 293
Anna Nicole Smith	89, 131, 152, 164, 293
Arnold Schwarzenegger	71, 139, 152, 219, 293
Aristotle	15, 288, 293
Arthur Schopenhauer	280, 293
Arthur Wellesley	62, 126, 164, 179, 295
Artistic Triad	293, 299
Avenue of Crowns	136, 172, 175, 193, 196, 199, 202, 293
Babe Ruth	71, 117, 153, 167, 177, 190, 201, 293
Basic Matrix	7, 10, 21, 22, 24, 54, 188, 210, 223, 226, 229, 230, 231, 293
Bernie Madoff	227, 293
Bible	128, 270, 294
Bill Gates	71, 294
Bill Clinton	62, 294
Billy Graham	55, 126, 153, 170, 173, 192, 195, 294
Binary	30, 31, 93, 94, 101, 191, 222, 273, 274, 276, 287, 294
Binary Masters	274, 294
Biset	294

Bishop Mandell Creighton	137, 294
Bistack	294
Bob Dylan	89, 139, 153, 173, 197, 294
Bob Hope	62, 117, 152, 173, 177, 190, 205, 222, 294
Book of Revelation	128, 294
Buddha	74
Calvin Coolidge	174, 179, 192, 197, 294
Cameron Diaz	67, 122, 153, 195, 294
Capstone	93, 295
Carl Sagan	164, 181, 199, 201, 294
Challenge #1	294
Challenge #2	294
Challenge #3	294
Challenge #4	294
Challenges	14, 47, 70, 72, 83, 90, 94, 148, 165, 212, 216, 230, 231, 239, 245, 250, 251, 256, 266, 273, 277, 283, 284, 295
Charan Singh	138, 169, 182, 203, 295, 303, 318
Charles Caleb Colton	137, 181, 295
Charles Darwin	76, 126, 151, 173, 181, 192, 201, 212, 225, 226, 231, 295
Charles Lindbergh	92, 117, 152, 169, 190, 224, 295
Charles Manson	227, 295
Christopher Columbus	295
Condoleezza Rice	164, 181, 201, 204, 295
Core Numbers	273, 295
Crown	30, 31, 116, 180, 202, 207, 233, 234, 235, 236, 275, 292, 294, 295
Danica Patrick	67, 111, 152, 173, 195, 207, 295
Destiny	29, 46, 295, 296
Dolly Parton	71, 139, 152, 179, 199, 207, 295
Douglas MacArthur	89, 111, 151, 173, 174, 197, 199, 223, 296
Dr. Phil McGraw	85, 153, 166, 181, 295

Parenting Wisdom   **King**

Duke of Wellington	62, 126, 295
Dyad	295
Edgar Cayce	89, 139, 153, 164, 204, 219, 295
Edna St. Vincent Millay	89, 126, 152, 199, 228, 295
Elizabeth Taylor	89, 114, 151, 173, 174, 199, 201, 295
Elvis Presley	92, 123, 139, 154, 169, 201, 219, 228, 257, 258, 259, 260, 261, 295, 324
Epochs	245, 246, 247, 248, 249, 250, 251, 296
Ernest Hemingway	54, 114, 152, 296
Expression (Exp)	7, 22, 23, 97 (Chapter 5), 296
Exuded Qualities	77, 296
Fate	154, 295, 296
Filter	143, 296
Frank Sinatra	71, 114, 123, 153, 222, 296
Garth Brooks	92, 139, 154, 181, 207, 222, 223, 296
Genera	24, 99, 209, 216, 217, 296
General George Patton	89, 126, 152, 171, 173, 190, 207, 212, 220, 221, 231, 296
George Armstrong Custer	62, 131, 154, 170, 174, 194, 228, 296
George Foreman	85, 117, 151, 173, 197, 219, 221, 296
George Washington	55, 131, 153, 173, 174, 192, 195, 221, 296
George W. Bush	171, 177, 199, 205, 222, 296
Gisele Bündchen	92, 169, 296
Grand Elemental	44, 89, 136, 179, 206, 236, 292, 296
Grand PC Couplet	296
Grand Pinnacle/Challenge Couplet	296
Grand Void	210, 230, 231, 296
Grand Voided Challenge	221, 223, 297
Heidi Klum	92, 106, 151, 297
Helen Keller	76, 106, 152, 170, 181, 192, 201, 212, 223, 224, 225, 226, 231, 297

Henry Wadsworth Longfellow	92, 126, 131, 153, 181, 204, 297
Howard Hughes	81, 126, 130, 131, 152, 164, 170, 194, 207, 297
IR Set – (Influence/Reality)	235, 236, 297
Isaac Newton, Sir	126, 130, 131, 212, 213, 226, 228, 281, 297, 303
Jack LaLanne	76, 152, 205, 219, 297
Jackie Evancho	81, 117, 151, 199, 205, 297
Jackie Robinson	85, 106, 153, 174, 179, 192, 207, 226, 228, 297
Jerry Rice	297
Jesus	116, 297
J.K. Rowling	76, 117, 154, 197, 207, 219, 297
John David Doey	52, 93, 100, 150, 156, 158, 159, 184, 185, 187, 229, 231, 234, 235, 241, 248, 249, 255, 297
John Donne	56, 297
John F. Kennedy	136, 152, 166, 181, 197, 201, 262, 297
John Muir	298
John Wayne	67, 136, 151, 174, 206, 221, 298
Kenny Rogers	164, 190, 201, 298
King's Numerology™	6, 7, 21, 44, 155, 166, 183, 280, 298
Larry King	55, 122, 152, 177, 179, 204, 206, 219, 224, 298
Learned Qualities	77, 298
Letter Groupings	24, 209, 298
Letter Timeline (LTL)	237, 238, 239, 242, 298
Life Linkage	266, 269, 298
Life Matrix	23, 109, 161, 245, 246, 298
Lifepath (LP)	7, 22, 23, 47 (Chapter 4), 49, 51, 53, 298
Lifepath Analogies	49, 298
Linkage	266, 269, 298
Lord Acton	137, 181, 298
Mariah Carey	123, 298

Marilyn Monroe	85, 117, 151, 174, 179, 195, 199, 212, 220, 221, 226, 228, 231, 257, 260, 261, 263, 298
Marion Jones	89, 136, 153, 219, 226, 298
Martha Stewart	89, 131, 152, 204, 205, 298
Martin Luther King, Jr.	126, 153, 174, 190, 192, 212, 223, 224, 232, 299
Mary Jane Smith	52, 93, 100, 150, 156, 157, 159, 184, 187, 229, 230, 233, 235, 239, 246, 247, 252, 253, 299
Master Artistic Triad	299
Master Number	30, 299
Material Nature (MN)	23, 183 (Chapter 8: Nature [Personality] Layers), 186, 187, 188, 299
Material Soul (MS)	22, 155 (Chapter 7: Soul [Desire] Layers), 159, 161, 162, 188, 299
Matt Damon	164, 192, 299
Michael Jackson	81, 123, 134, 136, 152, 169, 174, 192, 206, 257, 267, 268, 299
Michael Phelps	76, 131, 151, 169, 200, 207, 219, 299
Mohandas Gandhi	92, 114, 151, 169, 207, 299
Moses	116, 299
Mother Teresa	92, 126, 131, 153, 173, 192, 212, 222, 231, 299
Mount Sinai	116, 300
Muhammad Ali	85, 114, 151, 164, 169, 204, 207, 219, 225, 228, 300
Name Timeline (NTL)	98, 235, 242, 300
Naomi Campbell	89, 136, 153, 169, 195, 197, 228, 300
Napoleon Bonaparte	55, 117, 152, 170, 300
Natal data	28, 300
Nature (Natural Nature)	7, 23, 183 (Chapter 8: Nature [Personality] Layers), 184, 300
Nature Layers	183 (Chapter 8: Nature [Personality] Layers), 300
Number 1	300
Number 2	300
Number 3	300
Number 4	300
Number 5	300

Number 6	300
Number 7	300
Number 8	300
Number 9	300
Number of Man	37, 74, 197, 198, 262, 301
Number of Mankind	262, 301
Numeric Houses	301
Numerology	9, 21 (Chapter 2: The King's Numerology™ Basic Matrix), 27, 301
Oprah Winfrey	71, 126, 131, 151, 166, 174, 199, 207, 219, 222, 257, 265, 266, 301
Parenting Wisdom	7 (TOC), 24, 301
Percy Bysshe Shelley	137, 301
Patrick Swayze	85, 111, 154, 177, 181, 207, 301
PC Couplets	250, 252, 296, 301
Performance/Experience (PE)	7 (TOC), 141 (Chapter 6: The Performance Experience), 301
Peter Jennings	67, 122, 153, 301
Peyton Manning	76, 117, 154, 228, 301
Phil Mickelson	67, 152, 167, 179, 301
Pinnacle #1	301
Pinnacle #2	301
Pinnacle #3	301
Pinnacle #4	302
Pinnacle/Challenge Couplet	252, 296, 301, 302
Pinnacles	245, 250, 301, 302
Prince Charles	62, 139, 151, 164, 179, 190, 195, 222, 263, 302
Prince William	62, 139, 151, 164, 190, 195, 302
Princess Diana	85, 117, 151, 177, 181, 192, 197, 219, 231, 257, 262, 263, 264, 302
Pythagoras	11, 15, 27, 38, 128, 281, 282, 302
Quadset	302
Quadstack	302

Quaternary	302
Queen Elizabeth II	85, 139, 153, 207, 302
Quick Check Formula	185, 186, 302
Richard Lovelace	71, 302
Rodin's The Thinker	41, 302
Roseanne Barr	164, 302
Rudyard Kipling	302
Sarah Brightman	123, 302
Saint Charan Singh	138, 168, 182, 203, 303
Saint Dadu	79, 174, 194, 303
Saint Jagat Singh	303
Saint Sawan Singh	303
Sam Walton	81, 126, 151, 303
Sarah Palin	81, 134, 136, 152, 164, 170, 190, 197, 303
Serena Williams	92, 114, 151, 164, 303
Shaun White	92, 111, 151, 207, 303
Simple Letter Value Chart	24, 99, 209, 303
Sir Winston Churchill	303, see also Winston Churchill
Socrates	13, 303
Soul	7 (TOC), 155 (Chapter 7: Soul [Desire] Layers), 303
Stacking	260, 303
Steve Jobs	55, 106, 151, 207, 228, 229, 303
Subcap	93, 273, 303
Sylvester Stallone	81, 126, 151, 166, 179, 190, 303
Tao (Taoism)	31, 33, 58, 163, 273, 303
Ted Bundy	218, 226, 303
Teen Years	7 (TOC), 271 (Chapter 12: The Teen Years), 304
Theodore Roosevelt	171, 179, 304
Thomas Jefferson	76, 114, 153, 164, 304

The 1st Triad	see 1st Epoch-Pinnacle-Challenge Timeline [1st E-P-C Triad]
Tiger Woods	55, 139, 151, 197, 304
Timeline	304
Tom Brady	89, 153, 304
Tommy Lee Jones	89, 139, 153, 192, 229, 304
Triad	7, 23, 109, 245, 304
Triset	304
Tristack	304
United States of America	38, 76, 114, 124, 153, 173, 181, 194, 206
Voids	7 (TOC), 209 (Chapter 9), 304
Walter Cronkite	76, 131, 151, 164, 204, 226, 304
Warren Buffett	81, 131, 152, 166, 199, 228, 304
Whitney Houston	92, 123, 131, 153, 167, 199, 304
Womb Years	273, 304
William Shakespeare	85, 96, 126, 131, 152, 177, 181, 199, 204, 212, 224, 231, 304
Winston Churchill	29, 85, 124, 126, 152, 167, 170, 192, 207, 303, 304
Yang	31, 32, 34, 50, 58, 304
Yin	33, 34, 50, 56, 58, 304

Richard Andrew King
~ Books ~
www.RichardKing.net

The King's Book of Numerology
Volume 1 - Foundations & Fundamentals

The King's Book of Numerology, Volume 1-Foundations & Fundamentals provides complete descriptions of Basic Numbers, Double Numbers, Purifier Numbers, Master Numbers, the Letters in Simple and Specific form as well as the Basic Matrix, the numerological blueprint of our lives.

~

"*The King's Book of Numerology* series contains new information that informs and predicts more completely and accurately than any previously published numerological work. It brings back the empowered sciences of long ago, information long since lost upon this plane." ~ G. Shaver

"The best numerology book I've ever read." ~ M.W.

"I've learned as much about numerology from *The King's Book of Numerology* the last few days than I have in my past five years of study."

~ Frank M.

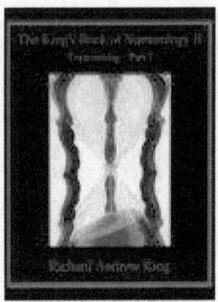

The King's Book of Numerology II
Forecasting - Part 1

The King's Book of Numerology II: Forecasting - Part 1 is dedicated to opening the door to the divine blueprint of our lives. That plan, that divine blueprint of destiny, is exact, precise, unchangeable, unalterable and . . . knowable, at least in general terms.

Once this awareness of a predetermined fate becomes established through application of numbers and their truths, our understanding and consciousness of life will, no doubt, change. We will begin to see ourselves as part of an immense spiritual super-structure far beyond our current ability to comprehend, understand or perceive. Life will take on new meaning and, perhaps, we will even begin to awaken to greater spiritual truths.

Subjects covered: Life Cycle Patterns, The Pinnacle/Challenge Matrix, Epoch Timeline, Voids, Case Studies and much more.

Blueprint of a Princess
Diana Frances Spencer - Queen of Hearts

The tragic death of Princess Diana of Wales - the most famous, the most photographed, the most written about woman of the modern world and possibly of all time - was one of the most shocking and saddening events of the late Twentieth Century. Not since the assassination of American President John Fitzgerald Kennedy in 1963, has such an event captured the attention of the world. On that ill-fated Sunday of 31 August 1997 and the following week until her funeral, there was much discussion and reflection of the Queen of Hearts, the People's Princess, England's Rose. But in all of the media news coverage, there was no discussion given to the cosmic aspects of her life and death. This book is dedicated to addressing those issues through The King's Numerology^{tm}. Its purpose and hope is to offer some consolation and explanation as to that one question so poignantly written on a card of condolence left with the multitude of flowers before the gates of Buckingham Palace... "Why?"

~

After learning from King's numerological teaching, it is impossible to conceive of going back to that 'twilight naive and foggy' state of being where one can only guess or hint at the truths, motivations and directions of one's life that is Pre-King. Not only do I recommend this book, but I suggest it and his other numerology books as absolutely necessary for the library of anyone even remotely interested in the science of numerology.

~Hunter Stowers

Messages from the Masters
Timeless Truths for Spiritual Seekers

In a time where there is more need for enlightenment than ever before, *Messages from the Masters: Timeless Truths for Spiritual Seekers* offers timeless truths for genuine seekers thirsty for spiritual nectar.

Masters are the Ph.D.s of the universe, the Light Bearers of the Divine Flame. Their knowledge and wisdom are supreme. They have no equal. Although appearing human, they are not. Masters are the exalted Sons of God. Their chief duty is to rescue souls, liberating them from the maniacal maelstrom and madness of the material world and returning them to their eternal Home with the Lord.

Messages from the Masters is a rich source of hundreds of quotes from a cavalcade of nine Perfect Saints throughout the last six hundred years: Guru Ravidas, Kabir, Guru Nanak, Tulsi Sahib, Swami Ji Maharaj, Baba Jaimal Singh, Sawan Singh, Jagat Singh and Charan Singh. The messages in this book focus on the importance of the Divine Diet, the priceless Human Form, Reincarnation, the World, the Negative Power and Soul Food.

Warning! *Messages from the Masters* is not for the faint of heart or the worldly-minded. Masters come into the world to sever our attachment to it, not make it a paradise. Although the epitome of love and wisdom, they shoot straight from the hip, pull no punches, favor no religion. Their universal message of soul liberation is reflected in the statement of Saint Maharaj Charan Singh: *Just live in the creation and get out of it*!

99 Poems of the Spirit

99 Poems of the Spirit draws from the writings of Perfect Saints, Masters, Mystics and Sacred Scriptures. Designed to lift the consciousness, mind and heart, all of the poems are original works by Richard Andrew King. Their purpose is to help connect the reader with the mystic side of life in order to enhance the process of self-realization while advancing on the spiritual path and climbing the ladder leading to the ultimate attainment of God Realization. It is a treasure chest of poetic spiritual gems offered to excite, educate and stimulate the mind and soul in the glorious journey of spiritual ascent.

A few selected poem titles are:

A Thousand Mile Journey
Animal Food
Awake, Dear Soul
Between Two Worlds
Cards of Life
Child of the Light
City of the Dead
Glittering Lights
Karma
King of Fools
Lady of the Light
Reaping Weeping
Serious Business
The Wheel
We Reap the Deeds
World of Fools

The Age of the Female
A Thousand Years of Yin

The Age of the Female: A Thousand Years of Yin highlights the profound and extraordinary ascent of the female in the modern world, placing her center stage in the global spotlight as presidents and leaders of nations, titans of industry, corporate executives, military generals, media magnets, doctors, lawyers and a whole host of other prestigious titles normally associated with the male.

Why has her rise to prominence been so rapid, especially in consideration of historic time? Why also has there been an increased interest in other people's lives in our society, in competitive athletics, personal data collection and the exploration of space and other worlds?

The Age of the Female: A Thousand Years of Yin answers these questions. It is an insightful and exciting read into these mysteries, offering compelling and irrefutable evidence through the ancient science and art of numerology that, indeed, the age of the female has arrived and the next thousand years belong, not to him, but to her.

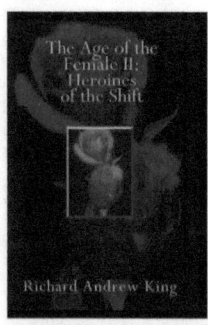

The Age of the Female II
Heroines of the Shift

The Age of the Female II: Heroines of the Shift continues the remarkable journey of the female's ascent in the modern world of the 2nd Millennium.

This installment is a general read in five chapters honoring the accomplishments of women in categories of female firsts, female Nobel laureates, female athletes, female icons and female quotations.

The achievements of the women featured in *The Age of the Female II: Heroines of the Shift* are deserving of respect and admiration. Their lives, challenges and successes are motivational catalysts for every individual to be the best he or she can be and to honor the very essence of what it is to be human.

The Age of the Female II: Heroines of the Shift is intended to be an inspiring and educational read for everyone, not just women but men, too, offering knowledge and insight of the depth, power and daring-do of women as their Yin energy rises upon the global stage in this millennium which destiny has irrefutably marked as the Age of the Female.

The Black Belt Book of Life
Secrets of a Martial Arts Master

The mystery and mystique of the martial arts is not only ages old, it's legend. Revered throughout the world, martial arts is a treasure chest of life secrets that transcend the boundaries of combat to include the expanse of life and living. Arguably, martial arts is a great system for teaching the integration of body, mind and spirit.

The Black Belt Book of Life: Secrets of a Martial Arts Master is not about physical fighting strategies and tactics. It is about concepts and principles we learn though martial arts training that can help us in the struggle of life and in the journey to conquer ourselves. In the end, a true Black Belt should be a realized soul who, having engaged the enemy – himself – finds himself, triumphant.

The Black Belt Book of Life: Secrets of a Martial Arts Master reveals many secrets of martial arts training, sharing these truths in quick and easy to read vignettes to benefit martial artists and the general public as well. It is a book for all readers, not just martial artists, both males and females, especially the youth of today who are in search of a foundation to guide their lives.

www.KingsKarate.net

Your Love Numbers
Discovering the Secrets of Your Life, Loves and Relationships

Your Love Numbers reveals the secret formula defining all great relationships and how to assess the love potential of any relationship.

Your Love Numbers reveals the mystery of love through the most ancient of all sciences . . . numbers, your numbers, calculated using only your full name and date of birth and those of the people you love! "Numbers rule the universe; everything is arranged according to number and mathematical shape," said Pythagoras. And, yes, everything, including love, can be measured in numbers!

Your Love Numbers is based on research by master numerologist, Richard Andrew King. Applying his unique and revolutionary new theories, love and attraction between people can be determined using very easy to learn concepts. With a little study and practice, all this can be done in a matter of minutes.

Your Love Numbers teaches you how to assess a relationship or potential relationship in minutes, saving you endless time, energy, effort and possible heartache in the end. By knowing ourselves and the people we love, our relationships will be potentially more rewarding, satisfying, productive, peaceful, lasting and loving . . . for everyone - our family, spouses, partners, children, friends.

www.YourLoveNumbers.com

Destinies of the Rich & Famous
The Secret Numbers of Extraordinary Lives

Why are rich and famous people rich and famous? Is it luck? Hard work? Advantage by family name? What makes them special? What secrets are the basis of their success?

- Why is Oprah Winfrey a billionaire entrepreneur?
- What gives Sarah Palin her Going Rogue persona?
- What caused Marilyn Monroe to be a sex goddess?
- What caused Princess Diana's tragic life and death?
- Why was Michael Jackson plagued by child issues?
- Why was Howard Hughes a disturbed, rich recluse?

Destinies of the Rich & Famous explores the secret numbers of the following famous global icons and explains through The King's Numerologytm why they are both rich and famous.

Dr. Albert Einstein	Marilyn Monroe
Amelia Earhart	Michael Jackson
Elvis Presley	Muhammad Ali
General George Patton	Oprah Winfrey
Howard Hughes	Princess Diana
John F. Kennedy	Sarah Palin

www.DestiniesOfTheRichAndFamous.com

To order books, go to

www.RichardKing.Net

and major online booksellers

Contact

Richard Andrew King

PO Box 3621

Laguna Hills, CA 92654

www.RichardKing.Net

Email: Rich@RichardKing.net

www.ingramcontent.com/pod-product-compliance
Lightning Source LLC
Chambersburg PA
CBHW021833220426
43663CB00005B/222